Mr. Sorkin Goes to Washington

Mr. Sorkin
Goes to Washington

Shaping the President
on Television's The West Wing

MELISSA CRAWLEY

McFarland & Company, Inc., Publishers
Jefferson, North Carolina, and London

LIBRARY OF CONGRESS CATALOGUING-IN-PUBLICATION DATA

Crawley, Melissa, 1971–
    Mr. Sorkin goes to Washington : shaping the president on
television's *The West Wing* / Melissa Crawley.
      p.   cm.
    Includes bibliographical references and index.

    ISBN 0-7864-2439-7 (softcover : 50# alkaline paper) ∞

    1. West Wing (Television program).   I. Title: Mister Sorkin
goes to Washington. II. Title.
PN1992.77.W44C73   2006
791.45'72—dc22   2006004314

British Library cataloguing data are available

On the cover: flag picture ©2006 Digital Vision;
Seal of the President of the United States

Manufactured in the United States of America

McFarland & Company, Inc., Publishers
  Box 611, Jefferson, North Carolina 28640
    www.mcfarlandpub.com

Per Alan.
Sono il vostro ammiratore più grande.

Contents

Preface

For me and for many others in Australia in 2001, *The West Wing* will always be associated with September 11. News of planes flying into the World Trade Center interrupted an episode of the series. One minute we were watching the fictional American presidency, and the next the real America was under attack. Because I was writing about the show and I am an American, people would share this "where were you when" memory with me. While I already believed in the show's effect on popular culture, their recollections gave its influence a new and poignant dimension.

This book, then, is a way to recognize the impact of television on our daily lives, but it's also an attempt to search out broader connections between media, politics and our past. How do we learn about the presidency, and what does television add to the process? Looking for answers to these questions, I turned to a series that I loved to watch. What began as a three year project to earn a Ph.D. in media turned into a broader analysis of how a unique writer's presidential stories recalled the early lessons of our political education. Aaron Sorkin's talent with language earned him many fans, but his representation of the presidency also contributed to the institution's enduring myth. In terms of the presidency, television is more than news, and this book is a testimony to the power of its fictions.

Lights, Camera, President

When television set ownership expanded throughout the United States, the president entered the lives of citizens in new and more revealing ways.

Television's cameras brought presidents to the public in celebration and in defeat, in triumph and in scandal, in life and in death. For their part, presidents used television to persuade, encourage, confess and repent. Television, however, has become more than a broadcast record of presidential history or a tool for presidential communication. Its entertainment formats also broadcast the president. If these formats "offer a mirror ... to the culture of the audience they seek to serve" (Paterson 1998, 57), then their presidential representations reflect the diverse discourses that shape the cultural and political meaning of the office and the man.

While scholarship recognizes television as an agent of political socialization in its news broadcasts, its value as a civic force outside its nonfiction representations of the presidency is often overlooked. While several studies address the impact of new media on American politics (Davis and Owen 1998; Diamond and Silverman 1997), their approach remains broad and functionalist. They examine how new media (defined to include talk radio, tabloid journalism, television talk shows and computer networks) impacts American politics, concluding that its reliance on politics as entertainment has more negative than positive potential. Their research, while usefully recognizing politicians' use of nontraditional media, ultimately addresses issues found in existing critical work. Alternatively, this book examines the contribution of television drama to the socializing forces that shape the presidency, as most Americans understand it. Specifically, it discusses how the representation of the president in the television drama *The West Wing* recalls the affective processes of political learning.

In the introduction to *The West Wing: The American Presidency as Television Drama*, editors John O'Connor and Peter Rollins comment that the series is a reflection of "America's best image of itself" (2003, 13). If the presidency as represented in the series reflects America's best self-image, then an examination of the president as a character is central to any exploration of the show's impact. The work collected under this title includes discussions on the show's didactic potential (Pompper 2003; Beavers 2003), its representation of White House politics (Levine 2003; Chambers 2003) and its depiction of race and gender (Lane 2003). When the show's fictional president is explored, it is through his relationship to the actual presidency as both institution and man (Hayton 2003) as well as his intellectual complexity, a status one author suggests is ultimately representative of a pure form of democracy (Finn 2003). Sorkin's presidential representation has also been examined as a "romantic vision" that "reflects the postmodernity of U.S. politics" (Parry-Giles and Parry-Giles 2002, 209). While this body of work raises important critical ideas surrounding the notion of the presidency in television drama, its focus on the president, specifically, is limited.

Critical discussion of *The West Wing* has also been widespread in newspapers and magazines. The comments range from praise for the program's ability to make presidential politics interesting to derision for its fantasy portrayal of a too perfect administration. While the fictional president is often a subject in these commentaries, the discussion is again limited to the success or failure of the show's dramatic depiction of his traits. In many cases, these traits are compared to real presidents, suggesting that the show's representation reaches beyond its fictional boundaries. These comparisons are useful because they demonstrate the show's contribution to the larger political and cultural understandings that surround the presidency. However, they often do not go beyond simple comparisons.

While the existing scholarly work on the series offers important insights, it does not significantly explore the elements of the politically socialized presidency that might inform the show's fictional representation. An important element of the series' impact is that the president as a symbolic meaning system exists outside the mediated encounter of the weekly fictional show. By recognizing that the show's impact does not exist independent of the political socialization processes experienced by most Americans, this book offers a new approach to the existing scholarship. It also contributes to previous work on media psychology (Gitlin 1980) and political psychology (Edelman 1988) as well as the field of political socialization, which has neglected the role of television outside the news. The president is chosen as the focus of political learning because he is the primary element of the political system that is disseminated by the media.

Chapter Outline

Because the end is often a good place to reflect on the beginning, this book opens with an account of Aaron Sorkin's departure from *The West Wing* and introduces the power of the presidential myth. A theoretical framework is outlined in Chapter One. Political socialization studies are examined with a focus on how the president is learned as an affective meaning system. As an agent of political learning, the media was initially understood to perform a secondary role. Studies later recognized that it played a more significant part in political socialization processes, particularly its television formats. The contributions of television's audiovisual formats to the political learning process are also discussed along with the role of information processing theory and its relationship to the sounds and pictures of television.

Chapter Two begins with a brief overview of the president in film.

As the president was a cinematic image before his television debut, the chapter discusses several films with a focus on the emotional qualities of the presidential character. The chapter then looks at issues surrounding the broadcasting of the president. Historically, the rise of broadcasting and the development of presidential communication are closely aligned. Radio broadcasts not only demonstrated the power of affective presidential rhetoric but also strengthened the idea that the president is the primary agent of government. When television made the president news, this image was further solidified in the public mind and presidents began to recognize and use television's power to emotionally connect with the viewer and voter. The president, however, was not limited to television news broadcasts. Early productions chronicled the lives and achievements of the nation's founding fathers. As television's entertainment schedule expanded, the trend would continue and grow to include satire and comedy. Like cinematic representations, television's depictions of the president often focus on affective characterizations.

Chapter Three introduces *The West Wing*, opening with a discussion of quality television conventions. This chapter examines the visual and textual style of the first four seasons of the series to analyze how these aspects of the production contribute to an affective representation of the president. In terms of visual language, the analysis focuses on the patriotic imagery of the series and the use of the Steadicam, which has become an integral part of the show's aesthetics. In terms of text, the analysis focuses on how Aaron Sorkin constructed the five senior staff characters. These characters drive the narrative, and their conversational exchanges and monologues highlight Sorkin's distinct dialogue and the series' affective tone toward political issues. More importantly, an examination of these characters reveals how Sorkin creates a tone that recalls some of the most basic traits of the socialized president.

A significant component of *The West Wing*'s impact on the representation of the president is its complex relationship with reality and fiction. This interaction is the focus of Chapter Four. While the presidency of the show is fictional, its characters often engage in contemporary political debates. This narrative structure provides the foundation for discussions of the show's didactic potential and has prompted real politicians to use the show as a forum to promote specific issues. While the fictionalized engagement of the show's characters with real policies may reflect the "cultural preoccupation" with the presidency and "its place in our national culture" (Parry-Giles and Parry-Giles 2002, 209), it also reduces politics and the presidency to affective rhetoric. As television drama, the series must rely on affective dramatic conventions to be successful. While it may be useful to initiate political discussion, its ultimate project is to construct compelling stories. When these stories enter public discourse, they contribute to the presidency as an emotional representation.

Chapter Five examines the character of President Bartlet. It is organized around three main identities: the paternal, the moral and the intellectual president. The chapter shows that each identity, while Sorkin's deliberate construction, also has a strong foundation in historical conceptions of the president. This suggests that Sorkin's dramatic construction may function as a significant agent of political learning but is not a unique addition to the processes of presidential socialization. Chapter Six concludes the book with a discussion of Sorkin's approach to writing and the ultimate contribution of the series to presidential representation.

Political learning studies suggest that the president is perceived from an emotional standpoint. Television drama is also an affective experience. Political television drama, then, presents a unique opportunity to examine the ways in which the affective experience of learning the president is reaffirmed in the emotional setting of fiction. In this context, the following analysis of *The West Wing* will demonstrate how the presidency is represented to the American people in ways that become part of the national story to which all citizens belong.

Introduction

In May 2003, the cast of *The West Wing* was filming the final episode for its fourth season. As the actors prepared for a scene where a Republican senator is sworn in to replace President Bartlet (Martin Sheen), they were asked to halt production and meet in the Roosevelt Room. Creator Aaron Sorkin and Executive Producer and Director Thomas Schlamme entered and announced that they were leaving the series immediately. Bradley Whitford, who plays Deputy Chief of Staff Josh Lyman, described the moment as "an emotional holocaust"; the announcement "was agony for all of us" (quoted in Murphy and Schwed 2003). Martin Sheen compared it to the loss of a parent. The cast, he said, "felt like orphans" (quoted in Cigelske 2003).

Most critics attribute the reasons for Sorkin and Schlamme's departure to a combination of over-budget production costs, late scripts and the 21 percent decline in ratings experienced during the show's fourth season (Weiner 2003). Executive Producer John Wells, who took control of the show, explained that his "preference was always that Aaron stay" but "as the ratings came down, there was more pressure on making the budget ... the pressure of that got to be a bit much for Aaron" (*ibid.*). Sorkin's work habits (in four seasons he wrote or co-wrote 86 out of 88 episodes)[1] meant that scripts were frequently late. The resulting production delays were estimated to have cost 3.8 million dollars during the series' fourth season (Murphy and Schwed). With costs high and ratings low, Sorkin was also under pressure from the network to write "juicier story lines" and change the show's focus from characters who were "too liberal for a country that had seemingly veered to the right" since September 11 (*ibid.*). While Sorkin's public announcement simply said that he will "never forget" having "the best job in show business" (quoted in Carter 2003a), other reports suggest that he told his writing staff he refused to "choose budget over quality" (Murphy and Schwed).

Surprise over the departures quickly turned to speculation as critics discussed the show's future without Sorkin and Schlamme. One of the most repeated concerns was how the series would work without Sorkin's talent for producing distinctive dialogue. Bill Carter wrote in the *New York Times* that the change would have an impact because the series has "always been a product of Mr. Sorkin's personal vision" (2003a). Sorkin's "intricately worked dialogue" and Schlamme's "innovative techniques" created a unique aesthetic that would be difficult to maintain without them (*ibid.*). Richard Just, writing for *The American Prospect Online* commented that the "show's genius was so particular, its narrative voice so distinctive, that it's hard to believe it will even be worth watching" after Sorkin's departure (2003). The fact that both Jeff Zucker, NBC's president of entertainment, and Wells have addressed the loss of Sorkin's narrative sound (a style one recurring cast member calls "Sorkinese")[2] suggests that the issue is significant. While Zucker accepts that audiences "may miss a little of the small talk in the hallway" because "nobody was better at the small banter ... than Aaron Sorkin" (quoted in Goodykoontz 2003), Wells admits that Sorkin's long speeches would be difficult to recreate as he wrote them "exceedingly well" (quoted in Smith 2003).

In addition to speculation over how the show would successfully replicate Sorkin's distinctive sound, critics suggested that the series needed to recover its political relevance. Typical of the sentiment were these comments:

> Overall, 9/11 and the arrival of the Bush administration made the doings of President Bartlet and his staff seem irrelevant. Who cared about diplomatic crises in a fictional Middle East when the actual U.S. military was gearing up for war in the real thing? Who wanted to hear "Wing" characters debate school vouchers and a graduated income tax when the real America was on Orange Alert? [Seitz and Sepinwall 2003].

For Seitz and Sepinwall, viewer numbers dropped in the fourth season because the show's verisimilitude was lost. Their comments were echoed by other critics who suggested that the ratings decline occurred because "Sorkin's heavily liberal leanings" were poorly received "at a time when the country was veering in exactly the opposite ideological direction" (Barney 2003). A show once celebrated by critics as "the very best show on network television" (Duffy 2000), "one of TV's most satisfying hours" (Bianco

2001) and "a zeitgeist show" (Waxman 2000) was punished for failing to align itself with the changed national mood.

While *The West Wing* has survived the loss of Aaron Sorkin, his work on the show confirmed its status as a landmark television series. In his scripts, the characters' rapid conversational exchanges and theatrical speeches created a narrative sound rarely heard on television drama, while his approach to political debate ennobled public service. However, *The West Wing*'s most significant contribution to public discourse was Sorkin's construction of the presidency as an emotional institution. Week after week, *The West Wing* asked viewers to recall the most basic lessons of their early political education.

Feeling Presidential

Everywhere else in the world, politics dominate culture. Not so in America ... Americans are held together only by ideas, the clashing ideas of opportunity and equality—as it were by a culture of hope.

(Theodore White 1983, 71)

The origins of the contemporary United States' presidency may be found in colonial America's disillusionment with powerful men.[3] Reacting to the power of colonial governors who depended on the Crown for policy direction rather than the people, the colonists grew increasingly dissatisfied with their lack of representation (Bailey and Shafritz 1988, 1). After the war for independence, the framers of most state constitutions answered the question of representation with the creation of weak executive branches and powerful legislative bodies. This pattern was repeated on the national level, as the government formed by the Articles of Confederation did not include a central chief executive; instead it relied on the Confederation Congress to be a legislative-executive body (*ibid.*). However, weak state executives and lack of clear leadership on the federal level soon resulted in politicians' calls for a stronger form of government that included a visible chief executive. Vigorous debate between those for a strong national executive and those fearful of repeating the excessive power of English rule led to the formation of a leader limited by a thorough and succinct list of qualifications and duties. The responsibilities of the now-named President of the United States were clearly intended to prevent the possibility of one man gaining too much power. Article II, Section 2 of the United States Constitution specifies that the president is commander in chief of the army and navy and will have power to make treaties, appoint ambassadors, judges and all other officers of the United States. Section 3 empowers the president to convene Congress, "to receive ambassadors and other public ministers" and to "take care that the laws be faithfully executed." Yet Americans compel their leader to rise above these restrictions. In him, they see the leader of White's "culture of hope." They see someone who is both the same and different from themselves.

In the political life of Americans, the "culture of hope" does not exist independently. The structure of feeling that Americans cling to as their national destiny has a focal point, a place of intersection where ideas meet. In the United States, capitalism forms an uneasy alliance with fairness and the citizenry look to a leader to watch over the precarious balance. This is the president's job. After all, as White argues, "a president is held responsible by the people for whether they have jobs or not, whether they eat or not" (1983, 427). The president is protector and provider, a shadow of a monarch long ago abandoned. The president is a structure of feeling.

For most Americans, the president is learned as a structure of feeling from an early age. Work on the primary stages of political learning suggests that feelings are central to civic education. Many children's understanding of the political system has little basis in information, is overwhelmingly positive and strongly emphasizes the president (Greenstein 1960). This civic orientation is often carried through to adulthood. Several core studies in the field conclude that for many, the processes of political education that are responsible for forming a positive idea of the president last throughout the developmental lifecycle (Easton and Hess 1962; Cleary 1971). This is not to argue that adults continue to view the president positively throughout their lives. Rather, research suggests that while children grow and cognitive evaluations lead to less dependence on a positive viewpoint of the president, the core values surrounding the presidency remain consistent (Dawson and Prewitt 1969). The primitive patriotism of early childhood may grow more sophisticated, allowing for critical views of the man holding the office, but, for many, the presidency remains a respected institution. Barber argues:

> It seems probable, for example, that such early feelings, if firmly established, would affect all later learning, perceptions and sentiments. That is, a child starts out with the feeling that his government is good. When new messages come in to the effect that the government is bad, they have to deal with that pre-established sentiment. The child who has learned the earlier lesson thoroughly is unlikely to give it up on the basis of a few negative experiences or facts [1970, 105].

The affective focus of political learning finds support in a cultural system that requires the presidency to be capable of greatness.[4] Buchanan notes:

if the presidency is to be equal to the task of handling such forbidding problems as war, economic collapse, or the threat of nuclear annihilation, it must be great—great enough to stand on equal terms with such larger-than-life challenges [1987, 26].

In Buchanan's conception, the ideology of greatness relies on two beliefs. For the majority of Americans, the presidency has the "potential to make extraordinary things happen" and the officeholder "should be able to realize that potential" (28). While both these beliefs have an intellectual component, they also contain an emotional element that is strongest in times of crisis. When the president confronts a national problem, he also captures the emotions of citizens. Many Americans rely on the president to reassure their fears or to assuage their anxiety in times of national turmoil. During heightened emotional states, the president is necessarily in a position of psychological strength. While this function of the presidency suggests its practical use, "the cultural meaning of the presidency also extends into the realm of emotion" (*ibid.*). Most people intellectually assign tasks to the presidency but they also feel something about those tasks.

Certainly, men have overseen the United States presidency who did not meet their "potential" to "make extraordinary things happen." Presidents have failed to achieve greatness and caused widespread public cynicism toward the institution. The war in Vietnam, the scandals of Watergate, Iran-Contra, Clinton's impeachment and the controversial 2000 election have all contributed to a declining view of the presidency. Waterman et al. argue that at the end of the twentieth century the presidency had "serious problems" (1999, 61). However, Buchanan suggests that events like Vietnam and Watergate were a temporary suppression of the idea rather than a permanent alteration (1987, 28). In his view, periodic reassessments of greatness only occur because of the "inadequacies of individual presidents" (*ibid.*). The concept of greatness maintains its power because the presidency as an institution survives the abuses of the men who occupy it.

Buchanan's theory also relies on the lessons of history. Various presidents live in America's national consciousness as symbols of greatness. Buchanan argues that this symbolism relies on contemporary perceptions of the individual president's role in historically significant events. He suggests that shared understandings and subliminal definitions of presidential greatness were forged by emotionally significant national experience (32). Washington, for example, inspires awe because of the "emotion-laden circumstances in which his qualities were displayed. The terrors of revolutionary war, the anxious beginnings of a new nation" (34). This discourse is promoted by the various elements of political learning—school, family, media—so that most citizens collectively share in the memory of Washington as a man of high moral and physical courage who epitomizes the characteristics of what an American president should be. In turn, an affective view of presidential character is applied to contemporary frameworks creating a shared historical understanding, what Buchanan calls "presidential culture" (25). This meaning system then becomes part of how most citizens understand the presidency. The national memory of presidential greatness is embedded with emotional significance, creating a mental map of the president.

Communication scholars Trevor and Shawn Parry-Giles argue that when critics like Buchanan focus on presidential greatness as measures of political power, they "tend to ignore the symbolic importance of the presidency as a cultural force in U.S. political life" (2002, 211). While this criticism may be justified, Buchanan's work does offer valuable observations about the nature of Americans' feelings toward the presidency. Feelings are difficult to discuss critically, but they form a large part of the symbolic system that allows the presidency to be a cultural force. Buchanan, who defines feelings in terms of leadership, contends that they are crucial to discussions of the presidency. He suggests that the "emotional, non-rational dimensions" of the institution need to be considered to "clearly understand citizen's evaluations of presidential leadership" (29). He notes that "emotion is the key, for without it leadership remains little more than management and does not inspire awe or become enshrouded in mystique" (1987, 30). While many people in the United States do not necessarily feel inspired by the president, he is clearly conceptualized as a leader. As Greenstein suggests, the president is "the most visible landmark of the political landscape, virtually standing for the federal government in the minds of most Americans" (2000, 3). Aside from feeling something about leadership, many people apply feelings to the institution. Buchanan offers several examples to support the argument that the presidency, as an institution, touches Americans' emotions, including the "strong emotional and physical reactions" when a president dies in office as well as the rise in approval ratings a president receives when inaugurated (29). As he suggests, this rise "can only be attributed to the psychological impact of ceremonial investiture, as the new president has had no chance to do anything except appoint some officials and give a speech" (*ibid.*). For political science scholar James Barber, political feelings are made up of a complex web of personal identifications, associations and understandings of the contemporary world (1970, 102). They are "part of a much broader map or pattern of feelings associated with family, work and social life" that often "run back into the past of the citizen" (103). Feelings about politics are not simple or easily isolated to specific factors. However, media, as a primary element in the majority of citizens' experience of the presidency, plays a significant role in perpetuating the institution's affective components.

In his essay, "Television Viewing as a Cultural Practice," Saenz suggests that television viewing "provides a prominent occasion for viewers' construction of culture" (1994, 573). Audiences, he argues, "carry out considerable rhetorical, political, poetic and cultural work" through the act of watching television, which itself "institutes a persistent social practice" (*ibid.*). Within this social practice, meaning is made. If culture is defined as a particular structure of feeling generated by groups of people, then part of the work of television audiences, in Saenz's formulation, is to construct an affective response from their viewing experience. A viewing experience of the president, then, would provide an occasion for this work to be carried out, whether the source was the reality of the news or the fiction of situation comedy or drama. Television, like political learning, employs affective tools to reach the public. Television, like culture, can represent a structure of feeling.

While most Americans will never encounter the president in their lifetime or see the inner workings of the Oval Office, they have what Saenz refers to as "implicit social knowledge" (575) of the president's role and his environment. For most people, the televised image of the president *is* the president. Living with television means encountering the president in a symbolic environment. This text of the president however, is read in relationship to other texts. Intertextuality "proposes that any one text is necessarily read in relationship to others and that a range of textual knowledges is brought to bear upon it" (Fiske 1987, 108). This does not mean that one text specifically refers to another but rather "intertextuality exists in the space between texts" (*ibid.*). The president on television, then, must be understood in relationship to the audience's cultural understanding of the president outside of media. This understanding exists as political learning but is also defined by the fact that the president is, for most people, always and only a media image. The representation of the president only makes sense in relationship to all the other images of the president that the audience sees.

Fiske, using Barthes' work, notes that the intertextual is the "prime site of culture" and "intertextual relations are so pervasive that our culture consists of a complex web of intertextuality, in which all texts refer finally to each other and not to reality" (1987, 115). In Barthes' theory, this implies that the real is only accessible through a culture's construction of the real, which in turn is only found in the products of culture rather than in reality itself (*ibid.*). A text may only be understood in relation to every other text in a culture rather than a specific reality. The sense that a text makes

to an audience may be a sense of reality, but it is not based on reality itself.
This intertextual process is activated by certain codes. As Barthes notes,
every text refers to "what has been written, i.e. to the Book (of culture, of
life, of life as culture), it (the code) makes the text into a prospectus of this
book" (1975, 20–1). A televisual representation of an event may only be
understood in relation to every other representation of the event that an
audience has viewed. As Fiske explains:

> So a representation of a car chase only makes sense in relation to all the oth-
> ers we have seen—after all, we are unlikely to have experienced one in real-
> ity, and if we did, we would, according to this model, make sense of it by
> turning it into another text, which we would also understand intertextually,
> in terms of what we have seen so often on our screens. There is then a cul-
> tural knowledge of the concept "car chase" that any one text is a prospectus
> for [1987, 115].

In Barthes' view, there are a number of these "cultural knowledges,"
which texts present to the reader and which the reader must use in order
to understand the text. Each narrative becomes a rewriting of these already
written knowledges (*ibid.*). Fiske, noting that Barthes was specifically interested in literature when developing his theory, suggests an application of
the concept to nonfiction texts such as the news in order to explain an
audience's understanding of a news item "not in terms of its relation to the
'real event' but as a prospectus of the already written (and thus already read)
'Book'" (116). Specific news items then are understood in terms of an audience's "cultural knowledge." Barthes' cultural knowledges are written in
terms of action. For example, he refers to "The Kidnapping," "The Meeting," etc. (Barthes quoted in Fiske, 115).

Applying Fiske's theory to nonfiction texts leads to a news narrative
of the president that becomes a rewrite of the already written knowledge
of the president in American culture. In this way, television depictions of
the president are represented in terms of existing cultural knowledges that
are infinitely based on texts with no roots in reality. The president becomes
pure image based on the cultural knowledge of the president, which is also
an image that exists in an unending circle of intertextuality. This would
imply that meaning is impossible to discover; however, as Fiske argues,
"meaning is necessarily infinitely elusive" (117). To overcome this, Fiske calls
for a shift in focus "from the text to its moments of reading; points of stability and anchored meanings (however temporary) are to be found not in
the text itself, but in its reading by a socially and historically situated viewer"
(*ibid.*). The meaning of the president then is not based in a reality but rather
in brief experiences—moments of historical memory that may change with
time and age but are strongly based on emotions.

For media theorists such as McLuhan (1964) and Baudrillard (1979, 1983), television is incapable of producing meaning because the message ultimately becomes subordinate to the medium. Whereas, in the past, the media were believed to reflect reality, they now, according to Baudrillard, form a "hyper" reality where the real is lost in representation. Society is so saturated with media messages that information and meaning "implode" and collapse into "noise" that becomes pure effect without content or meaning (Kellner 2002). This implosion of content into form allows Baudrillard to utilize McLuhan's media theory: "the medium is the message signifies not only the end of the message, but also the end of the medium" (Baudrillard 1983, 102). Baudrillard is suggesting that because the media and reality "implode," it is impossible to distinguish between media representations and the "reality" which they supposedly represent (*ibid.*). Media is thus incapable of communicating meaning in Baudrillard's conception and only appeals to the masses through pandering to their interest in spectacle, entertainment and fantasy. The masses, he claims, absorb all media content and neutralize (or resist) meaning only to demand and receive spectacle and entertainment, which further erodes the boundary between media and the "real" (*ibid.*). Subsequently, this media "implosion" into the masses renders meaningless any attempt to discover how the masses process the media.

Referring to McLuhan's distinction between "hot" and "cool" media, Baudrillard suggests that eventually all media become "cool." As Kellner argues:

> That is, for Baudrillard all the media of information and communication neutralize meaning and involve the audience in a flat, one-dimensional media experience which he defines in terms of passive absorption of images, or a resistance of meaning, rather than the active processing or production of meaning. The electronic media therefore on this account have nothing to do with myth, image, history, or the construction of meaning (or ideology) [2002].

In this account, television and the masses dissolve meaning. As a form of media, television "suggests nothing" and "is only a screen" that "transistorizes all neurons and operates as a magnetic tape—a tape not an image" (Baudrillard 1979, 220). This book claims the opposite stance and suggests that television is a significant communicative media.

CHAPTER ONE

Theorizing the Presidency

Learning the Presidency: The Political Socialization Studies

Scholarship on the United States presidency has existed almost as long as the office itself. The first study of the presidency as a social and political institution was written in 1825 by Augustus B. Woodward and entitled *The Presidency of the United States* (Heclo 1977, 1). Woodward's themes reflected operational concerns of the young institution and included commentary on how the president's staff and personal time should be organized, the management of leaks and intelligence activities, the organization of advisory systems, directions on leadership in foreign policy and the chief executive's relationship with Congress. At the turn of the century and more quickly after 1930, the presidency emerged as a specialized area of research. Many of the early works traced the history of the office (Stanwood 1898, 1912) while presidents themselves contributed to the critical inquiry (Cleveland 1904; Wilson 1914; Taft 1911; Roosevelt 1913). By 1977, a bibliographical survey of the existing presidential literature beginning from the mid–1930's listed almost 3,000 entries (Greenstein et al.).

While the early literature stressed executive politics and organizational issues, the scholarship of the late 1960s through the following decade marked a transition to public politics. Works that are regarded as the core of presidential scholarship emerged during this time and raised themes that continue to influence current critical thought (Neustadt 1960; Rossiter 1960; Cronin 1974; Schlesinger 1974). Research during this time focused on presidential power, selection and election practices, and popularity and public images. Presidential communication studies began as a serious field of inquiry and examined the president's relationship with his constituents as mediated through the press (Pollard 1964; Cornwell 1965; Stein 1969; Keogh 1972).

During the 1960s, critical thought regarding United States politics also shifted towards a psychosocial orientation. Scholars began to investigate the origins and development of a person's underlying cognitive attitudes toward politics and the president. The concept of socialization was borrowed from the behavioral sciences and applied by political scientists in an effort to understand civic learning patterns. Political socialization studies sought to explain how people acquire "certain predispositions toward the political world" (Riccards 1973, 1). Some definitions of political socialization found in early research centered on the individual, and others were based on the political system. Greenstein's work stresses the first model, defining political socialization as

> all political learning, formal and informal, deliberate and unplanned, at every stage of the life cycle, including not only explicitly political learning but also nominally nonpolitical learning that affects political behavior, such as the learning of politically relevant social attitudes and the acquisition of politically relevant personality characteristics [1968, 551].

Almond, however, views political socialization as a function of the political system. He argues:

> All political systems tend to perpetuate their cultures and structures through time, and ... they do this mainly by means of the socializing influences of the primary and secondary structures through which the young of the society pass in the process of maturation.... Political socialization is the process of induction into the political culture. Its end product is a set of attitudes—cognitions, value standards, and feelings—toward the political system, its various roles, and role incumbents. It also includes knowledge of, values affecting, and feelings toward the inputs of demands and claims into the system, and its authoritative outputs [1960, 27-8].

While Greenstein argues for the importance of both overt political learning and more subtle nonpolitical learning as significantly contributing to the individual's socialization process, Almond sees the process as a result of the needs of the political system. Almond's definition presupposes an emphasis on the acculturation of the individual with regard to existent systematic needs, which Greenstein's definition does not (Cleary 1971, 46). Almond's emphasis on acculturation leads him to further argue that political socialization "is the process whereby political attitudes and values are inculcated as children become adults and as adults are recruited into roles"

(1966, 24). However, according to Easton and Dennis, this view is limiting. They argue that assertions about the systematic implications of political socialization in a definition of the term narrow possible research alternatives by implying that socialization inexorably leads to conformity with existing standards of behavior (1969, 9–13). In a democratic society, citizens have the freedom to choose alternative civic behaviors that the system itself encourages. This is the liberalizing force of political socialization. Cleary notes:

> Political socialization is a liberalizing force when it opens options by developing an individual's information, understandings, and cognitive abilities, thereby building his capability to analyze a problem situation in broad perspective. The very essence of a democratic society demands that the focus of political socialization be on its liberalizing function [1971, 47].

While this liberalizing force may be a noble goal to strive toward, it is often difficult to reach. Most socializing agents assume particular sets of goals are important and should be fostered, often ignoring alternative values or standards of behavior. Pranger argues that most political socialization in the United States emphasizes the deliberate shaping of values supportive of acquiescence and obedience instead of the development of the educated man (1968, 44). This view finds support in the majority of citizens' understanding of the president. Socialization, in this instance, becomes a limiting rather than liberalizing force because it closes the options of individuals by fostering a value system that develops predispositions toward particular attitudes.

From an early age, most Americans are taught values that predispose them to view the office of the president in a particular way.[5] The process of political socialization then becomes a combination of Greenstein's and Almond's definitions. Political learning is both individual and institutional. Smith, Bruner and White developed one conception of the organizing principles of political consciousness. As Bennett explains, these researchers saw attitudes and beliefs both in the service of personality needs and as analytical devices used for making sense of the external world (1975, 19). Attitudes and beliefs form the bond between the individual and the social world. Lasswell argues that political behavior, stems from personal needs, drives and dispositions; in the case of political behavior these personal motives are directed toward public objects (1960, 24). The individual reaches a level of political understanding through various political and nonpolitical experiences. But this learning is always experienced within an environment that is predisposed to support a democratic system. The system's needs shape the experiences to fit particular attitudes favorable toward perpetuating it.

On an operating level, the political system of the United States is assisted by the individual's acceptance of the presidency as an institution founded on specific principles. While these principles are essential to the system's assertion that it works, nonacceptance on the part of the American citizen does not mean that the system fails.[6] Rather, the principles provide a necessary framework for the presidency that gives individual presidents the power to lead as well as the power to fail, while the institution itself remains intact.

In a brief summary of the origins of the political socialization movement, Dawson and Prewitt trace the core understanding of socialization to the field of anthropology, wherein an individual is "engaged in a new world of social relationships" enabling him to form a "political self" (1969, 16). In this view, political socialization functions as an opening onto the world of politics. An individual develops a political self through his relationships with the social world. Using the ideas of anthropologist George Herbert Mead, Dawson and Prewitt suggest that the political self may be thought of in the same terminology as Mead uses for the social self. Mead writes:

> The self is something which has a development; it is not initially there, at birth, but arises in the process of social experience and activity, that is, develops in the given individual as a result of his relations to that process as a whole and to other individuals within that process [quoted in Dawson and Prewitt 1969, 17].

For Dawson and Prewitt, the process of political socialization works to produce a political self. It is created rather than born.

The political self, under Dawson and Prewitt's conception, is shaped by several categories of knowledge and feelings on the part of the citizen. Political attachments and loyalties are feelings directed toward the nation that allow a person to say "I am an American," while specific knowledge about political institutions (for example, understanding that federalism is part of the United States Constitution) also form part of the political self (20). Dawson and Prewitt assign "transient views" to an additional category. These views allow a person to "react to specific political policies, programs, personalities and events" (*ibid.*). This conception of the political self is what accounts for citizens' attitudes toward the president as officeholder versus the president as political institution. President as officeholder allows a citizen to react in positive or negative ways because it is about a man who holds Democratic or Republican ideals and pursues policy to meet those beliefs. Alternatively, president as political institution reaches the core of attachment and loyalty to the nation.

Much of the political socialization research of the 1960s and 1970s analyzed the origins of political attitudes in children (Easton and Hess 1962; Greenstein 1965; Hess and Torney 1967; Easton and Dennis 1969; Andrian 1971) with the majority of studies agreeing that a child has strong orientations toward political compliance due to his experience in subordinate roles and this compliance begins before the child enters school. Easton and Hess' study of 12,000 elementary school children concluded that children generalize attitudes toward authority from their immediate experiences to perceived authorities who lie outside their direct experiences (1962, 242). They found that once children became aware of the political world, they transferred their experience of nonpolitical authority onto figures of the political system:

> The child not only learns to respect and admire political authorities, but with regard to many characteristics sees them as parents writ large [*ibid.*].

This positive outlook is a theme repeated by Hess and Torney in their study of American grade school children. They argue:

> The young child's involvement with the political system begins with a strong positive attachment to the country: the U.S. is seen as ideal and as superior to other countries. This attachment to the country is stable and shows almost no change through elementary school years. This bond is possibly the most basic and essential aspect of socialization into involvement with the political life of the nation. Essentially an emotional tie, it apparently grows from complex psychological and social needs and is exceedingly resistant to change or argument [1967, 213].

Greenstein reached a similar conclusion in his study of young children, reporting that favorable orientations toward the president as a central authority figure may result from the transference of feelings toward the parents to the political world (1960, 941). While these early studies usefully highlight the relationship between a child's experience of parental authority and his/her perception of presidential authority as a process of emotional transference, they fail to account for the negative side of the exchange. Nonfavorable outcomes are also likely to occur, as not all children share the same positive experience of parental authority. Resistance to their parents' authority is therefore just as likely to lead children to reject the president as a benign or respected figure.

Most early political learning studies placed the president as the main actor on the child's political stage. Dennis suggests that the president becomes the child's first real connection with the political world. He notes:

> [The child] begins as a political primitive with a vision of government as the embodiment of a man or a small set of men who constitute a yet dimly rec-

ognized form of external authority. Probably the first recognizable shadow that flickers across the wall of the cave of the child's unformed political mind is that of the president. He forms the initial visible object of the political world and from him, the child builds down, gradually incorporating more and more objects below him until the image becomes rounded and complex [1973, 79].

This connection, he suggests, remains constant through the developmental cycle, despite changing attitudes toward the government. As expected, children's knowledge about government increases as they grow older and they are more likely to view the government negatively. As children reach adulthood, various socializing agents influence their cognitive perceptions of the government, but early research shows that core values and attitudes do not change:

By the time a person reaches adulthood he has acquired a relatively stable set of basic political attitudes. While change might occur, it is more likely to take place with regard to feelings toward current authority figures than toward the political system itself [Easton and Hess 1962, 236].

Basic political orientations may be modified as the individual grows and is exposed to different values and belief systems, but the fundamental attitudes remain stable. Dawson and Prewitt argue that:

The persistence of basic views is of great importance for the overall development of the political self. These feelings serve as the foundation upon which subsequently acquired orientations are built. Political events and experiences later in life are interpreted within the context of these basic orientations. They serve as "political eyeglasses," through which the individual perceives and makes meaningful the world of politics [1969, 23].

For Dawson and Prewitt, the basic orientations that aid in the development of a person's "political self" are located in feelings. If, as Cleary's research suggests, children in the United States attach to personalities before they understand the nature and functions of the political system (1971, 53), then the resources they will use to inform their future interpretations of the president are similarly based on feelings. For the purposes of this research, the nature of these feelings is less important than the idea that they form the foundation from which the majority of the American public builds its understanding of the president.

Dawson and Prewitt suggest that the political socialization processes that form the political self operate on both an individual and community level (1969, 13). Nations, they claim, "perpetuate their political standards by inducting new generations into established patterns of thought and action" (*ibid.*). This in turn defines what United States citizens mean when they speak of the "American way of life":

> Majority rule, competitive elections, national loyalty, accepting the general rules of the game even when we dislike specific policies; all are part of the "American way." From one generation to the next these standards are passed on [*ibid.*].

Numerous scholars subsequently began to examine exactly how these standards were transmitted and by what specific agents of socialization.

Early studies reached various conclusions as to the main agent responsible for political orientations. Some saw the family as playing the most crucial role (Hyman 1959; Mitchell 1962; Davies 1965; Pinner 1965; Lane 1966; Wasby 1966; Flacks 1967; Hess and Torney 1967; Jennings and Niemi 1968, 1971; Jennings and Langton 1969; Hirsch 1971; Kubota and Ward 1971). The majority of these early studies noted that children's orientations toward politics were most often aligned with those of their parents. V. O. Key argued that the family's influence was long term: "There can be little doubt that family influences contribute to the shaping of basic values and outlooks, which in turn may affect the individual's views on political issues long after he has left the family fold" (1961, 294).

The child eventually leaves the total environment of the family to experience the social world, and this is where group influence finds a role in political learning. Peer groups were found to be significant socializing agents by some researchers who reported that an adolescent will begin to take politically related cues from his/her friends (Levine 1961, 596) and that these "primary group" interactions are "essential links in the complex process by which political norms are indoctrinated and party preferences implanted" (McClosky and Dahlgren 1959, 758). In the research, peer group influence was seen to effect the individual's broader notion of politics, as he began to personally identify with the members of his social family. The more intense this identification, the more the individual's political attitudes were influenced by the social group, whose norms provided reference points against which he measured his political behavior (Newcomb 1958, 266). Peer groups are most often encountered in educational settings and were found by many early researchers to have a more significant impact on political learning than a child's group of friends.

The school as socializing agent received much critical attention by early scholars (Ziblatt 1965, Hess and Torney 1967; Abramson 1967, 1970; Langton and Jennings 1968; Ehman 1969; Prewitt, Von der Muhll and Court 1970; Merelman 1971; Mercer 1971). In 1967, Hess and Torney argued that the school was the leading agent of political socialization, surpassing the family and peer groups. Their research, based on the Easton-Hess survey of 12,000 elementary school children, reached the following conclusions:

> The family transmits preference for a political party, but in most other areas
> its most effective role is to support other institutions in teaching political
> information and orientations.... The school apparently plays the largest role
> in teaching attitudes, conceptions, and beliefs about the operation of the
> political system. While it may be argued that the family contributes much to
> the socialization that goes into basic loyalty to the country, the school gives
> content, information, and concepts which expand and elaborate these early
> feelings of attachment [217–19].

Hess and Torney base this argument on their finding that their sample schools provided the most specific information related to political attitudes and values. They reach this conclusion by noting that the majority of children in their sample voiced the same political orientations toward leading government figures and political activities as a sample of their teachers. However, Cleary points out that "this congruence may be due to a common source in the society other than the school" as well as noting that "there are important dissimilarities in the political orientations of the children and the teachers" (1971, 65). While Hess and Torney may have overstated the case for the power of the school as a socializing agent, particularly by failing to discuss the political development of children who avoid school, other researchers made similar arguments for the influential role of educational institutions. Henry notes:

> The elementary school classroom in our culture is one of the most powerful
> instruments in this effort, for it does not merely sustain attitudes that have
> been created in the home, but reinforces some, de-emphasizes others, and
> makes its own contribution. In this way it prepares and conditions for and
> contributes toward the ultimate organization of peer and parent-directed
> attitudes into a dynamically interrelated attitudinal structure supportive of
> the culture [1963, 192–3].

Political values are transmitted to the child through classroom rituals, including pledging allegiance to the flag, in the hope that participation will form and cement patriotic feelings.

Research has also found that emotional orientation toward political understanding exists in textbooks used to teach the child the basics of government. In an early study, Litt analyzed textbooks used in a civics education course and reported that a "democratic creed" ("the rights of citizens and minorities to attempt to influence governmental policy through nontyrannical procedures") was the major political message. Fifty-two percent of the text was devoted to this idea (1966, 489). Litt found that teachers, school administrators and political leaders of the community articulated these values as well.

In a more recent study of civic education textbooks, Sanchez reviewed forty American government textbooks with a specific interest in the depiction of the president. His conclusions note that the president is often written about in emotional terms with little substantive information to validate his status. For example, both Eisenhower and Kennedy "earn high marks for the personal impact their charisma made on the office" (1996, 63) while the textbook authors ignore other, more controversial aspects of their leadership. Presidents, as represented in textbooks, have a long history of being portrayed as the domineering force of government.

In a 1974 study, Cronin argued that "textbook presidents" were portrayed as far more powerful than actual officeholders, while a 1982 update of the study by Hoekstra showed that textbooks were still creating unrealistic expectations of the president by listing the many roles he was expected to play (Sanchez 1996, 64). Sanchez's work found that textbooks are continuing to grade presidential performance according to unreasonable standards: "Most books still furnish students with an imposing checklist of roles ... with powers allegedly attached to these roles, the books create the image of a dominating officeholder who towers over the political system" (64). The early studies on school as a socializing agent should be considered in relation to the political climate of the decade in which they were written. However, the updated studies suggest that the ritual climate of the classroom continues to support an emotional view of the government and the president. For many students, this orientation to the political system and the president works to reaffirm early attitudes and values as taught by family and peer groups.

The Media as an Agent of Political Socialization

Most early studies of the media as an agent of political socialization relegated it to a secondary role, finding little evidence that it was a causal force in the child's development of political attitudes (Katz 1957; Hyman 1959; Lane 1959; Gerbner 1960; Key 1961; Dawson and Prewitt 1969). Most researchers agreed that the media, while an important source of political information, served to reinforce existing political orientations rather than create new ones. In his study of public communication, V. O. Key confirms this view: "It is safe to conclude that the major influence of the media upon political attitudes is by and large a reinforcement of the status quo" (1961,

396). Both Cleary (1971) and Dawson and Prewitt (1969) placed great emphasis on the work of Katz (1957) and Lazarsfeld (1955), who hypothesized that the media did not directly influence the population. Rather, it was "opinion leaders" who were more attentive to the messages from the media and subsequently passed on the messages they felt were important to those over whom they exercised influence. This was conceptualized as the "two-step flow" of communication wherein the opinion leader is the first step in the process of reception. This theory placed strong emphasis on family and peer groups as the agents of influence in the socialization process and gave media a secondary and limited role. Dawson and Prewitt make the following conclusions regarding media's role in political learning:

> First, more often than not the media act as transmitters of political cues which are originated by other agencies. Second, the information carried by mass media goes through a two-step flow. Third, the media tend to reinforce existing political orientations rather than create new ones. Fourth, the messages of the mass media are received and interpreted in a social setting, and in the context of socially conditioned predispositions [1969, 197].

Dawson and Prewitt show little support for the power of media as a primary agent of political socialization. However, their conclusions were based on a narrow perspective. While the studies conducted in these early years on the family, peer groups, and the school as primary socializing agents were based on empirical evidence, conclusions regarding media's role in the process were drawn from research generalizations based in the field of psychology. Media was studied from the perspective of having an effect, specifically on children.

In 1960, the most complete research supporting the view that media had little direct effect on social attitudes and behavior was proposed by Klapper. Using psychological principles of learning and dissonance theory, Klapper was the first to propose that the effects of communication were a reinforcement of existing predispositions due to selective exposure and mostly neutralized by the interpersonal influences of Katz's "two-step flow" of communication (Dennis 1973, 392). Klapper's generalizations were then cited in the political socialization literature of Dawson and Prewitt, who, in the absence of other evidence at the time, asserted that media content reinforces a child's political predispositions and media's effect is mediated by influences from interpersonal sources at home and in school (1969, 198–200). Klapper's theories, however, were based on the failure of the media to effect change in people's attitudes toward controversial issues. His narrow scope did not cover the idea that the most likely effects of the media in relation to political socialization would be in the acquisition of general political knowledge or a potential heightened interest in public affairs. This effect places media in a more direct role in the political socialization process.

In the early political socialization studies, media's role was also viewed as dependent on other variables. Hess and Torney (1967) treated media variables inferentially, linking past media findings to the behavior of the children in their sample (Kraus and Davis 1976, 21). In a critical review of Hess and Torney's work, Kraus and Davis note that the research presented many opportunities for Hess and Torney to explore the role of television on the political learning process but they dismiss it in favor of general conclusions. "They avoid television by discussing the election outcome and conclude 'that the election itself had a strong impact on many children and may in itself have been a socializing experience'" (*ibid.*). This lack of critical inquiry into media, specifically television, is evident in Easton and Dennis' work as well. They allude to media, televised debates and the drama of presidential campaigns, but they do not test for television exposure, content or general viewing behavior (23). Television is minimized and viewed as a dependent rather than independent variable in the political learning process. However, research in the 1970s reversed this trend and began to make significant claims regarding the power of media in political socialization (Chaffee, Ward and Tipton 1970; Hollander 1971; Dominick 1972; Rubin 1976; Atkin and Gantz 1978; Drew and Reeves 1980; Conway, Wyckoff, Feldbaum and Ahern 1981).

In their study of Wisconsin teenagers, Chaffee et al. hypothesized that public affairs media consumption would account for some change in political cognitions and behavior in comparison to parents, peers and the school. The results of their study indicated that there were causal effects between media and public knowledge. They concluded that "mass communication plays a role in political socialization in so far as political knowledge is concerned but its influence does not extend to overt behavior such as campaigning activity" (1970, 658). Dominick explored the role of television as a teacher of political facts and attitudes in children ten and eleven years old. Eighty percent of the sample named the media as a source of most of their information regarding the president and vice president (1972, 55). Atkin and Gantz's research put significant emphasis on the news as a source of children's political learning. Their work concluded that more than half of all children sampled watched television news regularly, and the news made a major contribution to their interest in and knowledge about political affairs (1978, 185).

Research conducted by Conway et al. reached a similar conclusion, arguing that news and levels of political knowledge reinforced each other and determined political attitudes and participation to a greater extent than other agents of the socialization process, including parents, gender and education (1981, 165). Research in the 1980s also examined the influence of media on political malaise and cynicism (Zimmer 1983; Paletz and Entman 1984); the influence of broadcast and print media on different types of political learning at different times (Chaffee and Tims 1982; Garramone and Atkin 1986); the influence of media use on political participation (Volgy and Schwarg 1984); and the interaction among media use, family communication and developmental stage on a child's political learning (Peterson and Somit 1982; Kuo 1985; Dennis 1986; Meadowcroft 1986; Tims 1986). These studies found patterns that suggest media may encourage family discussions about politics and encourage political learning from other sources.

In his review of this later political socialization literature, Buckingham (2000) contends that subsequent research has qualified some of the claims made regarding the power of news, particularly television news, in the process of political learning. Television news often represents children's first contact with the world of politics. It is at this stage that high exposure to television news is correlated with high levels of political knowledge, as discussed by Atkin (1981). However, in early adulthood, a reliance on television is increasingly associated with lower levels of political knowledge, while a divide grows between those who use television and print media and those who use only television (Chaffee and Yang 1990).

Later research also began to look at the importance of other variables in the political learning process that further qualify earlier claims. Studies have examined variables such as family communication patterns (Dennis 1986; Liebes 1992) and their relationship with ethnicity (Chaffee and Yang 1990; Austin and Nelson 1993) as potential mediators in political socialization. In this later work, high levels of news media exposure is correlated with high levels of participation in politics, but the influence of family, peers, and community variables is recognized as more significant than earlier thought (Andreyenkov et al. 1989; Robinson et al. 1989; Chaffee and Yang 1990). Buckingham argues that, despite the growing sophistication of this later research, it tends to rely on reductive measures of political understanding, which is then assessed through the recall of factual information in multiple-choice tests (1999, 173). He concludes that, theoretically, the studies position political socialization in a functional role wherein children are viewed as passive recipients of adults' efforts to place them in specific social roles. Political learning, then, becomes a process of transmission rather than an interactive exchange of ideas.

While research on broadcast news and the political learning of children found a correlation among the variables (with some qualifying factors), more specific studies of viewers' abilities to process television news present a different conclusion. In broad terms, this research has suggested that viewers learn little from watching the news. Robinson and Levy argue that television news "has a rather dismal record as a medium of information" (quoted in Buckingham 1999, 175). Gunter's research confirms this lack of comprehension. His findings conclude that viewers quickly forget the majority of what they see and often fail to understand it (1987, 35). Buckingham notes:

> In general, television news appears to be more effective in imparting information about key personalities than in communicating details about the main stories; and even when viewers can recall what happened or who was involved, they are much less able to retain information about the causes and consequences of events [176].

The research suggests that viewers do not concentrate on broadcast news; cognitive response is low or in some cases, nonexistent.

While the political socialization research suggests that television news has a significant role in the development of children's political understanding, the research on learning from television suggests that viewers have difficulty in remembering or understanding what they see. Buckingham argues that the conflict exists because both research methods focus on learning as individual cognition, and the social dimensions of learning are only addressed in terms of measurable demographic variables such as social class, gender and education, which are seen to influence cognition from the outside (*ibid.*). He proposes that this cognitivist emphasis causes a general neglect of the emotional dimension of news, in other words, its ability to entertain, outrage, upset, or calm the viewer (177). It would then follow that political drama programs that inherently produce these emotional attributes may be a logical area from which to examine the political socialization process.

Processing the Presidency

Television drama teaches lessons about the presidency through its narrative relationship to the affective components of political learning. Specifically, television's audiovisual format allows presidential information to be processed in particular ways. This process is related to Saenz's notion of the ways in which television functions as cultural practice. He argues:

"Culture," is an artifice characteristic of a particular historical moment when previously separate symbolic practices become subsumed under a new category of generalized knowledge, aesthetic appreciation, and meaning. Television's incitement to produce "culture" forms part of a larger, historically specific mode of social reproduction [1994, 579].

It is the contention of this book that the "culture" of political socialization, previously constituted by the "separate symbolic practices" of learned behaviors such as the pledge of allegiance and value systems based on feelings of loyalty and allegiance to democratic ideals, have been collated in *The West Wing*. The "generalized knowledge, aesthetic appreciation and meaning" generated by the series has incorporated fundamental socialization processes, which allow viewers to build a structure of feeling toward the president. This structure of feeling must also rely on a stored knowledge or "mental map" that allows the feelings learned in political socialization to be connected to the present. This "mental map" is the basis of information processing theory which suggests that specific schema develop early in a person's life that give him the ability to process current stimuli. Stored experience, or what Graber terms "stored historical knowledge" (2001, 15), enables a connection between the past and the present. When faced with the stimuli of the president, Americans must link his image with a stored mental schema to process the information effectively. Political socialization processes that are firmly rooted in emotional learning enhance this stored schema. The majority of Americans, in relating to their president, share what Saenz terms "a specific mode of social reproduction" of his image, and the television drama *The West Wing* facilitates this process through its themes and narrative devices. Viewers of the program are implicated in a moment of shared historical memory. They bring their political socialization to bear upon the televised experience. The cultural symbols of their collective memory unite to become part of a mental map that they may then apply to the reading of a particular television text.

In her work *Processing Politics*, Doris Graber (2001) proposes a new paradigm for understanding the connection between political learning and audiovisual media. Using information processing theory, she expands upon the existing research on schema formation and its relationship to audiovisual stimuli (Chase 1973; Bundesen 1990; Gazzaniga 1992; Eagly and Chaiken 1993; Kosslyn 1994; LeDoux 1996; Morton 1996; Calvin 1997; Gregory 1997; Carter 1998; Damasio 1999; Glynn 1999) and argues that critics of television base their judgments about the medium's benefits on the often poor recall of factual information by the average television news viewer. For Graber, the affective processes of learning have been overlooked, particularly in research that focuses on the factual recall of political information. The ability to process and interpret information, she suggests, also relies on the emotional connection between new stimuli and past experience. Information processing "takes advantage of stored experiences, linking the present with the past" (17). Applying Graber's argument to political social-ization research suggests that childhood learning of the president produces specific pathways that allow a person to connect future learning with his "stored historical knowledge" (15). In information processing theory, this knowledge is strongly associated with emotions because "people attach feelings and evaluations, such as liking and disliking, to objects and situa-tions at the moment of perception" (16). In addition, most people "create fresh images of their world primarily during their formative years and retain most of them throughout life, with only moderate amplifications and revisions in light of new experiences" (19). Templates are formed and used to process future learning. If, as the research suggests, these templates are emotional, then learning future information must also rely on a level of affec-tive processing.

Political socialization research claims that most people first negoti-ate the president as an affective figure. In turn, future information process-ing of the president would significantly depend on that past context. This does not mean that affective responses impair cognitive evaluations. As Graber explains: "When an emotionally charged image is processed, the brain simultaneously signals the center where emotions are processed as well as the centers where most reasoning occurs.... The various messages produced by emotional reactions are then processed cognitively" (36). Emo-tional responses to the president, then, are often accompanied by nonemo-tional thoughts. For example, as Graber notes, the emotions aroused by the president announcing that the country is going to war will also cause most people to consider the economic and financial issues associated with the decision (*ibid.*). Emotional responses (or learning) do not override rea-soning, rather emotions become an essential part of the ability to reason (Sniderman et al. 1991; Damasio 1994; Marcus et al. 2000). So how peo-ple come to feel about their president does not hinder their ability to cog-nitively evaluate him; rather, the two are intricately combined to work together.

However, for the majority of people, the fact that feelings come before cognitions when thinking about the president is significant because it priv-ileges audiovisual stimuli. In early childhood, before verbal learning begins in aural and written form, audiovisual learning is the most significant source of schema development (Graber 2001, 31). Images and sounds elicit emo-tions; pictures of starving children or a landscape devastated by war make people feel a certain way. This feeling may then be processed to connect to previously learned schema, which allow the person to combine feelings with thought. The audiovisual image of the president also arouses emotions, because as Graber notes: "pictures serve as cues for retrieving information stored in memory ... most messages contain symbols that tap into the audience's stored schemas to augment the meanings conveyed explicitly" (71). The president's image provides the cue to recall stored memories that read the president emotionally. Because the audiovisual image is the only image that most Americans will experience of their president, television, as the prime audiovisual source, becomes a significant force in how the president is continually learned throughout the life cycle. Television provides a vicarious experience of the president that can only be understood by referring to already stored schema. However, as Graber cautions, this interpretation is somewhat limited by the fact that the audiovisual message conveyed by television regarding an issue is selected by a journalist, who then controls the dimensions that are available for interpretation (82). But these dimensions often do not vary and ultimately contribute to a consistent picture. For example, in the majority of news broadcasts, the president is depicted in familiar ways. These audiovisual images arouse emotions in a viewer, who is then able to connect to past schema and interpret the image, most often in a way that reaffirms the early affective understanding of the president.

Schema is also important in Buchanan's understanding of public perceptions of the president. In his attempt to analyze how people organize their thinking about candidates and presidents, he turns to cognitive psychology and its understanding that all cognitions are schemas, or "the intelligence that selects and interprets the information that is admitted to the mind" (Goldman quoted in Buchanan 1987, 48). Buchanan uses a definition of schematic theory formulated by Kinder et al. that:

> depicts comprehension as a process in which new information is interpreted in terms of prior knowledge. Understanding is achieved by recognizing that new information represents a particular instance of a more general type. The news that President Carter has decided to invade Cuba, for example, may be interpreted by some as simply one more instance of a Democrat stumbling into war. Understanding the particular event comes about through the elicitation of a general interpretive framework or schema [1987, 49].

However, while Buchanan recognizes that schemas are cognitive structures, he stresses that they also utilize affective and normative stances as well. As he argues: "Schematic theories identify information as relevant for reasons of emotion and belief as well as for reasons of logic" (*ibid.*). This interaction of thinking with feeling and believing forms the basis of a citizen's reality perception. In Buchanan's conception, schemas form a more realistic explanation for how the public chooses among candidates and judges presidential candidates (*ibid.*). For the purposes of this book, schematic theory affords a more complete picture of how citizens learn the president and the subsequent role media plays in this understanding. While the interaction of cognition, affect and ideology are essential to schematic theory, this book sees the role of emotion as the superior theoretical component because the president is foremost an affective learning experience.

Interpreting reality through schemas, however, has limitations. Buchanan notes that the potential for error comes from schemas' tendency toward simplification (50). This simplification is necessary because people are able to process only a limited amount of information at any one time. Buchanan points to several studies that reveal the possibility of distortion in schema. One study argues that people focus on information that supports their previously held positions and filter out arguments that contradict them (51). Errors in comprehending and interpreting information may also be systematic. Buchanan points to Nisbett and Ross' research on attribution theory. Their work argues that:

> Attributions of abilities, opinions and responsibility for outcomes to others are supported by evidence that is vivid, concrete, emotionally or symbolically interesting and consistent with preconceptions. Rational or scientific evidence like statistics, facts and figures tends to be ignored [*ibid.*].

In their formation of presidential schemas, citizens tend to rely on information that is affective or emotionally satisfying to their previously established understanding of the president. As Buchanan argues, "in the assignment of praise or blame to presidents, strength of character and level of competence are likely to figure more prominently in evaluative conclusions than any mitigating circumstances, whether justified by the facts or not" (51). A citizen's affective schema formation often takes precedence over cognition when evaluating presidential performance.

To minimize distortion in schematic information processing, Buchanan calls for an aggressive examination of presidential theories "to ask what classes of information are stressed, ignored, created or distorted and why" (52). It is the contention of this book that the class of information most stressed in communicating about the president is that which focuses on the affective, thereby guiding schema formation to a specific conclusion. Presidency schemas work to reinforce preconceptions, affirm values and express feelings, in addition to registering and processing information (51). Schemas are the key to making sense of the presidency, both personally and socially.

CHAPTER TWO

Communicating the Presidency on Screen

The President on Film

The West Wing's emotional characterization of the presidency finds a contemporary parallel in cinematic representations of the president.[7] Early-twentieth-century newsreels gave the feature film audience a glimpse into the president's activities. In 1896, President McKinley made the first presidential film appearance, a practice he would continue over several years. Director James H. White showed McKinley at home in Canton, Ohio, in 1896, leaving church services in 1897 and reviewing the troops at the Pan-American Exposition in 1901. Both his inaugural speech in 1897 and funeral procession in 1901 were also captured on film. When television news services replaced the newsreel, Hollywood took over and the president was back in the cinema as the star of the show rather than a mere news highlight. Abraham Lincoln was the most popular president in film, having by 1989 been represented on-screen in 133 movies. Ulysses S. Grant was a distant second with 44 films, while George Washington, who, despite being the first president, only managed to win third place with 34 movies to his credit (Tooley and Schrof 1989, 62).

Lincoln is the subject of one of the earliest films to portray a president. In *The Birth of a Nation* (Griffith 1915), the president is depicted as an emotional figure. Griffith's film is a retelling of the history of the South, but the limited portrayal of Lincoln is significant. In the film, Griffith treats the president with reverence; Lincoln's first appearance on-screen is accompanied by the hymn "Glory, Glory, Alleluia." The scene ends with an emotional close-up of Lincoln, who is distressed and shown saying a prayer after he signs an executive order to enforce the Emancipation Proclamation. Throughout the film, Lincoln is portrayed as the benevolent and forgiving leader, in contrast to the vengeful Senator Stoneman, who wants to punish the South. Rogin notes that the contrast between the merciful president and the merciless senator serves to feminize Lincoln: "The maternal image of Lincoln was a common one, promoted by Lincoln himself. It drained the president of war's ferocity and anticipated his martyrdom" (1987, 199). This maternal characterization is carried through in Lincoln's assassination scene, where he is shown pulling a shawl around himself as he sits in Ford's Theatre, emphasising vulnerability and impending danger (212). Griffith positions Lincoln as the South's "greatest friend." He is not only a revered leader but also a personal companion who experiences pain and sorrow at the thought of his countrymen on the brink of war.

Emotional reverence toward the president is a theme more fully explored in the 1939 Frank Capra film, *Mr. Smith Goes to Washington*. In this film, Jefferson Smith, a newly appointed, idealistic young Senator discovers that he is the pawn of manipulative politicians. He heroically takes to the Senate floor and speaks until he collapses from exhaustion, his actions restoring faith in a corrupt system. The president, while not represented in this film directly, is seen through the eyes of Mr. Smith as the symbol of all that is good and right. Interestingly, President Lincoln is the focus of his emotional attachment. After a sequence of Smith visiting various presidential monuments, he ends at the Lincoln Memorial, which he describes with childlike excitement. "There he is ... just looking straight at you as you come up those steps, just sitting there like he was waiting for someone...." Mr. Smith relates to the president on a purely emotional level. In a refrain of Griffith's "greatest friend" conceptualization, Lincoln becomes Mr. Smith's companion, someone who is waiting for him to fulfill his destiny.

From the Second World War to the end of the 1960s, Hollywood continued the reverential depiction of the president. Wise and selfless, they were embodiments of strong moral virtue. Perhaps the epitome of this conception was the film *Fail-Safe* (Lumete 1964) in which the president, after an accidental bombing by an American B-52 on a large Soviet city, orders a nuclear strike on New York City in order to avert a full-scale Soviet retaliation. The moral fortitude of the president is made even more poignant as the audience learns that he is aware that the first lady is in New York and will be killed. In *Fail-Safe*, the president is the right man doing the right thing.

While *Fail-Safe* gave audiences a righteous president willing to make the ultimate personal sacrifice to save the world, another film of that decade was absurd in its depiction of presidential character. *Dr. Strangelove (Or: How I Learned to Stop Worrying and Love the Bomb)* (Kubrick 1964) portrays a juvenile American president who lacks critical thought. Faced with a rogue general who has ordered a nuclear strike on Russia because he believes the Communists are conspiring to "sap and impurify" American's bodily fluids, president Merkin Muffley, along with his advisers and the Russians, attempts to avert the disaster. Unlike the president in *Fail-Safe*, President Muffley is "well meaning but ineffectual" (Christensen 1987, 116). He is neither strong nor a man of action. Rather his pleasant tone and mild-mannered concern in the face of nuclear holocaust make him a ridiculous figure as his telephone conversation to the Russian Premier demonstrates:

> Clear and plain and coming through fine.... I'm coming through fine too hey. Well then as you say, we're both coming through fine.... Well it's good too that you're fine and I'm fine.... I agree with you, it's great to be fine.

The character maintains this attitude throughout the film, describing the General who started the crisis as doing "a silly thing." In another scene the president shouts: "You can't fight in here. This is the war room," when talks break down among the assembled advisers. The absurdity of president Muffley is successful because his actions and demeanor are in direct opposition to what an American audience understands a president to be. Ultimately, the character bolsters Americans' vision of a president by showing them what he is not. President Muffley may be easily dismissed as a farce that allows the audience's vision of the American presidency to go unchallenged.

As the Vietnam War escalated and ultimately failed to gain public support, and the lies of Watergate were exposed, the real life president became the wrong man doing the wrong thing. Film abandoned its reverential representations and began to depict the president in a harsher light. *All the President's Men* (Pakula 1976) did more than expose the corruption of the Nixon administration; it constructed the president as a sinister force, an untrustworthy, deceptive leader who would remain in power through lies and manipulation if not for two intrepid investigative journalists. While Nixon is depicted as unsympathetic, he is still subject to an emotional reading. His failures are failures of character. His values are warped, and the audience is encouraged to connect with the president by recognizing that he should be the opposite.

While the president was represented in various films of the 1980s, he was often a minor character. Perhaps American society was content to have an actor for president who often brought the movies to his office. President Ronald Reagan, former Hollywood actor and California governor, once famously quipped, "Go ahead. Make my day," promising to veto Congress when they threatened to raise taxes. The line, as many people recognize, is spoken by the character Dirty Harry in the film *Sudden Impact* (Eastwood 1983). In a recreation of one of his more famous roles, Reagan was often quoted as saying, "Do it for the Gipper," whether it was addressing the Olympic athletes in 1984 or urging people to vote Republican (Rogin 1987, 15). Rogin argues that President Reagan often merged his on-screen identity with his off-screen identity ultimately producing "Reagan the image" (3). Cannon suggests that Reagan's entire political life from governor to president was, in fact, shaped by his acting experience. He writes:

> Asked what kind of governor he would be, Reagan quipped, "I don't know, I've never played a governor." And when he left the White House twenty-three years later and came home to California he told Landon Parvin, "Some of my critics over the years have said that I became president because I was an actor who knew how to give a good speech. I suppose that's not too far wrong. Because an actor knows two important things—to be honest in what he's doing and to be in touch with the audience. That's not bad advice for a politician either. My actor's instinct simply told me to speak the truth as I saw it and felt it" [2000, 20].

The fact that Reagan believed in speaking what he felt (more often than what he thought) to the American public as their president is significant because it established a rhetorical style that relied on stories.

For Reagan, his persuasive abilities and success as a two-term president strongly relied on emotional rhetoric often steeped in remembered film plots. These fictional stories found an easy alliance with the symbols and myths of American politics. Reagan "derived his most potent rhetorical symbols from the apparently less exalted sources of our daily lives" (Erickson 1985, 4–5). Reagan's language was the language of film and television. His references were more than a construction of image; they served to connect him to the people through a shared cultural experience. On an emotional level, the president was the same as anyone who went to the movies.

Reagan reminded the public that the president could connect with them through popular culture. While the success of this relationship could be seen to be the catalyst for future presidents embracing nontraditional mediums of communication with the electorate,[8] it was not the first time a president used popular media to reach the people. From Franklin Roosevelt's fireside chats to Harry Truman's numerous addresses, presidents have employed radio broadcasts and television to communicate with the public, often using the lead-in of a popular program to maintain audience numbers. Reagan's rhetoric, as with other presidents' speeches, attempted to reassure the public and "make them feel part of a greater enterprise" (Cannon 2000, 96). Similar to any leader, he used emotion to persuade the public to accept his message. The fact that his narratives often originated from the fantasy of film, television and folklore resulted in a collective experience for the public; one which the majority of voters at the time chose to enthusiastically embrace.

The large number of president-centered films in the 1990s focused on the personal. The president was either a fantasy hero, capable of taking on extreme odds and winning through physical and mental superiority and a moral value system, or a malevolent figure who was punished for a corrupt value system. The films of the 1990s showed audiences the personal side of the president, while maintaining a reverence for the institution.

In the film *Air Force One* (Peterson 1997), the president is family man and action hero. When a group of terrorists highjack Air Force One, the president decides to stay onboard, protect his family and single-handedly thwart the attack. The motivation for the president's behavior comes from his desire to prove himself worthy of the office. As one hostage remarks: "It makes me so proud, Mr. President, that you stuck with us ... whatever happens." The president's choice is also constructed as right and moral. Unlike the terrorist leader, who is "a monster" regardless of his grievances, the president is "a great man," whose killing of several highjackers is always in self-defense. Even when engaging in morally suspect behavior, the president is redeemed through a higher value system.

Independence Day (Emmerich 1996) also depicts the president as action hero. However, this time he is fighting against alien invasion rather than earthly terrorists. Again, the president inserts himself directly into the fight. He takes to the skies as a fighter pilot, shooting alien ships before they attack Earth. While the film depicts the aliens as attacking major cities throughout the world, thus making the fight an international one, the only world leader that stands with the public is the U.S. president. He delivers rousing, emotional speeches to invigorate the troops of men. He is their leader who will deliver victory alongside them because that is the right and moral action.

In *Mars Attacks!* (Burton 1996), the president is again confronted with alien invasion. Unlike *Independence Day*, however, the president mistakenly chooses to welcome the Martian invaders rather than fight them. A comedic look at the importance of presidential image, *Mars Attacks!* has the president turn to Jerry, his press secretary, rather than his military advisers, for advice on handling the invasion. Consequently, the suggested strategy is for the president to take over the prime-time news broadcasts—a suggestion the president enthusiastically embraces:

> We'll go all needy on this. I'll wear my blue Armani suit. And Jerry, I'll need a good speech—statesman-like historical and yet warm and neighborly. Abraham Lincoln meets *Leave It to Beaver.* You know, that sort of thing.

While *Air Force One* and *Independence Day* position the president as moral action hero, *The American President* (Reiner 1995) frames the president as moral common man. In this film, the president is popular and respected among both his staff and the voters. He is willing to make political compromises, to "fight the fights we can win." A widower and single father, he romantically pursues a lobbyist in a way that makes him a regular guy. The president's romantic relationship, however, quickly comes under attack from his political opposition, who labels him a promiscuous womanizer. The strategy is successful, and the president's popularity drops. Fighting back, he refuses to be politically and personally compromised and delivers a speech declaring his passion for both the lobbyist and his job. Affectively, the film celebrates the presidency by finding a balance between private man and public leader.

A few films of this decade chose to recreate the lives of real presidents by focussing on the personal behind the presidential. Both the films *Nixon* (Stone 1995) and *Truman* (Pierson 1995) present a study of the man behind the office, particularly emphasizing the role of character in each man's struggle to find a place in history. Oliver Stone's interpretation of the presidency of Richard Nixon not only deals with the president's political life and choices but also concentrates on his personal relationships, ambitions and obsessions. *Truman* uses a similar focus on the personal to recreate the legacy of a president. While each film approaches its subject in diverse ways, both narratives ultimately uphold the presidential myth by creating an emotional connection between the memory of a president and the audience/citizen.

The films of the 1990s also showed the public a darker side of the president. In *Absolute Power* (Eastwood 1997), the president is characterized as morally bankrupt and wholly unredeemable. The plot revolves around a thief who witnesses a sexual indiscretion between the president and the wife of the president's close friend. The president is drunk, the affair becomes violent and secret service agents kill the woman. The resulting cover-up eventually leads to the president's death. Throughout this film, the president is never a sympathetic figure, thereby allowing the audience to distance themselves from his corruption. In turn, the presidency and all it stands for remains intact, and the man who disgraced its values is fairly punished.

Wag the Dog (Levinson 1997) is yet another film that depicts the sexual indiscretions of the president. Here, the president is caught in a compromising position with an underage girl. The situation is further compounded with the forthcoming election. In order to distract the voters from the scandal, the president's staff hires a Hollywood director to manufacture a war. The president in this film representation is only seen indirectly through his often out of focus appearances on television. He is utterly dismissed as a character and viewed merely as a product to be manipulated. Again the president is characterized as corrupt but reduced to such an insignificant state that the values of the institution are protected.

Presidents in film have been depicted as men of action, righteousness, moral fortitude and in the last decade, men capable of moral deceit. The common thread running through all these characterizations has been a personal one. The president is seen from a position of emotion. His inner thoughts and feelings have been either exposed and exalted or exposed and decried as unworthy. When the president fails to show remorse for morally unacceptable behaviour he is justly punished. More important, he is depicted as emotionally remote. The audience is not allowed to feel sympathetic. It is only when the president shows courage that the audience is able to connect with him emotionally, thereby protecting the presidency despite the man.

Broadcasting the President

The development of presidential communication and the rise of broadcasting in the United States share an intimate history. The first significant use of broadcasting in presidential politics was in 1923 with a speech by President Warren Harding. Delivered in St. Louis but simultaneously broadcast in Washington and New York, the speech marked the first time a radio network had been assembled to carry the president's voice across the nation. The speech "signaled a new era in broadcasting which would profoundly change the structure of radio and television in America" (Foote 1990, 1). Not only did the speech weaken the concept of localism on which American radio was built, but it also meant that the new national focus for broadcasting service would strengthen the presidency. As Foote explains, both broadcasting and the presidency significantly benefited from the new relationship:

A politician whose voice commanded attention in every corner of such a vast land simultaneously could build a strong national constituency. Conversely, a strong presidency contributed to a strong national broadcasting system. presidential speeches created a demand and the president provided one of the few sources of programming that could unite American interests.... Broadcasters could also use the presidency as a springboard for building and maintaining a network of radio stations before the American people ever saw a need for such a strong national system [2].

Network radio broadcasts gave the president unprecedented access to the nation, and broadcasters used this newfound power to secure their future development.

As the development of radio spread a network of stations across the country, the amount of airtime devoted to presidential and governmental communication steadily increased. Most Americans, however, still regarded the radio networks as entertainment rather than news outlets and the president became the key component in the broadcasters' efforts to raise their status (Foote, 8). Transmitting the voice of the president brought prestige. As former CBS president Frank Stanton commented, the networks were eager to broadcast the president of the United States "because it was a recognition of radio's place in the scheme of things" (quoted in Foote, 9). Carrying presidential and congressional speeches positioned radio in the role of public service provider. This position quickly developed into a highly competitive race as each network was eager to be seen as the nation's most serious news source. Washington became the center of news for the networks, and the president became their most valuable commodity. In courting the president, the networks virtually guaranteed him automatic access.

The issue of access reached a turning point with President Roosevelt's 1936 Sate of the Union Address. William Paley, president of the Columbia Broadcasting System (CBS), refused airtime to the Republican opposition.[9] Halberstam argues that the consequences of Paley's refusal meant that broadcasting "would be to an uncommon degree, a presidential vehicle" (1979, 37). Paley's decision meant that now the president had unchallenged access to the most influential means of communication in the country. As a result, by the end of the Roosevelt administration, every president had gained a right of access to all radio networks simultaneously, without worrying about a direct rebuttal from the opposition party (Foote 1990, 21).[10]

The rise of network radio not only cemented the president's importance in the everyday lives of the public but shaped his message to them as well. While he had to be responsible to maintain a consistent national message, his was often the only message. For the American constituency, listening to a single political voice, the president strengthened his position as the focal point of government. Through the development of network radio, patterns of presidential access were firmly established, as were Americans' expectations of presidential communication because entertainment was the lead-in to the primetime president. People expected the government to communicate on the same channel as their favorite programs. Politics became integrated into leisure, a trend that would resurface in the rise of presidential television.

The first regular television service in the United States began with NBC in the spring of 1939. As with radio, television looked to the president to garner prestige among the public. The policy of automatic access that the president enjoyed with radio continued with network television. As Foote notes: "The radio networks had been so accustomed to putting FDR on the air and had benefited so much from doing so that executives saw no reason to make radical policy changes with television" (25). As a result, the television networks facilitated President Truman's transition to the new broadcast medium. It was Truman's speaking style that began to change the way television approached presidential broadcasting and ultimately ensured future presidents' position in the public sphere.

Unlike Roosevelt, President Truman used his broadcasting opportunities to inform rather than emotionally persuade the public. Each of Truman's speeches covered a specific topic that allowed the news divisions to assess each broadcast on the basis of news value. Presidents continued to receive automatic coverage but networks saw their role in carrying the speeches less about public service and more about reporting the "big" story (Foote, 26). Using this logic, NBC and ABC Mutual decided not to carry President Truman's speech to a Democratic dinner in March 1952, fearing it "might be too political in an election year or that it would set off 'equal time' demands" (Fixx 1972, 248). As a result, CBS was the only network to broadcast the surprise announcement by President Truman that he would not be seeking reelection, setting off a wave of criticism by the *New York Times* over television's lack of "flexibility and alertness" in news coverage (cited in Foote 1990, 26).

The repercussions of this event would be felt throughout television broadcasting. The possibility of missing newsworthy presidential announcements shaped television coverage of the office to the extent that in future years the "networks would waste countless hours covering the trivia of the presidency.... From that time on, the president was always news" (Foote, 27). The combination of historically accepted automatic access and the fear of missing a newsworthy event created a broadcasting climate that effectively came under the president's control. While news coverage of the president was under the media's control, addresses to the nation were under the president's control. This power would be used to great advantage by future presidents, who would continue to exploit television to their benefit. One of the first politicians to successfully capitalize on television's potential to reach the viewers' emotions was Richard Nixon.

Comstock suggests that "the story of television's role in politics glibly told is the story of Richard Nixon" (1991, 94). The story of Nixon and television begins with a financial scandal and a cocker spaniel. In the middle of the 1952 Republican presidential campaign, investigative journalists reported that a secret fund had been established by a group of California businessmen for the campaign expenses of Richard Nixon, the nominee for Vice-President. In response, Nixon announced that he would offer a full explanation in a half-hour television broadcast. The speech, which aired on September 23, 1952, was a conventional attack on the opposition's policies framed with emotional appeals to the audience. Reciting an extensive list of his finances, Nixon lamented that his integrity and honesty were being questioned. The underlying effect was a sympathetic one; he was just like anyone in the audience who had to pay a mortgage and support a young family. Perhaps the most enduring image of the speech centered on the family pet:

> One other thing I should probably tell you, because if I don't they will probably be saying this about me, too. We did get something, a gift, after the election. A man down in Texas heard Pat on the radio mention that our two youngsters would like to have a dog, and, believe it or not, the day we left before this campaign trip we got a message from Union Station in Baltimore, saying they had a package for us. We went down to get it. You know what it was? It was a little cocker spaniel dog, in a crate that he had sent all the way from Texas, black and white, spotted, and our little girl Tricia, the six year-old, named it Checkers. And you know, the kids, like all kids, loved the dog, and I just want to say this, right now, that regardless of what they say about it, we are going to keep it [*Nixon Library Online*].

The broadcast concluded with Nixon appealing to the public to write and tell the Republican National Committee whether they wished him to remain on or be dropped from the ticket. The outcome was more than favorable, with the national committee claiming that the response "ran 350 to 1" to keep him on the ticket (Lang and Lang 1984, 20).

Nixon's direct communication with the voters led to a new era in campaigning. An issue of political morality was transformed into one of personal honesty (Lang and Lang, 21). The viewers' responses to Nixon's declaration of the "truth" was often based on their feelings toward him, as press reports of the time reveal: "The people who own dogs like I do are for Nixon. That story about the dog for his children made me love him," while another commented: "Nixon was so utterly sincere that no one could doubt his honesty" (*ibid.*). Issues became lost in impressions. What began as an investigation into possible corrupt campaign contributions ended with the televised image of an honorable all-American political candidate and the family pet. Nixon's future encounters with the medium would prove to be equally important for the relationship between presidential politics and television.

Nixon, of course, was not the first politician to use television, but his encounters with the medium mark significant moments in the transformation of political communication. For Comstock, Nixon's "Checkers" speech revealed what politics and television could achieve. In addition to the medium being used to make dramatic and direct appeals to the public, a strategy that Comstock notes future politicians with money for air time would increasingly use, television was significant in another way:

> The medium was used by many viewers to evaluate the character or whole man, a response made possible among all the media that reach the home only by the audiovisual characteristics of television [1991, 95].

Powerful pictures augmented powerful political rhetoric. Nixon's relationship with television demonstrated that presidential performance was important to Americans and in turn, a key to electoral success.

While the Eisenhower/Nixon ticket won the presidential election, television secured its place as the nation's premiere media outlet. Between 1952 and 1956, television sets were the must-have item for American households. The power and pervasiveness of television increased the president's dependence on it as a means of communication with the public. Eisenhower would not only telecast his addresses, but he would also broadcast parts of his news conferences and cabinet meetings to reach the growing audience. His choices accelerated the rise of presidential television (Foote 1990, 28). President Kennedy would continue to nurture this growth by proving to be an accomplished television performer in both his early campaign debate with Nixon as well as the telecasts of his live speeches and press conferences while in office. However, it was President Johnson who dominated the television networks. In his first year in office, he appeared on air more times than Kennedy had in three years and more than Eisenhower had in eight (Minow et al. 1973, 44). Still dependent on the president for news, the networks consistently gave in to President Johnson's (often unpredictable) demands for airtime, which gave him unprecedented exposure. Audiences would see the president interrupt the network news in 1965, only to speak for six minutes. Later, he would refuse to start an address on the hour and broke into the last five minutes of the popular show *Bonanza* (Foote 1990, 36). As they did with early radio broadcasts, the American audience came to associate presidential communication not only with news but with prime-time entertainment as well.

Throughout the next two decades, presidents continued to take advantage of their easy access to television with varying degrees of success. Both Presidents Ford and Carter would encounter powerful networks at a time when the presidency was considered weak. Their relations with television networks were often adversarial, with the broadcasters sometimes denying access, claiming that the speeches were not newsworthy. The networks, while growing more sophisticated in their news practices, saw their dominance of the airwaves weaken with the introduction of cable television in the mid–1980s. Audience share declined dramatically as viewers turned to new outlets for entertainment and news programming. The network prime-time share dropped from 91 percent in 1976-77 to 67 percent in 1988-89 (Foote, 152). Presidential television also suffered. As the networks lost their grip on entertainment programming, the audiences for presidential addresses also dropped (Foote, 153). The American public was turning to alternative programs outside the network. No longer able to depend on the lead-in audience, presidential addresses lost large numbers of viewers. Even President Reagan, "the great communicator," was not immune to the effects. His State of the Union speeches (when audiences are traditionally high) dropped from an 84 share in 1981 to just under a 50 percent audience share in 1989, meaning that more than 30 million viewers had defected to other programming during his presidency (*ibid.*). While the past decades may have seen presidential speechmaking lose its share of the prime-time audience, the president's relationship to broadcast media, (while at times adversarial) remains a significant aspect of his effort to lead public opinion. The campaign is the time when this effort becomes most important.

Campaigning for the Presidency

Research on the media and presidential campaigns is substantial. Scholars have focused on specific campaigns (McGinniss 1969; Hofstetter 1976; Wattenberg 1984; Robinson 1981, 1987; Robinson and Sheehan 1983; Robinson and Ranney 1984; Adams 1984; Nelson 1985; Alger 1987; Kessel 1988; Stempel and Windhauser 1991; Buchanan 1991; Denton 1994, 1998; Cavanugh 1995; Just et al. 1996;) as well as analyzing the broader connections between the media and the race for the presidency (Weaver et al. 1981;

Patterson 1982; Joslyn 1984; Arterton 1984; Schram 1987; Seib 1987; Graber 1989; Alger 1989; Taylor 1990; McCubbins 1992; Diamond and Silverman 1995). Campaign advertising has also received significant scholarly attention (Patterson and McClure 1976; Jamieson 1984; Kaid et al. 1986; Diamond and Bates 1988; Kern 1989; Garramone et al. 1990; Johnson-Cartee and Copeland 1991; West 1997; Thurber et al. 2000; Kaid and Johnston 2000). While many of the studies take an effects approach and try to discover how voters' choices are influenced by media coverage of a presidential campaign, others examine the ways in which politicians and media interact to shape the information made available to the citizen.

While the media have played an important role in presidential politics from its earliest years, the recent shift from party-centered to media-based political campaigns is a significant development. Patterson argues that this transition was the direct result of several changes in the nature of communication. In the early 1900s through 1968, close to one-third of the national convention delegates were chosen through direct primaries; the remaining delegates were chosen in state conventions where the selection rules advantaged party leaders (1980, 4). However, during the 1960s, media began covering the primaries with an intensity that legitimized them "as the democratic way to make choices" (Rubin quoted in Patterson 1980, 4). Patterson suggests that "whatever their contribution to the change, the media, as a result, have become the focus of the candidates' nominating campaigns" (*ibid.*). Primaries have since become the key to securing the presidential nomination, which means that a candidate must use the media to reach statewide voters. Meetings with the party leadership have been replaced by attempts to persuade the voter through the local media outlet (*ibid.*).

According to Patterson's argument, another factor that led to the media's increased role in presidential campaigns was a change in the structure of media outlets (*ibid.*). During the early years of the media's development, the party was responsible for communicating the candidate's message to the public. The print media, with its large number of local papers was not a suitable means of gaining national exposure (*ibid.*). Television also failed to provide the coverage a candidate needed as the network news, in the 1950s, had limited resources and often relied on the reports of print media, which usually focused on the events of news rather than the newsmakers (Patterson, 5). The change to thirty-minute newscasts in the 1960s, however, meant that the networks began to focus on national politics and personalities, which Robinson notes, met the publicity needs of presidential candidates (*ibid.*). Hoping to get a place on the evening news, candidates began to structure their campaign activities around the needs of television broadcasters.

In addition to the structural changes experienced by media outlets, Patterson notes that a decline in partisanship may also be responsible for an increase in the media-centric campaign. He argues that erosion of partisan loyalties has caused voters to increase their dependence on the media as a means of information (*ibid.*). Votes are no longer guaranteed along party lines, making them "less predictable, more volatile" and "more sensitive to short-term influences, such as an election's issues and personalities, which are transmitted largely by the media" (Patterson, 6). The media, then, becomes more influential in the voting process, which requires the candidate to increase his dependence on broadcast and print outlets.

The decline of party politics in the face of the media campaign is often cited as having serious consequences for American democracy. By stressing the candidate as an individual over the candidate as a representative of the party, the media campaign has been blamed for creating a superficial voting public who is ideologically uninformed and susceptible to shallow political decisions based on the character traits of candidates. Aldrich suggests that the technology of television has precipitated this change in presidential campaigning because without it the candidate could not create the brand name that is necessary to win voting coalitions (1992, 64). However, McCubbins argues that brand names (which he defines as "a cue or signal that conveys information about the quality of a product [candidate]") are the result of experience rather than television as Aldrich's argument suggests (1992, 31). He observes that in politics, brand names have a long history:

> For example, nearly every voter at the time knew something about George Washington, Thomas Jefferson and Andrew Jackson. Indeed, their brand names were so strong they still operate today. Most Americans probably could not begin to name specific policies advocated by Jefferson, but they could say something about what he stood for; moreover, they might know something about his personal life, in much the same way that Americans have some knowledge of politicians' personal lives today [*ibid.*].

While McCubbins' argument does support the point that television is not the catalyst for producing the brand name phenomenon in the candidate-centered campaign, he fails to note that media still has a significant role in the process. As Heale's work suggests, voters in Washington's age knew something about him through campaign biographies. Not every voter was able to have an experience of Washington outside that which the print media provided for them. For Americans today, Washington's brand name might have been created through political socialization outside of media, but it lasts, in part, because media perpetuates it.

Mickelson suggests that television has become the driving and motivating force behind the transformation in campaign methodology despite the contributions of technologies such as the computer, fax machine and airplane. He argues:

> Trips are planned around television opportunities. Direct mail calls attention to television appearances. Campaign statements are timed to coincide with television deadlines.... It has compelled campaign managements to devote more care to strategic planning and more attention to budgets. It has put a premium on fund raising [1989, 4].

In addition to these developments, Mickelson suggests that television has come to dominate the choice of candidates as well, "who increasingly are being selected on the basis of their skills in performing before the camera" (5). These skills would strengthen the earlier personalization of political candidates that radio broadcasts had started.

While the presidential campaign of 1952 saw television replace the traditional whistle-stop as the most effective method to reach voters, it still remained secondary to print media in the view of candidates and campaign managers (Mickelson, 55). Candidates used television for thirty-minute paid speeches rather than the evening news broadcasts, while political correspondents filed reports that resembled radio "think pieces" (*ibid.*). The success of television's New Hampshire primary coverage was forgotten, despite the popular response it received. A television critic working for the *New York Times* urged candidates to recognize the lessons learned from the 1952 telecast:

> Up to now, they have thought of television primarily in terms of guest appearances of the purchase of time over which they would have control.... But the New Hampshire primary showed that television's complementary role of independent reporter may be of even greater significance.... The most rewarding and absorbing film "shots" from New Hampshire were the informal and unprepared scenes which caught the human equation in the raw and told their own stories in terms of character and personality [Gould quoted in Fixx 1972, 17].

Despite the candidates' slow acceptance of television's power to shape their campaigns, television of the 1950s was instrumental in reshaping the process of running for public office (Mickelson 1989, 55). In a sense, the 1950s saw the birth of the media campaign. As Mickelson argues, television during those years "focused attention on the primaries, showed vast numbers of Americans how exciting a national political convention can be, and furnished close-ups of the fall campaign that brought a new dimension to politics" (*ibid.*). In the following decade, television began to solidify its position in presidential campaigning. Various technological and economic innovations created a more attractive climate for politicians and broadcasters alike as each saw their advantages increase through the television environment.[11]

The partnership between television and presidential campaigns is a complex one. In-depth critical analysis of the relationship is beyond the scope of this book, yet it is important to consider television's early role in framing the president for the American people. Television dictated that presidential campaigns conform to the expectations of its audience, who viewed the medium as primarily entertainment. Campaign managers therefore responded by packaging the candidate into appealing programming formats. Public appearances were carefully choreographed to provide the maximum emotional impact, the sound bite dominated the newscasts and a candidate who appeared polished and personable won the attention of the public. Symbols rather than information became important, a development which can be traced throughout decades of presidential campaigning. The 1960 presidential debate between Richard Nixon and John Kennedy is often cited as the moment that the television image gained a prominent place in the American political mind. In a commonly repeated anecdote, the people who heard the debate on the radio are said to have believed Nixon won while those who watched the event on television gave Kennedy the victory, due reportedly to his more impressive appearance.

President Reagan's reelection campaign in 1984 also relied on the impact of the television image. Campaign managers for President Reagan believed in the power of the image over everything else. In the television program *Campaign! Forty Years of TV in American Elections* (Channel 4, 1988), American network news anchor Lesley Stahl recounts a story in which she reported on the Reagan campaign's masterful use of television.[12] The report, using images of Reagan from the news footage of his four years in office, criticizes the campaign for manipulating the public through pictures. Stahl encourages the audience to become aware of the reelection strategy (which was to show President Reagan in patriotic settings or actively engaging in activities that would seem to defy his age). Contrary to Stahl's expectations, the response to the story from a senior White House official was praise. In her words, he commented: "When you run powerful pictures of him before flags and balloons and smiling children, the public doesn't hear you" (*ibid.*). During the 1988 election campaign between Vice-President George Bush and Michael Dukakis, a news organization was again reporting on the seemingly transparent strategy of the candidates' manipulation of the television picture. The British news broadcaster Channel 4 ran a story that showed how the Bush campaign's constant placing of the vice president at events "where he appeared associated with weapons, soldiers and patriotism" was more appropriate to an audience's expectations of political television (Evans 1988). In contrast, Dukakis was shown meeting small crowds in the rain and accepting gifts from local associations in his home state of Massachusetts. The reporter comments that Dukakis is engaging in "small time campaigning that gets governors elected but doesn't win the White House and doesn't provide exciting TV images" (*ibid.*).

While news stories such as these show that broadcasters are aware of a presidential candidate's manipulation of the photo opportunity, their participation in televising the image perpetuates the mutually beneficial relationship between television and presidential politics. Broadcasters want dynamic images of candidates; candidates need to present themselves in a visually enticing way that will ensure coverage of their message. Audiences have been conditioned to receive their presidents in the environment of entertainment. If, as was the case in 1988, presidential candidates want to compete with the Olympics and the World Series, they need to be entertaining, a response that is encouraged as much by the audience as it is by television. Rosen notes:

> It's possible to enjoy the campaign in a way that has nothing to do with politics. It's possible, for example, to react to the candidates as you would TV hosts or new characters introduced into a sitcom. And it's also possible to look at the campaign as a sporting event where somebody slips up, somebody makes a crucial mistake, somebody scores. And certainly the networks and journalists invite that response as much as a political one [Evans, 1988].

A presidential candidate appears on television in prime time in order to reach the largest share of the audience. This strategy, however, also means that the candidate is intimately associated with entertainment and must present himself on the terms that the prime-time audience expects.

In the program *Television and the Presidency*, historian Theodore White suggests that the relationship between the medium and the institution mixes "reality with art and entertainment with history" (1980). Broadcast media's role in the presidency has amplified the public's relationship to their leader by changing the nature of political communication. Radio brought the disembodied president into the family living room; television made him whole. Television changed the nature of the election process by transforming campaigns and conventions. Nominating conventions grew from "deliberate bodies choosing candidates" to spectacles where audiences became spectators in the "orchestrated anointments" of a chosen individual (Comstock 1991, 101). Media strategists rather than party bosses developed intricate campaign choreography wherein every movement the candidate makes is conducted for the network news. In an interview for *Television and the Presidency*, Jody Powell, former Press Secretary to President Carter, noted that a candidate's schedule is "controlled more by how it will look on the news that night than any other single factor" (1980). In controlling a candidate's schedule, television also succeeded in controlling the candidate. Winning the presidency became as much about the projection of image as it did about policy initiatives or party allegiances. Television, as Comstock observes, "has become a larger part of the story" (1991, 103).

The President in Television Drama and Comedy

While presidents used television to secure their place in history, television mined the presidential past for dramatic stories. If, as Paterson suggests, television drama production "offers viewers national images and myths" (1998, 62), then its relationship with the presidency would seem to be a natural one. The president is both an image that symbolizes the country and a mythic representation of the nation's history. The battles and triumphs of presidents were recreated in much of television's early drama production and continued throughout its development as the live, prestige dramas of the 1950s gave way to the miniseries and docudramas of later decades. As with their theatrical counterparts, these productions recreated both the personal and the public lives of the presidents. While many of these depictions are limited by the creative treatment of facts and one-dimensional characterizations, others are credited with creating more faithful portraits of the nation's leaders. However, even television's complex treatments of presidential personalities routinely depend on narratives that offer simple associations. In his work on the PBS production of *The Adams Chronicles*, Scott Stoddart suggests that the Adams' family was constructed as a symbol of national values. Specifically, the production's creators "engage the audience in a saga of human proportions, rather than in a history lesson peopled with an aloof patriot and his family" (2003, 33). In turn, the production's thirteen-episode structure is used to "equate the Adams family with America—the start of the Adams saga is the start of America" (*ibid.*). This type of basic frame is employed throughout television's representations of various presidents. Despite the notion that "images of President Lincoln embody our nation's mixed historical memory about the meaning of the Civil War" (Schwartz quoted in Rommel-Ruiz 2003, 77), the president is most often simplified as an honest and humble leader whose talented oratory skills and paternal guidance freed the slaves and united the country. Washington is portrayed in similar terms. Although scholars suggest that he is "one of the most misunderstood and elusive men in history" (Leibiger 2003, 20), the first president is most often depicted as a heroic military leader whose inspirational character forged a nation. Television's treatments of twentieth century presidents rely on equally basic frames. Truman's plainspoken image shaped many of his television representations, while Kennedy's image as a young "idealist warrior" (Herman 2003, 309) (who was also prone to commit marital infidelity) informed many of the television narratives depicting his presidency. By defining presidents in basic terms, television drama perpetuates a simple approach to experiencing the presidential image that often relies on the audience's emotional knowledge of the officeholder. While these myths are a product of more than the television experience, they are sustained by its retelling.

While television's drama formats recreate the presidency's triumphs and tragedies with basic and affective frames of presidential character, its comedy formats provide outlets for satire, parody and (in recent times), a candidate's self-promotion. On June 3, 1992, presidential candidate Bill Clinton appeared on the late-night talk show the *Arsenio Hall Show*. Eventually sharing the stage with his wife Hillary, he reflected on the impact of the recent L.A. riots and discussed his plans for "reconnecting people to the American dream." In a memorable moment, he joined the studio band and played the saxophone, a performance that was consistent with his attempts to court young voters. In 2000, presidential candidates Al Gore and George Bush joined talk show hosts Oprah Winfrey, Jay Leno and David Letterman, where they shared good-natured jokes and their campaign messages. Both candidates also entertained audiences on *Saturday Night Live*, spoofing themselves in the lead-up to the 2000 election. With these appearances, the candidates revisited a long association between the presidency and television's comedy formats.

Presidents have been the subjects of television variety programming since the early days of broadcasting, most notably on the *Jack Paar Program*, broadcast on NBC from 1962–1965. Parr's show featured impressionist Vaughn Meader, known for his impersonations of Kennedy. In a skit for a 1962 broadcast, Meader answered random questions from the studio audience as if he were Kennedy at a press conference. The joke is later replayed in a sketch where Meader is seated at the Kennedy family dinner table. During the course of the meal, the "president" takes mundane questions from his family, including wife Jackie and brother Bobby, and answers them with the same tone and formality he would use with the press. The scene's humor comes from a gentle mocking of the president's distinctive accent rather than an attempt at biting political or personal commentary.

While not strictly satirical, the early sketches of Kennedy on the *Jack Paar Program* offered a start to television's irreverent look at the president. The trend would be continued and amplified by another comedy-variety program broadcast in the 1960s called *That Was the Week That Was*. Presenting topical satire in the form of one-liners, songs and skits, the program debuted on NBC in 1964. Originally a BBC program, the American version of TW3 (as it was popularly known) featured David Frost as a principle performer. Sharper than earlier comic treatments of presidential politics, TW3 offered satirical sketches of presidential candidates that often combined comments from studio performers with footage of the candidates. In one skit on the April 20, 1965, broadcast, the show's performers suggest that the answer to the Republican Party's 1965 attempt to change its image is to put on a topical humor television show with Barry Goldwater and Richard Nixon as hosts. Eventually, the political satire of TW3 pushed the show into numerous battles with network censors that ultimately resulted in a forced hiatus in the weeks before the 1964 presidential election (Marc 1997, 102). Cancelled after one season, TW3 returned for a special broadcast on April 21, 1985, and continued its presidential satire, this time with skits on Ronald Reagan. In one sketch mocking the president's intellect and childlike demeanor, Nancy suggests that the couple get some sleep because Reagan is meeting "one of the most important men in Latin America tomorrow." The president replies, "Oh! Ricardo Montalban. I hope he brings Tattoo!" a reference to *Fantasy Island*, a popular television series of the time.

The topical political satire of TW3 would be repeated by two other shows during the 1960s. *Rowan and Martin's Laugh-In* and the *Smothers Brothers Comedy Hour*. Though different in pace, *Laugh-In* was fast sight gags, mini-sketches and one-liners, while the *Smothers Brothers* focused on developed sketches and musical numbers, both programs reflected the growing antiestablishment feeling of the decade. *Laugh-In* would occasionally direct its one-liners to presidential politics. In perhaps the most ironic statement by a future president, Richard Nixon, then a candidate, made a cameo appearance and said the show's popular catchphrase "Sock it to *Me?*" The hosts of the *Smothers Brothers*, more caustic in their satire than the creators of *Laugh-In*, would engage in many fights with the CBS network over their social commentary. In one controversy, blacklisted folk singer Pete Seeger performed a song entitled "Waist Deep in the Big Muddy," whose political undertones were clearly intended as a criticism of President Johnson and the Vietnam War (Spector 1985, 160). The political process also came under comic attack from show regular Pat Paulsen, who ran the fictitious "Pat Paulsen for President Campaign."

With the cancellation of the *Smothers Brothers*, presidential satire on television declined until NBC debuted *Saturday Night Live* in the fall of 1975. Featuring live sketches, *SNL* reintroduced television audiences to presidential comedy with skits focusing on the clumsiness of President Ford. As played by comedian Chevy Chase, Ford would appear throughout the show's first two seasons as bumbling and accident-prone. Ron Nessen, Ford's press secretary, quickly became aware of the show's growing popularity and saw the skits as a good public relations opportunity. He commented later that "you win by showing you can laugh at yourself" (quoted in Hill and Weingrad 1986, 180). Nessen eventually appeared as guest host with President Ford, taping a few lines for the broadcast, including the show's signature opening, "Live from New York, it's Saturday Night" (Hill and Weingrad, 182). The impact of *SNL* on Ford's defeat during the 1976 election is unclear, but for those involved, including Dick Cheney, Ford's chief of staff, Nessen and many of the show's cast members, the impressions were believed to be a significant contributing factor (*ibid.*). Presidential satire, specifically the impersonation of presidents, became a fixture on *SNL* that exists today. Throughout the years, comedians have played presidents from Ford to George W. Bush. While the Ford impersonations were based on slapstick, the later impersonations were more authentic in terms of voice and mannerisms. Comedian Rich Little described his impersonations of Richard Nixon as a product of the president's visual quality. The president, he notes, was "very uncoordinated, very flat-footed, walked like he never took the hanger out of the coat" (quoted in Bland and Lofaro 2001, 72). Dana Carvey's impression of George Bush for *SNL* was popular with both viewers and the president, who even asked Carvey to perform the impersonation at the White House shortly after he lost reelection (*ibid.*). In 2000, the impersonations of George W. Bush and Al Gore by Will Ferrell and Daryl Hammond, respectively, prompted the real-life candidates to join the show and poke fun at themselves. Perhaps Bush and Gore recognized what Ron Nessen had understood years earlier. Presidents (and candidates) who were seen to embrace *SNL*'s satire could deflect some of its impact, demonstrate their sense of humor and (more strategically) reach a large segment of potential voters.

In 2001, the first situation comedy featuring a standing president as its central character premiered on the cable channel Comedy Central. Canceled after eight episodes, *That's My Bush*, created by Matt Stone and Trey Parker, was a satirical take on the Bush presidency. While the Associated Press suggested that the series was "juvenile, coarse and impishly determined to offend, critics at the *Washington Post* called it "tasteless, appalling and funny as hell" (quoted in Armstrong 2003). The show's claim to humor aside, most commentators agree that it was more a parody of the situation comedy form rather than a parody of the president. While *That's My Bush* did satirize the president personally and politically (various episodes spoofed Bush's position on abortion and the death penalty), the humor derived more from the idea of the president as the bumbling head of a household rather than the incompetent leader of the nation.

Television's dramatic depictions of real presidents allow the viewing public a form of intimacy with their leader. This closeness, however, often confirms rather than disrupts widely held knowledge about the president. That is, television's presidents often act in ways that are culturally accepted. Washington is heroic, Lincoln is just and Nixon is deceitful. Despite the complex nature of their characters, presidents, as represented by television drama, are most often true to the public's social and cultural expectations of them. When television satirizes the president, the man behind the institution is both scrutinized and humanized.

While television's entertainment formats have made significant contributions to the affective depiction of real presidents, until the Fox series *24* and NBC's *The West Wing*, its portrayals of fictional presidents have been less successful, often lasting one season or less. Shows featuring fictional presidents in primary roles are 1985's *Hail to the Chief*, featuring Patty Duke as the first female president, and the 1987–1988 Fox Network production *Mr. President*, with George C. Scott in the title role. (In 1967, the president was even an animated crime-fighting hero in *Super President*).

While the main focus of *24* is the counter-terrorism work of agent Jack Bauer (Keifer Sutherland), the series also portrays a black president, David Palmer (Dennis Haysbert) who must deal with public and private crises. In the show, President Palmer is faced with corruption, betrayal and deception both from within his administration and his family. The character however, is consistently depicted as ethical, moral and self-sacrificing. In season one, he is a presidential candidate who willingly risks his political future by honestly revealing a damaging family secret. He bravely divorces his treacherous wife and in seasons two and three continues to put his faith in Agent Bauer. Together, the two characters try to pursue the right course of action in the fight against nuclear bombs and deadly viruses. When Palmer is involved in scandal, it is usually as an innocent betrayed. Over the course of the series, he has been characterized as a betrayed husband, friend, brother and boss who nevertheless maintains an inherent goodness. Similar to *The West Wing*'s President Bartlet, the fictional President Palmer is a flawed but admirable man who represents noble presidential traits.

It is well understood that the power of politics is as much about emotion as it is about cognition. Emotional responses have been shown by various studies to be significant factors in the decisions of voters (Kagay and Caldiera 1975; Kinder and Abelson 1981; Abelson et al. 1982), and when this power is combined with the visual image, emotions often surpass cognitions. In their study of the facial gestures of leaders, Sullivan and Masters showed videotaped excerpts of all candidates in the 1984 presidential election to selected groups. They found that changes in viewers' attitudes were more likely to be influenced by emotional responses to reassuring displays than by cognitive variables such as party identification or assessment of leadership responsibilities (1988, 345). While the subjects' emotional responses were integrated with other sources of information (including the nature of the display and the context in which it occurred), their affective responses were paramount and "if reinforced, [could] become part of more enduring dispositions toward candidates" (346). Early political socialization and the processes involved in formulating and understanding the president as a symbolic meaning system contribute to this emotional endurance, as do the moving pictures of television.

Hart argues that television tells the audience that politics can be reduced to pictures (1994, 7). This reduction suggests that television's images are a poor substitute for the power of the written word. Where written language is able to convey in-depth details about presidents, pictures and sound merely communicate superficial images. Creating images for presidential candidates, however, has long been a goal of the written word. Heale's study of nineteenth-century presidential campaigns suggests that the power of campaign biographies relied on creating images as strong (and superficial) as those later provided by television. Throughout the nineteenth century, the same stories and anecdotes about presidential contenders were repeated in campaign literature across the country:

> Biographers of Jackson never tired of telling the celebrated story of how the Hero, as a doughty teenager in the revolutionary war, had defiantly refused to clean a British officer's boots. William Henry Harrison was forever being extolled for introducing the Land Act of 1800, young Jimmy Polk never failed to shine both in classics and in mathematics while at college.... The same words appear in sketch after sketch: Polk's serious expression was often relieved "by a peculiarly pleasant smile" [1982, 159].

Creating a political image through the campaign biography became an essential means of communicating candidates' personalities to the vast constituency who did not see or hear them. In addition, it "simplified and idealized" the candidates, "tailoring [them] as far as possible to the expectation of a mass and highly diverse electorate" (Heale, 161). Emotive language espousing the hopefuls' grand achievements became the precursor to the later audiovisual image that would try to accomplish the same goal.

Because television's images of the president are usually mediated by the news, the president as a meaning system is analyzed in the context of reality. This reality, however, is problematic and has prompted researchers to call for new perspectives. Griffin argues that the focus of research should not be on the relationship of news to reality. Rather, inquiry should examine "the form and structure of the image/text that is created for us daily" (Griffin 1992, 125). Using this framework, the ways in which the president is constructed audiovisually has direct implications on an audience's understanding of him, not through a mental comparison with reality but rather through a mental recall of already planted schematic cues. The details of news stories change daily "but the framework into which they fit—the symbolic system—is more enduring. And it could be argued that the totality of news as an enduring symbolic system 'teaches' audiences more than any of its component parts" (Bird and Dardenne 1989, 69). The pictures of the news teach a citizen the enduring symbolic system of the president. Graber suggests:

> People learn which large scenarios certain visuals suggest regardless of whether these scenarios are even related to these visuals during a particular news presentation. Through well-chosen and widely familiar cues, pictures can illustrate, as well as evoke, rich images of what it means that a dictator is ruthless ... or that pollutants are poisoning their environment [2001, 72].

Familiar visuals of the president addressing an excited crowd waving flags evoke images of what it means to be presidential. The content of the address can change along with the man giving it, but the cues arouse scenarios of patriotism or nationalism, which ensure that the president endures as a symbolic system largely based on emotion.[13] This argument is contrary to many media theorists' perspectives that pictures do not offer specific meanings to an audience, rather they are polysemic and each individual audience member is free to interpret meanings as they choose. The debate over communication accuracy, though, is less convincing than it appears. Graber argues:

> Picture language deals in stereotypes that have become part of specific cultures and subcultures. Because the time available for individual stories is brief, television news producers must tell them with a limited vocabulary of familiar audiovisual clichés that the audience can process quickly. Given the rapid pace of words and pictures, the audience has no time for reflection, for careful searches for alternative meanings or for close scrutiny of pictures to detect hidden cues [78].

Graber is not suggesting that personalized interpretations do not exist among television viewers, rather she is confirming that most viewers, having been educated in the audiovisual language of television, are able to extract shared meanings. An audiovisual of the president may be interpreted by a viewer in the context of his party affiliation or policy attitudes, but the overall meaning of the president as a cultural knowledge will be shared with other viewers. An audiovisual representation of the president will tap into other stored audiovisual images to aid the observer in comprehending meaning—a meaning that is often emotionally arousing. A citizen's understanding of the president is limited to audiovisual cues that elicit past audiovisual memories that are subject to a complex web of intertextual and emotional interpretation.

Hart argues that where politics is concerned, television has become America's "emotional tutor" (1994, 10). Presidents take an active role in this process because they "try to dominate people's emotional lives with their own lives" (28). Evidence suggests that many presidents engage in emotional dialogue when performing the job. Studying the rhetorical strategies of major presidential addresses from the late 1940s to the 1980s, Hinckley notes that:

> Presidents say they are moral, not political, leaders. They do not negotiate with Congress or win elections or engage in much specific activity at all. Instead, they believe and feel things. They take positions and tell the American people what is good, whether in public or private life [1990, 87].

By positioning themselves as men who "believe and feel things," presidents are able to perform their symbolic role as healers, defenders and protectors of the nation.

Barber sees the focus on feelings as the cause for the "disillusionment trend" that adults experience with the president wherein he initially enjoys a period of high support then progressively declines in favor (1970, 106). As he explains: "Great things are expected of the president, and when he is unable to deliver, a process of disappointment sets in, a sense that the president has not done what he could and should do, given all of that favorable feeling" (*ibid.*). While Barber sees this disappointment as a psychological process, proponents of the rhetorical presidency argue that it is strongly influenced by the media, who contribute to the gap between what the president is expected to do and what he actually accomplishes while in office. DiClerico suggests that the media's contribution to this division lies in the impact it has on both public expectations and presidential performance (1993, 115). In terms of public expectations, DiClerico offers this example of a description of President Reagan from *Time* magazine:

Reagan's face was ruddy, in bloom, growing younger by the second. His size seems an emblem of his modesty.... The voice goes perfectly with the body.... It recedes at the right moments, turning mellow at points of intensity. When it wished to be most persuasive, it hovers barely above a whisper so as to win you over by intimacy, if not by substance. This is style, not sham [116–17].

The first President Bush received the same treatment in the press in the early weeks of his administration. Having previously been described as a clumsy public speaker with no clear goals for the country, the press later reported on the public's warm feelings toward him. In one report, the public was described as being "fond" of the president's "tendency toward malapropisms and scrambled syntax" (*ibid.*). Rather than continuing the early attacks on the president's lack of vision, he was later described as "super-charged in his energies and curiosities" with "few ideological convictions other than a basic decency, patriotism and a desire for people to be accommodating" (*ibid.*).

The honeymoon period between a new president and the media is common as the nation moves through the cycle of leadership. A new leader offers new hope. As the cycle progresses, the public reaches a stage of disillusionment, when the president inevitably fails to live up to previously established inflated expectations. Occasionally, journalists recognize their role in the process: "In selling ourselves an ideal president who does not and never can exist, we are once again repeating the destructive process of buildup and letdown that we have suffered through so often in the past" (quoted in DiClerico 1993, 118). While the process may be experienced as destructive, it is a necessary movement in the cycle of the presidency. It is a pattern that permits White's "culture of hope."

The president as an ideal allows the public to continually accept the symbolic dimensions of the institution. As an object of emotion, the president is held responsible for the quality of life experienced by citizens despite having very little constitutional power to effect policy. As a president moves through his four-year term, the public is usually disillusioned because they realize that the ideal cannot exist. Yet each new election offers the promise of renewal. The president, as symbol rather than fallible man, is reborn. The political socialization process that frames the president in the affective ultimately manifests itself in the media as most journalists share the same presidential learning experience as their fellow citizens. As Barber contends, the pattern of disillusionment felt by the public toward the president is a psychological process, but one that cannot be wholly separated from the media's influence. Because the president is initially learned emotionally, citizens may come to have exaggerated expectations (which are often facilitated through the media) and be disillusioned when he fails to meet them appropriately. Televised politics continues this reliance on emotional learning.

In the absence of dialogue, interaction and exchange between the president and the public, television has become a "delivery system for intimacy" (Hart 1994, 11). The intimate nature of television and its relationship to politics is often overlooked in critical work. While several scholars have recognized the need to examine politics in terms of the personal (Lowi 1985; Ansolabehere et al. 1993), their analyses remain grounded in functionalist perspectives. The effectiveness of election campaigns is often discussed in terms of audience share numbers, market size and demographics. In many of these approaches, television's role in politics is reduced to its visual style. If television is "above all else a human experience" (Hart 1994, 10), then a significant key to understanding television's meaning systems is to examine how its representations generate this experience. To understand human experience is, in part, to understand feelings. As politics is also an affective experience for many people, television's presidential power lies in its ability to activate structures of feeling. For Hart, "a truly rich understanding of modern governance must ask what politics feels like when we watch it" (*ibid.*). In the following chapters, this book analyzes *The West Wing*'s representation of the president to begin to answer the question.

CHAPTER THREE

A *West Wing* Primer

Beginnings

Aaron Sorkin began his career as a playwright and, at the age of 28, had his first major success with *A Few Good Men*. The military courtroom drama, whose protagonist is a young, idealistic Navy lawyer fighting a systematic cover-up, ran on Broadway for 497 performances. He followed this with an unsuccessful off-Broadway production called *Making Movies*. The production of *A Few Good Men*, however, attracted interest from Hollywood, and Sorkin adapted a screen version that was directed by Rob Reiner in 1992 and nominated for four Academy Awards and five Golden Globes, including Best Picture and Best Screenplay. Over the next few years, he wrote the films *Malice* (Becker 1993) and *The American President* (Reiner 1995). After treatment for an alcohol and cocaine addiction, he concentrated on small writing contributions to the films *The Rock* (Bay 1996), *Enemy of the State* (Scott 1998) and *Bulworth* (Beatty 1998). As Sorkin recalls in the introduction to *The West Wing Scriptbook*, the idea of writing a television script became a troubling one:

> I didn't want to start writing something of my own because to do that I'd have to start writing something. I love writing but hate starting. The page is awfully white and it says, "You may have fooled some of the people some of the time but those days are over, *giftless*. I'm not your agent and I'm not your mommy, I'm a white piece of paper, you wanna dance with me?" and I really, really don't. I don't want any trouble. I'll go peaceable like [2002a, 3].

Despite his reluctance to face the white page, Sorkin pitched his idea for *The West Wing* after it was suggested by a friend that *The American Pres-*

ident would make a good television series if he concentrated on the senior staff of the White House (Sorkin, 4). Using the film as inspiration, Sorkin credits the overly long *The American President* script for providing him with "little shards of leftover stories" for *The West Wing* pilot ("Fans Get Look" 2001). With a deal in place, producer John Wells and Warner Brothers studio approved the pilot script. The network, however, rejected it. Executives at NBC argued that television shows about politics in Washington would not find an audience. They were also concerned about the political climate of the time, which was focussed on the Clinton/Lewinsky scandal, and felt that audiences would respond negatively to a political drama about the president and his staff. The script was put on hold and Sorkin was approached to create a series based on an earlier idea that took a behind-the-scenes look at a cable television sports show. *Sports Night* was broadcast on the ABC network from 1998 to 2000. Although critically acclaimed (Thomas Schlamme, director and executive producer, won an Emmy for it in 1999), the series failed to gain the audience numbers desired by the network and was cancelled after two seasons. During the run of *Sports Night*, the extremely profitable series *Seinfeld* ended on NBC and several of the network's executives were replaced. As Sorkin recalls: "The unthinkable happened: Somebody forgot to tell Scott [Sassa] and Garth [Ancier] you can't do a show about Washington and politics. They ordered *The West Wing*" (2002, 6).

The hour-long series premiered in September 1999 and at its height was watched by twenty million viewers every week (Byrne 2002). The show follows the work of the senior staff of the fictional Bartlet administration. A liberal Democrat, President Josiah (Jed) Bartlet, played by Martin Sheen, is an idealistic politician who inspires his equally idealistic and earnest staff. The series has won over twenty Emmy Awards, including four for Outstanding Drama Series. The show has also won the Producers Guild Award, Directors Guild Award, Writers Guild Award, Screen Actors Guild Award, Golden Globe, Humanitas Prize and the Peabody. *Entertainment Weekly* named it "TV Show of the Year" in 2000.

Much of the commentary surrounding the show suggests that its early popularity was a sign of public disappointment in real presidential politics. While the series may reflect a wish for noble public servants, the image of a benevolent president and his loyal staff also reflects a basic component of the majority of Americans' early political socialization. *The West Wing* recalls and reaffirms this learning through a specific production and narrative strategy that consistently asks the viewer to *feel* something about both politics and the presidency.

Quality Television and The West Wing

With references to Shakespeare and Graham Greene, visits to rare-book stores and oblique Latin episode titles like "Post Hoc, Ergo Propter Hoc," the show is so achingly high end that you almost expect the warning "Quality Television" to start flashing below the picture.

(Peter De Jonge describing *The West Wing*
in the *New York Times*, October 28, 2001)

Because *The West Wing* is strongly identified with the characteristics of quality television, it is useful to examine the series from this perspective before initiating a critical discussion of its plots and characters. While quality television is a debatable notion, it usually refers to a show's production values, narrative aesthetics and success at reaching a high-income audience. The idea began with the development of the independent production company, MTM Enterprises, which was established in 1970 by actor Mary Tyler Moore, her then-husband Grant Tinker and manager Arthur Price. MTM's flagship program, the *Mary Tyler Moore Show*, was to have a significant impact on the nature of network comedy and drama productions. The show's narrative style, emphasis on the workplace and focus on the needs of the quality audience created a legacy found in some of the most highly rated television drama programs broadcast today. *The West Wing* is one of quality television's most successful beneficiaries.

While the narrative contributions of the MTM style to network television programming are significant, it is also important to analyze them within a historic and economic context. In the 1970s, the networks began to change their views toward both programming and ratings practices, ultimately setting the stage for MTM's future success. Media scholar Jane Feuer argues that the early development of MTM was dependent on a marked shift in the networks' conceptions of the audience:

> The crucial change that began to occur around 1970 was a de-emphasis on numbers and a greater emphasis on "demographics." ... The constitution of the audience had been a factor during the 1950's "golden age" of TV dramas, when "upmarket" productions were used to entice the well-to-do to buy television receivers. However, during the 1960's the emphasis in ratings was on numbers alone. Without the shift toward "demographic thinking," it is unlikely that MTM would ever have gotten off the ground [1984, 3].

The shift to "demographic thinking" occurred, in Feuer's view, because of the shift toward spot advertising, which changed the networks' relationship to their advertisers and in turn, their audience (*ibid.*). Rather than sponsoring an entire show, advertisers would purchase thirty- or sixty-second spots on a specific program, creating a profit boom for networks, who could now charge higher prices for advertising time on popular shows. Profit and popularity became inextricably linked. Production companies, who by 1960 had taken over as creators of television programming from the advertisers, would be successful if they could produce shows that attracted viewers in a high spending demographic. During the 1970s, market research discovered that young, urban adults, (with a special emphasis on females) aged 18 to 49, were the major consumers of the types of products promoted on television (Feuer, 3).

The drive to capture this profitable audience demographic led to significant changes in program direction for all the networks of the time but specifically CBS, whose strategy was to replace almost all of its existing top-rated programs. The impetus behind the move was that the programs, while guaranteeing CBS the majority of the top-ten-rated shows of the 1970–71 season, were appealing to rural audiences consisting of children and adults over fifty rather than the younger, more demographically attractive urban audiences (Feuer, 4). To entice this demographic, the networks launched programs that they felt would be relevant to the young adults of the time. Program plots revolved around young, idealistic adults who worked to serve downtrodden social groups.[14] The programming change however, failed for CBS and by the 1971–72 season it was replaced with similarly themed but less overtly issue-based productions (*ibid.*).

Despite audiences' initial unenthusiastic response to the "relevance drive" in programming, Feuer suggests that its importance lies in the influence it had on the "two most significant" production companies of the 1970s: Norman Lear's Tandem Productions, producer of the controversial *All in the Family*, and MTM, the producers of the *Mary Tyler Moore Show* (*ibid.*). Both of these programs would signal a significant shift in the topics and style used in network situation comedies by addressing what was considered relevant to the quality audience. Having now been identified by their highly prized spending habits, this young, urban audience was the target of narratives previously not considered appealing to viewers. The producers, wary of the earlier failure of too much relevance, retooled their programs. They still attempted to reach their target demographic through culturally specific issues that were relevant, but now they shaped those issues into story lines expressed in workplace and relationship situations. Unlike previous situation comedies and dramas where the family household was central to the narrative, the workplace became the feature setting where other topics were explored. MTM's initial production established the precedent for this workplace format and appealed to the networks by being traditional enough to maintain popularity among a general audience and innovative enough to capture the attention of the quality demographic.

MTM's the *Mary Tyler Moore Show* was originally conceived as a vehicle for Moore to extend her popularity from the successful *Dick Van Dyke*
show, where she played Dyke's flighty but lovable wife. Responding to the
climate of the time, the new show ventured into more controversial waters.
Moore was cast in the role of a divorced woman living and working as a
news reporter in Minneapolis whose best friend was a New York Jew played
by Valerie Harper.[15] While some scholars argue that the *Mary Tyler Moore
Show* was truly innovative programming for its decade (Bedell 1983), others suggest that it was not "so fresh or distinguished a series that it could
be said to have uplifted situation comedy as a form" (Brown quoted in Feuer
1984, 6). Feuer argues that while the show's position in the "relevancy" programming of the decade emerges in retrospect, the importance of the show
is found in its ability to depict the "'feel' of a culture undergoing the
upheavals of a decade" (8). In her view, a large part of the reason for the
show's success was due to the controversial political content of *All in the
Family*,[16] which "took the onus off the innovative aspects of the *Mary Tyler
Moore Show*, but also allowed MTM to push a little harder in later seasons by breaking down some of the taboos that had existed at the time both
shows went on the air" (7). *All in the Family*, a comedy that centered on
the gruff and racist attitudes of an older white blue-collar worker and his
lovable, long-suffering wife, dealt with social and political attitudes that
were an unusual and controversial basis for situation comedy. Both shows
achieved ratings success for CBS, but the *Mary Tyler Moore Show* was perceived differently from the Lear programs because, in Feuer's view, it "was
also defined *against* the Lear comedies, as a show which dealt with 'reality' but not with explicitly political themes" (7). The "reality" of the *Mary
Tyler Moore Show* would be repeated in future productions from MTM
including *Lou Grant, Hill Street Blues, WKRP in Cincinnati*, and *St. Elsewhere*, among many others. MTM quickly developed the image of the
quality production company with shows that reproduced a distinctive style.

The mainstream press of the 1970s and 1980s often discussed MTM
as a production company of quality, thereby strengthening the label. *New
York Times Magazine* wrote: "MTM has a reputation for fair dealing,
and, by prime-time standards, high quality" (cited in Feuer, 32). This
ideal stretched to production practices and choice of actors as well. Feuer
notes:

> Articles in the trades and in popular magazines and newspapers have demon-
> strated that MTM would spare no expense in the visual style of its pro-
> grammes, putting "quality" above financial considerations. Long after other
> sitcom producers had switched to videotape, MTM continued to seek the
> "quality" look of film. And MTM hired a different breed of television actor

... all of whom had their roots in improv companies ... rather than main-stream television acting [*ibid.*].

The freedom MTM afforded and encouraged among its creative staff was also often cited in the press as a component of its quality output. Feuer argues that these factors allowed MTM to be conceptualized as a corporate "author" whose "conditions of creative freedom enabled [it] to develop an individualised 'quality' style" and whose "corporate signature may be deciphered from the texts themselves" (33). In essence, MTM became a brand name with a highly recognizable and often copied product line stamped "quality."

If, as Feuer suggests, MTM's quality brand name may be uncovered in its products, then the structural characteristics of the *Mary Tyler Moore Show* offer a solid base from which to analyze the components of quality television. MTM's contribution to the situation-comedy format was to emphasize character development rather than rely on a simplistic problem/solution structure (Feuer, 34). Newcomb suggests that this change created a new category for the genre: the "domestic comedy" (1974, 52). The domestic comedy, he argues, focuses on the personal; the problem that must be solved is rooted in mental or emotional states, and the family is the stable force. Often, the form may be extended when the problems faced by the families take on political or social importance (*ibid.*). Feuer suggests that these changes "transformed the problem/solution format of the sitcom into a far more psychological and episodic formula in which—in the hand of MTM—the situation itself becomes a pretext for the revelation of character" (35). Because the narrative revealed more developed characters, the plot was able to move from a simple structure based on sight gags and one-liners to a more complex engagement with the audience. The emphasis on character that the MTM formula initiated through the *Mary Tyler Moore Show* gave the audience characters that were perceived as more authentic than any previously seen in the genre:

> For the generation of women who came of age with Mary and Rhoda, these characters seemed "real" in a way no other TV character ever had.... The MTM women caught the cultural moment for the emerging "new woman" in a way that provided a point of identification for the mass audience as well. The MTM women could be read as warm, lovable TV characters or as representations of a new kind of femininity [36].

Connecting the audience with characters in psychologically meaningful ways rather than relying on stereotypical traits means that "character comedy in the hands of MTM became synonymous with 'quality comedy'" (*ibid.*). In this conception, appealing to the quality audience required characters that possessed a certain level of psychological realism. However, as Feuer argues, "the sitcom remains forever on the far side of quality for this reason, since a certain amount of stereotyping is necessary to get laughs" (37).

While MTM's formula was innovative in its approach to character development, quality in the context of situation comedy is limited to the requirements of humor. The *Mary Tyler Moore Show* and future MTM television productions found a balance between what Feuer terms "empathetic laughter" (*ibid.*) or laughing along with a character one identifies with, and humor that relies on feeling superior to a stereotypical character. But the comic methods used in MTM programs most often "produce the laughter of recognition, an identification that is especially acute for the 'sophisticated' audience" (41).

Despite the limited parameters of quality allowed by the situation-comedy format, MTM productions can be argued to have transformed the way audiences related to characters by changing the nature of their feelings towards them. Not only did the audience laugh with a sense of mutual recognition, but they responded to other MTM character innovations as well. One typical comic situation found in the format is when a character claims to have the ability to behave maturely but then acts childishly instead; another is what Feuer refers to as "comic reversals of expectations" where the audience is set up for a predictable pattern of sentimental comment and response but is surprised by an atypical response (43). These changes in the situation-comedy format cemented MTM's reputation as the production house of quality television. As the company expanded into drama programming, the innovations used in the *Mary Tyler Moore Show* resurfaced and expanded in new directions.

The transition to dramas for MTM occurred with *Lou Grant*, a spin-off program, whose title character was Mary's boss on the *Mary Tyler Moore Show*. *Lou Grant* took the original ideas pioneered by Moore's program, which included the ensemble cast of coworkers and a dialogue based around a literate style of writing (Feuer, 45), and added more drama-based plots. The program "took the work-family concept from the sitcoms, added a heavier strain of drama and an emphasis on public issues, and began to expand the narrative..." (*ibid.*). This narrative expansion would continue in future MTM programs such as *Hill Street Blues* and *St. Elsewhere,* whose multiple plot structures, large ensemble work-family casts and blend of drama and comedy with a realist treatment of often controversial issues would become the trademark for quality in drama programming.

The legacy of quality conventions initiated by MTM programs in terms of structure, themes and appeal to a specific audience demographic are clearly found in the narrative format of *The West Wing*. (The show can also be considered a direct descendent of the quality family tree. Its executive producer, John Wells, is also executive producer of the medical drama *E.R.*, which owes much of its production style to MTM's hospital drama *St. Elsewhere*.) A workplace drama that concentrates on the senior staff of the United States president, the plot structure of *The West Wing* relies on literate discussions of relevant political and social issues coupled with a psychological realism that often gives viewers an insight into the characters' personal motivations. It follows the quality convention pioneered by MTM of combining comedy and drama while dealing with controversial topics of current social concern.

An example of the level of dialogue and humor that the show often reaches is evident in a debate between Sam Seaborn (Rob Lowe), and the Chief of Staff's daughter, Mallory (Allison Smith), over the issue of school vouchers in an episode from the first season:

> SAM: Public education has been a public policy disaster for forty years. Having spent around four trillion dollars on public schools since 1965, the result has been a steady and inexorable decline in every measurable standard of student performance to say nothing of health and safety. But don't worry about it because the U.S. House of Representatives is on the case. I feel better already!
>
> MALLORY: Wow.
>
> SAM: What?
>
> MALLORY: For someone who's trying to date me, that was pretty snotty ["Six Meetings Before Lunch"].

In quality drama, one of the goals of this literate style of writing is to reach an educated demographic. This audience is considered quality by advertisers who are attracted to the group's disposable income. In terms of meeting this standard of quality, *The West Wing* has been extremely successful.

In the series' second year, an article in the *New York Times* noted: "The show has been the most upscale series on network television, not only in terms of its writing and the issues it tackled but its audience. It is seen by more adults ages 18–49 who earn more than $100,000 a year than any other network series" (Weinraub 2000). It was also reaching a segment of this audience in its first year, as the trade magazine *Variety* reported. The show tied with the popular series *Ally McBeal* in capturing the largest audience among households earning $75,000 or more in addition to beating every prime time show on all networks in the coveted bracket of adults aged 18 to 49 who live in households earning $50,000 or more (Bierbaum 1999). Despite reaching this coveted demographic, the show was ranked thirtieth among network programs in its first season, rating an average of fourteen million viewers, prompting the president for research at its home network NBC to call it a "solid performer" rather than a "breakout show" (Wurtzel quoted in Weinraub 2000). The "solid performer" exceeded all network expectations when its second season premiere episode drew 25 million viewers and brought NBC its highest rating for the period in eleven years (Millman 2000).

A Note on the Issue of Quality

While a clear connection can be made between the quality traditions pioneered by MTM's style and the structure of *The West Wing*, the term quality deserves more critical scrutiny. Quality is a complex and elusive term that has generated significant critical debate. Its meaning depends on aesthetic judgments that in turn rely on specific contexts. Quality may be viewed from a cultural as well as an institutional perspective. In relation to MTM, quality is defined in terms of program characteristics that are traced to a specific production style, but it is also dependent on an institutional perspective of what constitutes a desirable audience demographic.

In the United Kingdom, a significant debate over what constituted quality in television occurred in 1989–90 when a number of scholars attempted to analyze the issue and reach a consensus. The debate, while prompted by legislative issues, was still approached in aesthetic terms, which resulted in a diverse array of opinions. The Broadcasting Research Unit (1989) published a range of essays by academics, program creators and writers who all presented different perspectives. In addition, Mulgan (1990) discussed the concept by recognizing the quality elements in previously ignored genres including soap operas and talk shows, and Brunsdon (1990) approached the debate from within an established academic paradigm of critical deconstruction. Gunter argues that despite the vigorous debate, all these arguments failed to formulate a constructive framework for regulators to use in examining licensees in an "equitable and transparent fashion, with the interests of the consumer centrally integrated in the assessment" (1993, 53). While recognizing that quality is an abstract concept, Gunter suggests that ultimately quality depends on the viewers' judgements:

> Quality cannot be measured purely in terms of audience size. Nor can reliance be placed solely on the intuitive judgement of program makers or

other broadcasting professionals. Viewers have their own expected standards for television programs. It is the audience to whom those charged with safeguarding the public's interest must turn in order to measure the quality of the viewing experience [59].

The idea of quality in television broadcasting is in many ways an easily challenged construct that has been formulated by either scholars' aesthetic judgements and critical analysis or broadcasters' beliefs in their intuitive sense of the desires of the audience in a high consumer spending bracket. Despite the elusive meaning of the term, MTM effected a change in the narrative structure of situation comedies and dramas in the United States. These changes can be found in some of the most popular programs in American television history.

Staging the Presidency

From the first image projected on screen, *The West Wing* asks the viewer for an emotional reaction. The images and music of the show's title sequence work as an emotional cue for the audience, who is positioned to connect the pictures and sound of the sequence with the learned meaning of *presidential*. Visually and aurally, the opening of the series stands as a signifier for patriotism, power and nationhood. This is evident from the sequence's signature image: a billowing American flag superimposed over a picture of the White House. The music accompanying this patriotic symbolism is a snare drum—a marching beat, which associates the flag and the White House with soldiers, armies and independence. Lasting only a few seconds, it is separate from the main score of the sequence and calls the audience to attention. The viewer is immediately confronted with the sights and sounds of the symbolic heart of the United States. He is prepared to enter the political world of Democratic President Jed Bartlet.

Each week, the American flag and White House opening image leads to a review of previous plot points before a teaser scene opens the current episode. The main title sequence then explodes onto the screen with a "smash cut" and a rousing orchestral score. The signature, sheer image of the American flag returns and remains throughout the sequence, blowing across the screen, revealing the actors in scenes from the show along with black and white photographs of them in character. The scenes portray the characters in action in the workplace, and the photographs show them in earnest or contemplative moments in their offices, on the telephone, in meetings or in other work moments. This juxtaposition between the action and the still photograph connects the characters with both a political present and a political past. While they are shown in the present context of the fictional Bartlet administration, the still images create the impression that the characters are part of the historical record of the presidency. These photographs suggest a living political archive, a confirmation of the characters' places in the history of a presidential administration.

The fictional connection with historic symbols of the presidency is also evident in the sequence of photos and scenes that introduce President Bartlet. In the final black and white still photograph of Bartlet, he is standing over a table in the Oval Office with his head bowed, facing away from the camera toward a window. This image replicates a famous Oval Office photograph of President Kennedy where he is standing at a table facing a bank of windows. His hands are resting on the surface of the table and his head is bowed as he reads a newspaper.[17] The striking similarity between the two photographs serves as a visual cue for the audience to retrieve the memory of the famous Kennedy image, thereby connecting the fictional President Bartlet with a past American president. The faceless image conveys a quiet isolation, a sense of the gravity of the presidency.

For those viewers who do not have knowledge of the Kennedy photograph, the title sequence provides other visual presidential cues. The interior of the Oval Office, the seal of the president, his official motorcade and helicopter are all flashed across the screen, viewed through the waving curtain of the American flag. These visuals, cut together in this context, recall the symbolic system that conveys the president. The familiar images evoke stored knowledge, and meaning is generated. The audience is encouraged to recall their understanding of the real presidency and connect the fictional President Bartlet to it.

The main title's score also contributes to the power of the presidential symbolism. The theme, written by W. G. "Snuffy" Walden, is a combination of orchestra and electronics. Walden describes it as a "big sweeping expanse of music" with a "heroic feel" (Lambert 2000). Wanting music that underscored the power of the presidency, Walden notes that the theme is "a little bit of Taps, a little bit of gospel and a little bit of [Aaron] Copland" (quoted in Elber 2001). These influences come together to form music that not only elicits a feeling of grandeur but signifies American values. Copland's influence, in particular, contributes to the Americana feel of the theme, as his signature sound brought together traditional American folk melodies from across the United States. The result for Walden's theme is an epic and expansive piece of music that reflects the rhythms of American life and the values of an idealized American culture. Combined with the patriotic images of the title sequence, the score prepares the audience to enter the world of the American president.

The center of this world is the West Wing of the White House, the location of the Oval Office—the seat of presidential power. The audience is introduced to this space in the pilot episode after the teaser scenes that show each of the senior staff receive the message "POTUS in a bicycle accident." The tease in these opening scenes is that the audience does not see the workplace of this workplace drama and only learns that POTUS stands for President of the United States immediately before the title sequence begins.

The tease that opens the premiere episode continues into its first act as the camera follows Leo McGarry (John Spencer), Chief of Staff, arriving for work. An overhead shot focuses on the bronze seal of the president in the floor of the Northwest lobby of the White House. Leo works his way through a security post, stops in the lobby to speak to a staff member and continues across to a far door. The audience is observer here, watching the action in a long shot from behind the character. When Leo walks through the door, the audience's position changes as the camera walks along with him on his brisk journey through the hallways of the inner staff offices. The impression is a workplace of controlled chaos, with staff and aides walking in and out of the frame from all sides. Leo greets people, gets updates on various situations and carries on a conversation with his deputy Josh Lyman (Bradley Whitford) while moving through the corridors. He eventually makes his way to the desk of Mrs. Landingham (Kathryn Joosten), the president's main secretary and general guardian of White House decorum. She follows him as he enters an empty Oval Office. The audience has a quick glimpse of the office as Leo circles the space, drops a file onto the president's desk and exits through the opposite door.

In Sorkin's view, the scene is important as a visual signature for the series. As he notes in *"The West Wing" Scriptbook*, the scene "would stamp a visual style that the show would adhere to forever" (2002a, 8). Predominately, that style is the fluid "walk and talk" look that is achieved through the use of a Steadicam. A camera stabilization device, the Steadicam isolates the camera from the small movements of the operator. This allows the operator to combine a steady image with the freedom of movement required by a handheld shot. Typically, the Steadicam shots of the series cover 360 degrees, which permits the show to deviate from the standard three-wall television production set and function as a fully enclosed space. The result is a voyeuristic, all-access look at the president's work environment. As Smith suggests, the Steadicam tracking shot, while not used the most, is the "dominant consistent pattern of technique, used to distinguish the particular look and ambiance" of the series (2003, 133).

The visual aspect of the series is the creation of cinematographer

Thomas Del Ruth. Oppenheimer suggests that among cinematographers, it is Del Ruth who has done the most to pioneer the use of the Steadicam in series television (2000). As the cinematographer for the pilot episode of *ER*, the first series to extensively feature Steadicam movement, Del Ruth's shooting choices "changed the way people thought about staging and shooting a weekly program" (*ibid.*). No longer restricted by the narrow range of movements of more traditional shooting techniques, directors using the Steadicam can create more dramatically interesting scenes. The handheld movement of the camera creates the impression that the audience is following unconscious action rather than rehearsed action being staged for the camera (Millington and Nelson 1987, 116). This provides a sense of realism for the characters and their workplace, as compelling for the action of a hospital emergency room as it is for the Oval Office. The shots appear to be unplanned, which seems to place the characters in a documentary framework, supporting the impression that they are real people (*ibid.*). In *The West Wing*, this illusion is further supported by the show's use of the single, continuous shot. The continuous shot like the one that follows Leo walking through the West Wing offices is a feature of the series. The technique is repeated to great effect in the episode "Five Votes Down." One of the longest continuous shots of the series, it runs for four minutes and follows the president as he moves from a crowded ballroom to meet his staff in a hallway. It continues with the president and staff through the hall, down a flight of stairs, through a kitchen, down another flight of steps, through an underground tunnel and into an alley where his car is waiting. Del Ruth notes that the shot included over five hundred extras and almost all of the major cast members, who passed off constant dialogue over several hundred yards (Oppenheimer 2000).

Millington and Nelson suggest that this type of single, continuous shot is "essentially an actor-centred production strategy," which ensures that it is the actors' performance that "dictates the pace and rhythm of the scene" (1986, 117). The pace and rhythm of the actors is an important element of *The West Wing* because it mirrors the pace and rhythm of the dialogue. As the actors move briskly in and out of offices and up and down corridors, so too does the speed and rhythm of their conversations. For *The West Wing*, this results in a "very fast-paced show" that does not take on a "maniacal form of camera movement" (Del Ruth quoted in Fisher 2000). Del Ruth's technique has the camera moving at pace with the actors but rarely calling attention to itself. The story moves forward visually as well as dramatically. The result is a style that not only recalls the pace of Del Ruth's earlier work on *ER* but also reflects his understanding of *The West Wing*'s narrative:

This would have been an easy show to [place] into a reality format visually, which I had done with the pilot for *ER*. But I always felt this show was a presentation of an optimistic White House, a Camelot for the masses. To help sell that idea, we wanted a softer, veiled image that had a golden quality, as well as strong backlighting and contrast [quoted in Oppenheimer 2000].

While the use of the Steadicam does contribute to a sense of a real workplace (in terms of pace), Del Ruth's visual interpretation stresses the Bartlet White House as a romantic environment. For him, the narrative of the series is mythic, a modern-day version of Camelot, wherein loyal servants are guided by a righteous king. This sensibility is realized through specific camera and lighting choices that establish an emotional atmosphere.

The use of fluid camera shots that move from one scene to the next on a different set is complemented by a lighting design that sees the characters walk through circles of light and shadow. Del Ruth suggests that the camera movements contribute to the feeling of urgency and kinetic energy among the Bartlet staff, a feeling he believes is directly related to their proximity to the president (Fisher 2000). The actors' movements are punctuated by Del Ruth's use of "hot lights" in the ceiling. As the actors move underneath them, even at a slow pace, the light hits their heads and creates the impression that "they're flying at hypersonic speed" (*Official Companion* 2002, 36). The audience, then, is encouraged to visually associate the characters' energy and pace with the presidency. The impression is a White House that is alive with the vigor and vitality of smart, passionate people who work for an equally intelligent and dedicated leader. The pools of light through which the characters move also contribute to the pace of the series by adding tension to the atmosphere of a scene. Bartlet or a member of his staff is often in and out of shadow, suggesting a visual clue to the lighter and darker side of their personalities. Del Ruth suggests that his use of shadow is a deliberate one that creates a "subtext about the shadowy side of government," which heightens the viewer's sense of drama (*ibid.*). While the audience may not always have the ability to acknowledge the visual clues, Del Ruth believes they may respond to them emotionally: "They may not see it, but they feel the mood..." (quoted in Fisher 2000). This subtle effect of lighting is also used specifically for the character of the president.

Del Ruth notes that while he does not use signature lighting for President Bartlet, he does approach the character in specific ways. For the pilot episode, Del Ruth shot all the scenes with the president in amber gold light, which he believes conveyed the duality of Bartlet as a father figure and a man "surrounded by an aura of power" (quoted in Fisher 2000). He also notes that the color of the light functioned as a "form of reverence for the office that we all feel" (*ibid.*). In other scenes, Del Ruth combines specific camera and lighting techniques to highlight characteristics of the president that are revealed by the plot:

> If a scene puts the president in a heroic light, we subtly change the camera angle and lighting to reflect that. Other times, he isn't bathed in the most favorable light when elements of his personality come in conflict with those that are around him. Each scene has its own meter, tempo and style. We use composition, angles, lens choice, focus and colors to punctuate story points [*ibid.*].

The audience is positioned to experience Bartlet in ways that both soften and strengthen the power of the presidency. Yet they are always guided by Del Ruth's lighting and camera choices to approach the institution with a sense of reverence.

Del Ruth's lighting design for the series is continuous because the same sets are used from week to week. While he implements minor changes in the direction and quality of light, he believes that continuity is essential because "people expect a certain elegance in the White House" (*ibid.*). This expectation is not for a sense of reality (in fact, Del Ruth has only seen the real White House from the outside); rather, he suggests that the sets are important for what they reveal to the audience about the characters. He offers the example of the Roosevelt Room set as his favorite because the space is a "great environment for meetings" due to its openness, color and sense of depth (*ibid.*). For Del Ruth, the deep rich colors of the room suggest to the audience that the characters that meet there are serious, passionate people gathering in an elegant space that is worthy of the important nature of their work. The sets contribute to a specific vision of the White House, one that is enveloped in rich colors and soft pools of light and shadow that reflect the dynamic work of the powerful.

In addition to introducing the production's visual style, the continuous shot of Leo from the pilot episode establishes the pace of the show's dialogue. The characters speak in a quick rhythm that has become one of the most discussed attributes of Sorkin's scripts.[18] Critics have called the style everything from "intelligent, compelling and wonderfully engaging" (Welty 2000, 34) to "chat-happy ... windy preaching" (Levesque 2000). Sorkin has called his characters "hypercommunicative, which is to say they can't shut up" (quoted in Welty 2000, 34) and attributes the rhythm of his writing style to his background in musical theater. His goal with *The West Wing*'s dialogue is to imitate the rhythm, tone and pitch of music. As he explains it:

I think about the music of one line, of an entire scene or an entire episode which will follow the patterns of movements in longer pieces of music.... Now you have to marry all that to a story that you're telling. But the sound of it is terribly important [*Official Companion* 2002, 34].

The direction of the show specifically responds to this notion of music and movement. Schlamme comments: "Aaron writes musically. In some ways, what I'm trying to do visually is follow the orchestra a little bit" (*ibid.*). Following the actors' movements as they briskly move through the West Wing offices, Schlamme's camerawork choices emphasize his feeling about the documentary nature of the series: "I'm not a documentary filmmaker, but I like trying to incorporate that look, that sense of urgency and the feeling of being a fly on the wall in another world" (quoted in Hope 2002). The visual and aural pace of this "backstage access" creates the illusion that the audience has access to the private workings of America's most public symbol of presidential power. More importantly, this workplace is visually and aurally defined as energetic. The result is a representation of a White House that retains its aura of power and prestige while simultaneously allowing the public to not only claim a personal space within it but feel something about that claim.

Team Bartlet

For many Americans, politics is a way of speaking, not a way of living. For them, governance has less to do with constitutional rights than with politicians' rhetorical addictions.

(Roderick Hart 1994, 87)

An examination of *The West Wing*'s aesthetics, argues Greg Smith, should start with Aaron Sorkin's dialogue (2003, 127). For Smith, Sorkin's technique of moving between "rat-a-tat interchanges" and "florid speechmaking" results in "a distinctive voice for the show" (*ibid.*). This textual style functions on several levels. As Smith suggests, it stamps the show as uniquely Sorkin's and allows the series to use "mini-scenes" (defined as breaking a single scene into separate, smaller parts) to achieve its multi-plot structure (128). In addition, Sorkin's dialogue

is distinctive in that it breaks up single conversation between two characters into multiple topics, thereby conveying information quickly while mirroring the complexity of the *West Wing* world [*ibid.*].

Within the multitopic conversation are what Smith terms "snippets" or "extraordinarily brief dramatic units that together comprise a complete conversational interchange" (129). Smith uses an example from "In Excelsis Deo" to illustrate this structure when C. J. (Allison Janney) and Sam (Rob Lowe) abruptly move from a discussion about hate crime legislation to one about their respective secret service code names. The lack of transition "condenses a great deal of information about the daily lives of characters" and creates "dialogue efficiency" (130). Snippets also give the show humor. In "Lies, Damn Lies, and Statistics," this snippet takes place between Toby (Richard Schiff) and C. J.:

TOBY: Since when are you an expert on language?

C. J.: In polling models?

TOBY: Yeah.

C. J.: Nineteen ninety-three. Since when are you an uptight pain in the ass?

TOBY: Since long before that.

As Smith suggests, this type of snippet humanizes the characters by alternating between the "high seriousness" of their work and "moments of low silliness" (*ibid.*). Matching the rhythm and pace of the characters' dialogue with Steadicam tracking shots allows the audience to follow pairs of actors as they move in and out of the frame, beginning and ending conversations in one continuous flow. In this way, the viewer is visually and verbally encouraged to feel what it's like to work in the West Wing.

For Smith, the snippet/Steadicam structure allows the series to "accomplish one of its most distinctive purposes: to connect the personal with the political" (133). Throughout the series, political discussions are integrated with personal exchanges in quick flows that encourage the viewer to blur the boundaries between the two. However, the personal nature of the characters' conversational exchanges, whether in snippets or normal speech, do more than make a connection between the personal and the political. They create a highly affective narrative that consistently privileges emotions over cognitions. The political debate that propels each week's episode is often reduced to basic emotions that recall patriotic attitudes or teach simplified moral lessons. The outcome is a subtext that may leave the viewer with an emotional residue, encouraging an affective response to politics in general and the president in particular.

In an online interview for *NewsHour with Jim Lehrer*, Sorkin explains that the five principal characters that serve his fictional president are the ideal public civil servants; the series is his "valentine to public service" (September 27, 2000). Various interviewers and writers agree, commenting that *The West Wing* is a series that "extols the values of public service"

(Smith 2000) and "presents politics as the last and certainly the most honorable profession" (Wolff 2000). While President Bartlet is shown dealing with various advisers and secretaries, it is his interactions with the senior staff that form the show's basic narrative. The series is a workplace drama in the literal sense—the story lines are framed in the workplace of the West Wing—and in the sense that the personal lives of the staff are subordinate to their jobs and are usually only referred to if they further a work plotline. The principal characters who form the senior staff to President Bartlet are: Leo McGarry, Chief of Staff; Josh Lyman, Deputy Chief of Staff; Toby Ziegler, Communications Director; Sam Seaborn, Deputy Communications Director and C. J. Cregg, Press Secretary.[19] The narratives of Bartlet's senior staff reflect their status as true believers in the presidential ideal as it is preached in the sermon of early political learning. In addition, the characters' relationships with Bartlet are consistent with a collective American consciousness that conceptualizes the presidency from an affective position. This is not to say that the narrative abandons cognitive constructions of the presidency. Rather, it is the characters' reduction of the cognitive to the affective that underlies the political discourse of the show. The characters consistently define their approach to both political work and the president by their emotions. In this reduction lies the power of the presidential mythos.

Leo McGarry

The "Pilot" establishes the character of Leo McGarry (John Spencer) as an affluent and authoritative politician. A Caucasian man aged in his late 50s to early 60s, he is introduced in a scene that opens with an exterior shot of a large and stately home. Once inside the house, the viewer sees the character in a formal living area, reading the paper and being served by a maid. The audience hears rather than sees his wife as she calls to him that POTUS is on the telephone. A few seconds later as the teaser scene ends, the audience is made aware that the acronym refers to the President of the United States. While the audience is still unclear as to Leo's exact role in the narrative, he is firmly established as a figure of power and influence.

This impression is further clarified with the opening scene of Leo's arrival for work. The attention he receives from the various staff moving in and out of the frame, his confident stride through the halls and corridors and his easy access to the Oval Office all clearly mark his political authority. As head of the senior staff, Leo exhibits many of the traits of culturally constructed masculinity. He is a self-assured leader, autonomous and in control. His exchange with the president's secretary in the premiere episode also establishes the level of informality he shares with President Bartlet. As the series progresses, Leo's back story is developed, and the audience learns that the two men are old friends. The relationship, in fact, has seen Leo through some dark personal moments. In one episode he tells Bartlet: "When I was lying on my face in a motel parking lot, you were the one I called" ("He Shall, from Time to Time..."). The president, as the audience learns in the same episode, feels a strong bond with Leo as well, referring to him as his "best friend." This friendship is an important narrative device because it allows the idea of president to be understood on different levels. Throughout the series, Leo addresses Bartlet with a mixture of respect for his position and the familiarity of a best friend. Leo's sarcasm to his friend Jed is the source of much of the show's humor. More important, the friendship gives Leo the ability to speak candidly to the president, which prevents the character from becoming a cliché of authority. The two men's personal relationship gives Bartlet a personality outside that of the president but still maintains a high level of respect for his position. The audience, then, is able to conceptualize the president on the more personal level of friend in addition to the more familiar level of authority figure.

As the first season develops, the audience learns that Leo is a recovering alcoholic and Valium addict. On the surface, this narrative device seems to conform to familiar dramatic conventions used with political characters—a politician is suddenly revealed to have a secret, dark past. However, Leo's status as an addict disrupts this image and provides an opportunity to frame the presidency as a source for redemption.

Leo's addiction treatment is discovered when a Republican congressman accuses one in three White House workers of regularly using drugs. Unaware of Leo's past Valium abuse, the senior staff decides that they must publicly respond to the Congressman's accusations. It is Josh who uncovers the Congressman's true agenda and realizes Leo's secret. His response establishes the emotional tone that frames the addiction story line: "You're Leo McGarry. You're not gonna be taken down by this small fraction of a man. I won't permit it" ("The Short List"). Josh's response is one of feeling rather than reason. He places himself in the role of protector; he will succeed where Leo has failed. While this show of support for Leo is recognition of his powerful political status as well as loyalty to a coworker and mentor, it also reflects Josh's affective stance toward the presidency. Leo's potential disgrace must be prevented because it stains the whole of the Bartlet administration. To take down Leo is to destroy an invaluable part of the presidency itself.

Bartlet's reaction to the situation is brief, yet it confirms Leo's value to the presidency. Realizing he is powerless to prevent the news of his treatment from reaching the public, Leo informs the president, who responds: "You fought in a war, got me elected and run the country. I think we all owe you one, don't you?" ("The Short List"). Bartlet's statement to Leo not only positions the audience to feel something about Leo's situation, but also connects Leo with a national value system. In a society whose values include independence and career success, Leo has exceeded expectations. He is a veteran, a protector of freedom, whose postmilitary career has made a significant contribution to governing the nation. Leo's status as an addict is supplanted by his status as a veteran, which makes him worthy of respect. The valor and authority that form his identity as soldier replaces the vulnerability and weakness that characterize his identity as addict. Not only does the president respect and admire him, but Bartlet's use of the third person also seems to speak directly to the audience to concur. As Bartlet the man forgives Leo his transgressions, so too does Bartlet the president. Bartlet owes Leo, as does the nation.

Bartlet's response to Leo's situation also articulates Sorkin's sense of the presidential ideal. Bartlet is framed as a politician who recognizes that his power as president is a shared one. The audience sees the character as both a kind and loyal man whose first thought is for the well being of his friend as well as a humble leader who understands that the presidency is larger than one individual. Bartlet's response is characteristic of a president who puts his staff's needs before his own, who forgives individual weakness and celebrates individual contribution and who shares his power with those around him. In Sorkin's conception of politics as workplace drama, the president becomes the ideal employer.

Leo's addiction story line resurfaces in several episodes. It is significant because it is a personal issue that is used not only to drive plotlines, but also to reveal an overall theme of *The West Wing*. In addition to being characterized as the presidency of redemption, Bartlet's White House is a place of integrity, fairness and doing the right thing because the presidency demands nothing less. This is most apparent in an episode entitled "In Excelsis Deo" when Josh and Sam decide to prevent Leo's secret from being exposed.

In the "Pilot," Sam unwittingly sleeps with a prostitute who services many high profile politicians from both parties. Josh wants her to reveal any liaisons she has had with Republicans to use as leverage against the Congressman attacking Leo. However, Leo is outraged by the idea and adamantly forbids them from proceeding:

JOSH: Lillienfield's coming down the mountain Leo. This is no joke.

LEO: You don't have to tell me it's no joke Josh. It's my life. All I'm saying is we don't do these things ["In Excelsis Deo"].

Sorkin bases Leo's refusal on the character's belief in the superior morality of the Bartlet administration. The Congressman is characterized as an unscrupulous political player while Leo's rejection of his colleagues' actions positions Bartlet and his presidency as the opposite.

In this episode, as well as the previous one that introduces Leo's addiction history, the audience is positioned to view Bartlet's administration as one that follows a higher standard. It is characterized as a presidency set apart, a presidency that forgives. More important, it is depicted as a presidency that does not reduce itself to unethical behavior to gain political capital.[20] However, Josh and Sam do reduce themselves to unethical behavior. They disobey Leo and pursue a questionable course of action. They plan to blackmail their political enemies and disregard Leo's mandate that they, by sheer virtue of being members of the Bartlet administration, are above this type of behavior. Yet Sorkin redeems them because they were willing to engage in dirty tactics for their friend. They are doing the wrong thing but for the right reasons. The audience is free to forgive the characters for falling to the level of their political enemies because their cause is a noble one.

This concept is one that is repeated throughout the series of *The West Wing* and is significant because it establishes a feeling about the Bartlet presidency. The overriding narrative of the Bartlet administration is about pursuing a course of action for a noble cause. It is about selfless politics. It is about giving the audience faith that the men and women who work in the White House are good people trying to do the right thing. The implication is clear: If the audience believes that a president's staff has these qualities, it is easy to apply them to the president as well.

Josh Lyman

Leo's deputy is Josh Lyman, played by Bradley Whitford. As with the rest of the senior staff, the character is Caucasian and in his mid- to late thirties. In Josh, Sorkin creates a masculinity similar to Leo's character; he is confident, aggressive and in control. For Whitford, the character is "smart, oversensitive and full of rage" (quoted in Moore 2000) yet Josh is also fiercely loyal. This is evident in Leo's addiction story line from the first season, as well as several episodes from the fourth season. In "Guns Not Butter," Bartlet suggests that Josh is willing to sacrifice a lot to "avoid disappointing Leo," a sentiment that Josh echoes in a flashback scene during the episode "Debate Camp" as well as in a scene from "Game On." In the episodes, he tells Leo respectively, "we're going to do better for you boss" and "we're gonna make you proud." In the character's loyalty, Sorkin establishes the idea that the Bartlet presidency is one that inspires unwavering dedication.

Josh's loyalty is matched by his passion, a trait that Sorkin introduces in the first episode of the series when Josh reacts to a politically explosive situation with feelings rather than logic. The plot centers on Josh's forced apology to influential religious conservative Mary Marsh (Annie Corley), who he insulted while a guest on a political television news show. Josh learns from Leo that "the president's pissed as hell" at him for his arrogance and he may be fired. To ease the situation, Toby insists that Josh meet with Marsh and other members of the religious right, including Reverend Al Caldwell (F. William Parker), who has a working relationship with the administration. Toby's demand puts politics above personal conviction. Josh's reaction is the opposite:

> TOBY: Come to the meeting and be nice.
>
> JOSH: Why?
>
> TOBY: So C. J. can put it in the papers.
>
> JOSH: Al Caldwell's friends with bad people. I think he should say so for the common good, screw politics, how 'bout that ["Pilot"].

Again, Sorkin has a character stress the right thing over political expediency.

Josh offers his apology as the meeting begins, but relationships quickly deteriorate when Marsh makes a thinly veiled reference to Josh and Toby being Jewish, commenting on Josh's "New York sense of humor." While Josh remains calm and tries to deal with Marsh, Toby brings the insult to everyone's attention. The meeting quickly goes out of control, and one of the conservative participants attempts to focus the discussion by declaring that the Bartlet White House concerns itself more with the First Amendment than it does with the First Commandment. He then misquotes the First Commandment, mistaking it for the Third.

Sorkin uses this scene to redeem Josh by allowing the religious conservatives to expose their ignorance. The audience is positioned to laugh at their mistake. This reaction is strengthened by the president's entrance. Having overheard Toby being asked to state the First Commandment, Bartlet interrupts the meeting by quoting it. Everyone stands and falls silent.

A brief exchange then follows between a member of the religious right and Bartlet:

> VAN DYKE: May I ask you a question, sir?
>
> BARTLET: Of course.
>
> VAN DYKE: If our children can buy pornography on any street corner for five dollars, isn't that too high a price to pay for free speech?
>
> BARTLET: No.
>
> VAN DYKE: Really?
>
> BARTLET: On the other hand, I do think that five dollars is too high a price to pay for pornography ["Pilot"].

Rather than framing the scene to provoke a cognitive response from the audience, Sorkin disrupts it with humor. Any potential for substantive argument is displaced by a joke. The political issues the group represents become subordinate to the feelings this scene generates about them. As they are repositioned as bad, Josh is framed as good.

Sorkin uses Josh to reflect a feeling about the Bartlet presidency through story lines that emphasize the character's relationship with the staff and other political players. Rarely does Sorkin contextualize the presidency through Josh's relationship with Bartlet. Throughout the series, interactions between the two characters usually take place in the presence of other members of the senior staff. Josh's behavior toward the president is depicted as professional and advisory but also humorous and irreverent:

> JOSH: An hour with you in a rare bookstore? Couldn't you just drop me off the top of the Washington monument instead?
>
> BARTLET: It's Christmas. There's no reason we can't do both ["In Excelsis Deo"].

Occasionally, the two characters interact on a more domestic level, with the president taking on the role of father figure. In one episode, Bartlet consoles Josh over his father's death ("In the Shadow of Two Gunmen, Part I"), while in another he refers to Josh as his son ("Two Cathedrals"). This domestic aspect of their relationship is also alluded to in the "Pilot." After Bartlet admonishes the Christian right group, Josh leaves the room with the rest of the staff, seeming to have successfully avoided a confrontation with the president over his actions. However, Bartlet calls him back and firmly warns him, "don't ever do it again." Finn argues that in this episode "the tones surrounding Josh's misbehavior resolve into a 'wait till your father gets home' motif that Bartlet is quick to satisfy" (2001). This is important because it simplifies the president. In the scene, he becomes a basic figure of authority for Josh and for the audience, representing one of the most fundamental aspects of American's early political socialization. The fictional president becomes associated with the qualities of the real president, as they are learned by most Americans.

Toby Ziegler

As he does with the characters of Leo and Josh, Sorkin constructs Toby Ziegler (Richard Schiff) as a character who fights to uphold the ideals of the Bartlet administration and blurs the boundary between the personal and the political. However, Toby's relationship to the president is more complex. Toby's character prevents Sorkin's ideal version of the presidency from being reduced to pure cliché because the character functions as a constant reminder of Bartlet's failure to live up to the ideal. While Sorkin allows Leo to address Bartlet candidly and even engage in argument with him, Toby is the only main character who routinely confronts Bartlet over his failings. Through Toby, Sorkin connects Bartlet's failures to the presidency so that man and institution are not easily separated.

In order to make Toby's rough relationship with Bartlet credible, Sorkin often frames the character as an agitator. Toby's masculinity is, again, similarly constructed to that of Leo and Josh. He is assertive, in control and excels professionally. While Sorkin occasionally allows Leo and Josh to reveal feelings of insecurity, he rarely gives the audience the vulnerable side of Toby. The character is defined by his logical, stoic approach to situations as well as his lack of fear in confronting those in power. In various episodes, Toby challenges a congressman's concern over a pending trade bill:

TOBY: You're concerned about American labor and manufacturing?

CONGRESSMAN: Yes.

TOBY: What kind of car do you drive?

CONGRESSMAN : A Toyota.

TOBY: Then shut up ["The White House Pro-Am"].

Toby publicly criticizes the Indonesian president ("The State Dinner") and threatens a group of jaded network television news directors with a justice department investigation into antitrust violations, if they pursue their plan not to broadcast the majority of the national conventions:

There isn't going to be a horserace to cover either in New York or San Diego. But we gave you the airwaves for free 70 years ago and 357 days a year you can say who's up and who's down, who won the west and lost the south. But what's wrong with eight days, not every year but every four years, showing our leaders talking to us? Not a fraction of what they said but what they said ["The Black Vera Wang"].

Toby's role as malcontent provides a narrative tension about Bartlet's presidency that is often left unresolved, yet his speeches also articulate an ideal version of government that recalls the basic tenets of early political learning.

In an episode from the first season, this vision becomes clear in a speech to the president and Josh about the upcoming State of the Union address:

But we're here now. And tomorrow night, we do an immense thing. And we have to say what we feel. That government, no matter what its failures in the past and in times to come for that matter, government can be a place where people come together and where no one gets left behind. No one gets left behind—an instrument of good ["He Shall, from Time to Time..."].

The speech articulates the ideals that the American presidency (as defined by political socialization) promises—a fair and good institution that is responsible to all citizens. In an episode from the fourth season, Sorkin focuses this vision by directly connecting it to Bartlet. In "20 Hours in America Part II," Toby tells Josh and Donna:

If we choose someone with vision, someone with guts, someone with gravitas who's connected to other people's lives and cares about making them better— if we choose someone to inspire us then we'll be able to face what comes our way and achieve things we can't imagine yet.

The president, then, is someone who rises above the natural inclination of a politician to give the people what they want to hear. More importantly, he is a leader who is not afraid of his feelings.

Sorkin continues these themes through Toby and Bartlet's interactions, which become more confrontational as the series progresses. In a key scene from season one, Toby uses his frustration with Bartlet during a pickup game of basketball to express his feelings about the president's weakness:

This is perfect, you know that? This is the perfect metaphor. After you're gone and the poets write 'The Legend of Josiah Bartlet,' let them write you as a tragic figure. Let the poets write, "He had the tools to be a leader of men, but the voices of his better angels were shouted down by his obsessive need to win" ["The Crackpot and These Women"].

Toby's words frame Bartlet as a man struggling against a nature that does not meet the expectations of the presidency. This failure of character has important implications for the viewer's reaction to the institution of the president. Toby consistently establishes a vision of the presidency that Bartlet fails to realize through personal weakness. Yet Sorkin also constructs Bartlet's weakness as sympathetic. Later in the episode the president tells Toby

> I know I disappoint you sometimes. I mean I can sense your disappointment and I only get mad 'cause I know you're right a lot of the times....

By admitting that Toby is right, Sorkin allows Bartlet to recognize his failure to meet his potential as president. However, in the recognition he is forgiven for the failure because the audience understands that he wants to do better. This becomes clearer as the exchange continues:

> BARTLET: The other night when we were playing basketball, did you mean what you said? That my demons were shouting down the better angels in my brain?
>
> TOBY: Yes sir I did.
>
> BARTLET: You think that's what's stopping me from greatness?
>
> TOBY: Yes.
>
> BARTLET: I suppose you're right.
>
> TOBY: Tell ya what though sir, in a battle between the president's demons and his better angels, for the first time in a long while, I think we might just have ourselves a fair fight.

By admitting his failure, Bartlet is seeking the redemptive power of the presidency. To do this, he separates himself from the institution in order to be saved by it. However, Toby reconnects Bartlet with the presidential legacy by legitimizing his role within it. Toby's remarks ask the audience to recall the legacy of past American presidents and place the fictional Bartlet among them. His suggestion that perhaps Bartlet stands apart from these men because he has the potential to overcome his demons elevates the narrative's presidency to the institutional ideal as it is learned in early political socialization. While the presidency is a study in flawed men, it is an office that endures in spite of these men. This idea is an essential component in the acceptance of presidential power. The institution remains and is renewed with each new man who enters the Oval Office.

With the Bartlet White House, Sorkin offers the fantasy that the institution and the man may embody the presidential ideal simultaneously. One of the main functions of Toby's character is to act as guardian of this myth. Through his narrative, the audience is encouraged to believe in the ideal. As a surrogate for the viewer, Toby's frustration with the president's failure to make a positive impact may be understood to mirror the public's disenchantment with government. Yet Toby maintains a belief in the institution of the presidency. In other words, he articulates the vision of an ideal president that rests on the premise of a fair and just leader who speaks the truth and guides his people righteously. In this way, he recalls the optimism of early political learning and his narrative encourages the viewer to do the same.

C. J. Cregg

In *"The West Wing": The Official Companion*, Sorkin admits that the character of C. J. Cregg (Allison Janney) "was the most underwritten role in the pilot" (2002, 101). While it took Sorkin several episodes to develop the character, Janney notes that she wanted to play C. J. because she "loved the quick banter" of Sorkin's pilot script (*ibid.*). The only female member of the president's senior staff, C. J., in Sorkin's view, represents an image of women rarely seen on television. He notes that "unlike a lot of young female characters in films and television today, C. J.'s life isn't about 'When is Mr. Right going to come along and save me from this?' She is constructing her world for herself" (*ibid.*). While C. J. is depicted as independent, assertive and a strong member of the Bartlet family, the character is also frequently portrayed as a victim of her emotions. C. J. is Sorkin's clearest example of the link between the personal and the political as the character's feelings consistently inform her work.

While Sorkin claims that C. J. represents a strong form of female empowerment, he often makes her appear emotionally vulnerable. C. J. is the one member of Bartlet's staff who must continually prove her value. She is the only character who regularly displays anxiety over her abilities to work for the president. This is evident in a flashback episode that recounts the staff's recruitment for the Bartlet campaign wherein C. J. expresses concern that she may not be qualified to perform the role ("In the Shadow of Two Gunmen, Part II"). This self-doubt is absent from all the other characters' histories. In various plot points, Sorkin informs the audience that Leo has successfully served in political appointments. In fact, the vice president refers to him as a "world class political operative" ("Post Hoc, Ergo Propter Hoc"). Josh and Toby are also characterized as experienced political players ("Celestial Navigation," "In the Shadow of Two Gunmen, Part I"). C. J. and Sam are the only senior staff to be recruited from nonpolitical work, yet Sorkin only portrays C. J. as questioning her abilities. Sam is a corporate lawyer who expresses no anxiety about his capacity to work on the campaign or his qualifications to (later) fulfil the role of Deputy Communications Director.

The flashback narrative, while revealing C. J.'s earliest expression of self-doubt, does not introduce the theme. Sorkin uses the character's inexperience to position her as an outsider early in the first season. In "Lord John Marbury," the senior staff decides to purposely misinform C. J. about the level of hostilities occurring between India and Pakistan, causing her in turn to publicly dismiss a member of the press who questions her regarding the facts of the story. Leo tells her the truth the next day, and she is devastated by her treatment of the reporter. He unsympathetically responds that there will be times she should expect not to be informed. Toby attempts to offer a more consoling explanation, reasoning that the story was not ready to be reported. She dismisses his excuse and argues that they have undermined her fragile relationship with the press and severely affected her credibility. Toby admits the truth:

C. J.: You guys sent me in there uninformed so that I'd lie to the press.

TOBY: We sent you in there uninformed because we thought there was a chance you couldn't.

C. J. is isolated because her colleagues lack confidence in her ability to make the hard decisions that are a harsh reality of political work.

Sorkin mirrors this view of C. J. through the character's own actions. In "Let Bartlet be Bartlet," she blames the staff's low morale for her failure to stop the press from reporting on a damaging memo that is critical of the administration. The self-doubt this failure generates underlies the following two episodes, wherein she is clearly depicted as fragile and professionally weak. In one, she makes a critical mistake when speaking to the press about regulations governing the FEC ("Mandatory Minimums"), and in the other she feels ostracized by Leo, who chooses not to convey her opinion on a polling issue to the president ("Lies, Damn Lies, and Statistics"). C. J.'s lack of confidence in her professional abilities is continued in season two. In addition to recounting the anxious tone of her recruitment history ("In the Shadow of Two Gunmen, Part II"), Sorkin shows her stressed to the point of sleeplessness over a mistake she believes she made in a press briefing ("In This White House"). While these depictions support the idea that Sorkin continually collapses the space between the personal and the political, they also suggest that C. J.'s characterization is not as strong as Sorkin claims.

However, as Sorkin develops the character, C. J. becomes more politically sophisticated. In an obvious replay of themes introduced in the "Lord John Marbury" episode, C. J. successfully lies to the press. This time, she even chooses to deliver the misinformation to a reporter with whom she shares a romantic interest ("What Kind of Day Has It Been"). In other episodes, the president seeks her opinion on an issue and includes her in his jokes ("The Portland Trip"), she scolds Leo for failing to see her on professional terms: "I'm not your daughter. I'm the White House Press Secretary," ("Inauguration Part II"), and she earns the respect of her male colleagues. When Toby makes a critical mistake that C. J. warned him against, Josh recognizes and credits her restraint: "You had a lot of opportunities to say I told you so and score some points with Leo. You're a class act" ("The Leadership Breakfast").

While Sorkin develops C. J.'s political skills, he maintains the character's highly emotional views on issues. This invites the viewer to relate to several of these issues through C. J.'s feelings. In one episode, C. J. is asked about a news story in which Saudi Arabian schoolgirls were left to burn to death because the religious police deemed they were inappropriately dressed and could not be saved by male rescue workers. She responds:

> Outraged? I'm barely surprised. This is a country where women aren't allowed to drive a car. They're not allowed to be in the company of any man other than a close relative. They're required to adhere to a dress code that would make a Maryknoll nun look like Malibu Barbie.... Seventeen schoolgirls were forced to burn alive because they weren't wearing the proper clothing. Am I outraged? No. This is Saudi Arabia, our partner in peace ["Enemies Foreign and Domestic"].

While Sorkin allows C. J. to take an affective view of policy here, he also reminds the audience that they share an equal responsibility for "our partner" Saudi Arabia. Sorkin uses C. J's monologue to confront viewers with their role in the tragedy and to heighten the emotional component of a political issue. The scene is also important because it has implications for Sorkin's presentation of the presidency. If Sorkin uses Toby to represent political learning in its most basic form, that is, a conception of politics that holds the president accountable for the triumphs and failings of the nation, then he employs C. J. to represent later-stage political socialization. Moving beyond an understanding of the president as the sole instrument of government, she assigns the citizenry its role in politics, implicating the public in policy outcomes.

Sorkin continues to encourage an affective response to politics through C. J. in "The Women of Qumar." Perhaps his most emotional depiction of the character, Sorkin shapes the episode around C. J.'s reactions to the administration's approval of an arms sale to the country of Qumar. The Qumari government systematically mistreats and denies women basic human rights. C. J.'s reaction is foreshadowed by President Bartlet's comments in the opening scene. Briefing Toby about the sale, he tells him to inform C. J. but have her pass the information off to the Department of Defense. When Toby questions this decision by suggesting that the DoD's handling of the release indicates that the White House does not want the public to give it much attention, the president establishes the emotional tempo of the episode. He replies, "Every time we make one of these deals with a place like Qumar, I feel the women around here look at me funny." He continues by specifically referring to C. J., "C. J.'s going to be cool with this right? ... She knows who the good guys are right?" As the episode progresses, it is C. J.'s emotional reaction to the decision that forms a strong narrative undercurrent that flows into one of the minor subplots and ultimately explodes in a confrontation with the National Security Adviser.

Growing increasingly upset over what she feels is the administration's hypocrisy in advocating gun control and championing the rights of women, yet selling arms to a repressive regime, C. J. interrupts a veteran's group that is meeting with Toby to discuss their objections to a Pearl Harbor exhibit. Asking them to imagine that their efforts to defeat Germany had failed and the Nazis existed as a recognized government in the European Union, she poses this scenario:

> You're protesting because you think the Smithsonian isn't paying proper respect to what you and the soldiers of the Tenth Armored, Third Army risked and lost your lives for six decades ago. How would you feel in the hypothetical I just described, if I told you that in my press briefing at the end of the day, I was announcing we were selling tanks, missiles and fighter jets to the Nazis?

Toby reacts by firmly asking her to step outside. Once in the hallway, her anger surfaces: "Look. You know, if I was living in Qumar, I wouldn't be allowed to say 'Shove it up your ass, Toby,' but since I'm not—shove it up your ass Toby!" C. J.'s emotional state reaches its most extreme point at the end of the episode when she confronts the National Security Adviser, Nancy McNally (Anna Deveare Smith):

> NANCY: I understand you're troubled by the arms sale? The Nazis were a bad analogy. We're not fighting a war with Qumar.
>
> C. J.: Well, this isn't the point, but we will. Of course we will. Of course we will be fighting a war with Qumar someday and you know it, so, well, at least we'll be familiar with the weapons they're using.

When Nancy protests that the United States needs the air base in Qumar for refueling and radar purposes, C. J. protests that in reality, the base is just convenient. This leads her into admitting the real reason the sale upsets her: "They beat women, Nancy. They hate women. The only reason they keep Qumari women alive is to make more Qumari men." Nancy is unmoved by this reasoning, and C. J.'s emotional state grows increasingly unstable. Her tactics change, and she tries to appeal to Nancy, who is an African American, with an analogy to apartheid:

> It's the twenty-first century, Nancy. The world's gotten smaller. I don't know how we can tolerate this kind of suffering anymore, particularly when all it does is continue the cycle of anti-American hatred. But that's not the point either.... The point is that apartheid was an East Hampton clambake compared to what we laughingly refer to as the life these women lead. And if we had sold M1-A1s to South Africa fifteen years ago, you'd have set the building on fire. Thank God we never needed to refuel at Johannesburg.

However, this provocation fails to move Nancy, who responds mildly: "I'm doing the best I can." The unexpected reaction causes C. J. to reach her emotional breaking point. Close to tears she chokes out slowly and deliberately: "They're beating the women, Nancy." Nancy responds by walking away. C. J. raises a hand to her forehead, controls herself and calmly and professionally delivers her briefing to the press.

In her work on the series, Lane suggests that "*The West Wing* dramatizes the moral ambiguity and complex, layered relationships between the private and public spheres" (2003, 32). "The Women of Qumar" is a clear example of this narrative technique, as C. J. struggles with her personal attitudes and her work obligations. While the plot suggests that the relationship between the two is complicated, the final confrontation between C. J. and Nancy simplifies the connection. What begins as an intellectual position dissolves into an emotional collapse, an outcome Sorkin prepares the audience for throughout the episode as C. J. grows increasingly distressed. This characterization is consistent with the underlying tone of the series that the personal and the political are not easily separated. This tone, however, is not significant because Sorkin creates it. Rather, its power lies in how Sorkin achieves it.

"The Women of Qumar" is one example of many story lines in which Sorkin uses a character's feelings about politics to define politics. In Sorkin's scripts, the connection between politics and the personal is clearly blurred, yet his dependence on the dramatic power of emotions means that thinking something about political issues is consistently abandoned in favor of feeling something about them. The confrontation between C. J. and Nancy is between emotions and logic. C. J. protests on behalf of her feelings for the mistreatment of women. Nancy responds with Qumar's practical uses. C. J. represents compassion, empathy and humanitarian duty. Nancy is positioned as the cold, heartless representative of government. Sorkin constructs a simple fight with clear right and wrong. Because he gives logic less time than feelings, Sorkin allows C. J.'s position to be stronger. The character's desperate pleading is compelling and made more convincing when she accuses Nancy of hypocritical thinking. In addition, Sorkin prevents C. J.'s near breakdown from being dismissed because he returns the character to her professional role at the conclusion of the scene.

Sorkin repeats his focus on the emotional nature of the private/public theme in C. J.'s relationship with the president. In one of the third season's main story lines, the president announces that he has multiple sclerosis, a secret that he has kept for many years. Shortly after the MS news breaks, Haiti undergoes a military coup and the president decides to invade. In a typical pressroom scene, C. J. is briefing reporters on the situation. The room is chaotic and the reporters grow increasingly aggressive in their questions about the president's multiple sclerosis. C. J., who regularly conducts the briefings with a calm air of authority, begins to lose control of the meeting and grows increasingly confused by the barrage of questions being shouted at her. Responding to a reporter who questions the president's state of mind and his ability to make a rational decision regarding Haiti, she says with visible frustration: "To be honest with you Carl, I think the president is relieved to be focussing on something that matters" ("Manchester, Part I"). The entire room falls silent. The reporter asks if he heard her correctly. She tries to fix the gaffe but is unable to think or speak clearly and abruptly leaves the room. Toby and Sam, having heard the mistake, are shocked. Sam expresses their disbelief:

> He's relieved he might have to send troops into battle? He's relieved he might have to put lives at risk and kill Haitian civilians because it takes his mind off of having lied to the electorate?

Believing that her mistake at the briefing is irreparable, C. J. offers her resignation to Leo. He refuses it but does keep her from the pressroom for several days. Visibly depressed, she moves through her duties with little enthusiasm. Her attempts to get the first lady and the president together for a photo opportunity before the official launch of the reelection campaign lead to a confrontation with Bartlet:[21]

C. J.: I was told you wanted to see me.

BARTLET: Yeah. Don't be a marriage counselor. It pisses me off okay?

C. J.: I'm sorry?

BARTLET: You know what I'm talking about

C. J.: Sir—

BARTLET: That part of my life doesn't belong to you.

C. J.: Sir, I was simply putting together what I thought was the best press event. The First Lady is an excellent speaker—

BARTLET: Alright. I'll see you out there.

Before leaving, C. J. sees this as her opportunity to tell the president what she really wants:

C. J.: Sir, I think if you get a bump in the polls after today's speech, as we expect you will, sir, I think it'd be a good time for me to resign.

BARTLET: Yeah?

C. J.: Well, to leave earlier would have been strategically—

BARTLET: Yeah, okay.

C. J.: Look, the press says—

BARTLET: That's nonsense to me and I don't care.

C. J.: Well, you might not care—

BARTLET: Of all the new jobs we've created there are single mothers working two of them at minimum wage. There are school districts where less than half the students graduate and a kid born in Harlem is more likely to go to jail than a four-year college. They're bringing guns to school C. J.!

C. J.: Don't you dare lecture me Mr. President! Don't you dare do it.

The scene reaches an emotional breaking point, and both characters stop speaking, seeming surprised that they have raised their voices at each other. There is a tense silence between them, and C. J. turns away. The president's demeanor changes as if he has just thought of his words for the first time. He tells C. J. that he was never supposed to win the presidency. He was an acknowledged underdog, but then "you guys came along." He admits it was a mistake to keep her from the last press conference. The president's personal aide interrupts to tell C. J. that they need her at the event. Bartlet responds: "I need you too."

Sorkin begins this scene with C. J. believing that the presidency has been dishonored by her actions; specifically, she has failed to control her emotions. Again, the personal and the political are blurred, but this time C. J. has not found the balance necessary to perform her job. Sorkin then shifts the focus onto Bartlet's personal failure when C. J. confronts the president over his choice to privilege his feelings over those of his staff. Hearing Bartlet define the presidency in terms of the staff's collective mistakes without acknowledging his recent betrayal of their trust, C. J. admonishes him for shaming the institution and failing their presidential family. Bartlet appears unsympathetic because he attempts to separate the personal from the political. It is only when the president recognizes that this separation is wrong that Sorkin redeems the character. When Bartlet recognizes his mistakes as well as C. J.'s worth, Sorkin restores the president as a likeable character and gives validity to C. J.'s feelings.

While the confrontational scene between Bartlet and C. J. allows Sorkin to use C. J. to explore the affective dimension of the president's relationship with the personal and the political, he assigns C. J. a level of emotion that is not a regular component of her relationship with the president. Unlike Toby, C. J.'s passionate opinions about the administration's policy decisions are not routinely a challenge to the president. While C. J.'s view of government is as equally affective as the other senior staff, her usual response to its failings is to blame abstract political pressures or herself rather than directly confront the president (as Toby would do). Through C. J., Sorkin adds a new dimension to his portrait of the ideal presidency that recalls the mature stages of political socialization, wherein the president is not held solely accountable for the successes and failures of government.

Sam Seaborn

The West Wing narrative comes closest to representing the mythic presidency, the larger-than-life ideal leader, through the character of Sam Seaborn (Rob Lowe). With this character, Sorkin articulates a vision of politics that recalls the earliest learned notions of the president and government as instruments of good. Sam's politically innocent conduct asks the audience to remember their most basic conception of the presidency and government as institutions that lead by example and strive to enrich the lives of all citizens. While Sorkin uses Toby's voice to mold Bartlet into this vision, he uses Sam to create a version that partially exists outside of the president. It is as much about the idea of a great country as it is of a great leader.

Sam is the most sensitive and politically naïve of the principal characters, and Sorkin often feminizes his masculinity. Previously a successful attorney on the verge of being made partner in his law firm, Sam in the Bartlet administration is defined by his junior status. His relationship to the other male senior staff is often characterized by his attempts to please them and seek their approval. Of all the principal male characters, only Sam is allowed to consistently express his feelings or respond to issues emotionally. While Sam is recognized for these traits by his male colleagues, he is also separated from their form of masculinity, as his emotions often mark him as weak, a characterization that Sorkin uses in several episodes throughout the series.

Sam's emotional nature is introduced in the pilot episode. Specifically, his affective perception of the presidency is evident in the long monologue he delivers to Leo's daughter. Forced to give a tour of the White House to Leo's daughter's fourth grade class, he hastily tells the children that the White House "was built several years ago, mostly ... out of cement" and that the chairs they are sitting on were "fashioned from the lumber of a pirate ship." When the children's teacher, Mallory, stops him, he pleads with her to tell him which child is Leo's daughter, reasoning that if he can make her laugh, at least one part of his bad day might be salvaged. Mallory is not interested. Sam tries to gain her sympathy:

> SAM: Ms. O'Brian, I understand your feelings, but please believe me when I tell you that I'm a nice guy having a bad day. I just found out the *Times* is publishing a poll that says a considerable portion of Americans feel that the White House has lost energy and focus. A perception that's not likely to be altered by the video footage of the president riding his bicycle into a tree. As we speak, the Coast Guard are fishing Cubans out of the Atlantic Ocean while the Governor of Florida wants to blockade the Port of Miami. A good friend of mine is about to get fired for going on television and making sense, and it turns out that I accidentally slept with a prostitute last night. Now would you please, in the name of compassion, tell me which one of those kids is my boss's daughter.
>
> MALLORY: That would be me.

This monologue introduces Sam's understanding of the presidency, one that will form the basis of his relationship with Bartlet, as well as the audience, as the series progresses. A true believer in the sanctity of government, Sam believes that the criticisms of the Bartlet White House are only a perception, while the truth of their work is different. Throughout the series, Sam will be the voice of this optimistic vision, urging the audience to be converted.

The energy and focus that Sorkin uses to characterize Sam's work comes from a differentiation between the right side of an issue and the winning side of it. In this, Sorkin creates Sam as the "anti-politician" politician, confirming his innocent status. Contrary to the typical political text that depicts a self-serving politician concerned only with taking the quickest path to reelection, no matter where it leads, Sorkin writes Sam as a character whose only concern is staying on the path if it moves in an honest direction. In many story lines he has Sam argue aggressively for this idea. Early in season one the audience sees this for the first time.

After telling his boss's daughter that he accidentally slept with a prostitute, Sam realizes that he should confide in other members of the senior staff. He confesses to Josh and later to Toby that he has feelings for the woman and would like to see her again. Josh is surprised and suggests that the White House needs to avoid the inevitable bad press, while Toby cynically wonders why the administration needs an opposition party when they do so well sabotaging themselves ("Post Hoc, Ergo Propter Hoc"). Despite their warnings, Sam maintains a friendship with the woman. When C. J. finds out, the ensuing confrontation reveals the crux of Sam's character:

> C. J.: You work in the White House, Sam. You work fifty feet from the Oval Office and you're consorting with a woman—
>
> SAM: Consorting? I'm friendly with a woman. I like this woman. This woman poses no threat to the president. And it's very likely that owing to my friendship, this woman may start living her life in bounds, insuring for herself a greater future, and isn't that exactly what it is we're supposed to be doing here.

C. J. thinks she has figured out Sam's motivation:

> C. J.: You're there to help her see the error of her ways.
>
> SAM: I am there because I like her. I'm there because it's there I'd be if this were alcohol or drugs. I'm not sleeping with her. This isn't tawdry.
>
> C. J.: I don't care what it is. I care what it looks like.
>
> SAM: And I care what it is. And I think it's high time we all spent a little less time looking good—
>
> SAM & C. J.: and a little more
>
> C. J.: time being good? ["A Proportional Response"].

Sorkin connects Sam's behavior to the broader conduct government should support. As Sam wants to point the woman toward a greater future, so too should the government want it for her, for all its citizens. In this, Sam becomes an agent of the ideal administration. His faith in the government's role and his part in it is so strong that even when faced with the potential that his actions could cause damage to the president, he does not relent. When C. J. tries to explain her true point: "You have to let me protect you and you have to let me protect the president," Sam is still not convinced:

> Can I go now, C. J.? 'Cause what I think it's about is you, once again, letting the character cops win in a forfeit, because you don't have the guts or the strength or the courage to say "We know what's right from wrong and this is none of your damn business."

After accusing C. J. of not having the courage to see it from his perspective, Sam vents his frustration to Josh, arguing that he knows the difference between right and wrong. Josh responds that Sam knew his position would hold him to a higher standard. Sam replies: "I don't mind being held to a higher standard. I mind being held to a lower one."

Sorkin's characterization of Sam, as introduced in this early story line and maintained throughout the series, continues the recurring theme of personal issues merging with political ones. However, Sorkin also uses Sam to complicate the dynamic. As with the other principal characters, Sam defines politics by his emotions, but he also demands that the presidency adhere to a specific value system. Rather than isolate this value system to the character, Sorkin assigns it a broader cultural meaning so that Sam's affective (and personal) positions are often the right ones. The audience is encouraged to focus on Sam's noble goals rather than judge the morality of prostitution.[22] Sam is not fighting for "prostitute Laurie," he is fighting for "citizen Laurie," whose government should be responsible for helping her reach her potential. The idea uses the presidency to articulate a value system that is appealing because it does the right thing. In addition, the presidency has as much responsibility toward the citizen as the citizen has toward it. As the episode concludes, Bartlet underscores this theme when he speaks to Charlie, the young man who will become his personal aide. Discovering that Charlie's mother was killed in the line of duty by cop killer bullets, Bartlet asks if he would like to "come help try" to get them banned ("A Proportional Response"). Working for the presidency is framed in personal terms. In Sorkin's conception, it is an institution that responds to citizens' emotional needs because that is its mandate.

Sorkin's portrayal of Sam as a character who is committed to a pure vision of politics—one that is strongly informed by his emotions—resurfaces in several later episodes that show him unwavering in his ideals, even in the face of power. An example of this occurs midway through the first season in "The Short List" when the character confronts a Supreme Court nominee the Bartlet White House has been courting.

Having discovered a university paper written by the administration's nominee to the Supreme Court that argues against privacy as a guaranteed right, Sam strongly believes that the candidate should be dropped from consideration. While the nominee believes that the Constitution must be taken literally, Sam disagrees and makes his objections known in clear terms by quoting a member of the 1787 Georgia delegation:

SAM: "If we list a set of Rights, some fools in the future are going to claim that the People have only those rights enumerated and no more."

HARRISON: We're you just calling me a fool, Mr. Seaborn?

SAM: I wasn't calling you a fool, sir. The brand new state of Georgia was.

Later, he presents his case to Toby and the president:

> It's the next twenty years. Twenties and thirties it was the role of the govern-
> ment. Fifties and sixties it was civil rights. The next two decades are gonna
> be privacy. I'm talking about the Internet; I'm talking about cell phones. I'm
> talking about health records and about who's gay and who's not. Moreover, in
> a country born of the will to be free, what could be more fundamental than
> this?

With this speech, Sorkin again connects Sam's personal convictions
to the administration as a whole. Sam's vision of the nation's future should
be the government's vision. More important, Sam's argument relies on the
affective, asking Toby, the president and the viewer to recall basic notions
of patriotism. In fact, the entire scene depends on creating an emotional
atmosphere, first toward the judge, then toward Sam's patriotic declaration.

Asked by the president to defend his position, the scene begins as the
nominee confidently claims that for litigation purposes, the Constitution
must be interpreted strictly according to its text, which does not mention
a right to privacy. Sam reacts with his quote from the Georgia delegation,
and the judge suddenly becomes impatient and arrogant. He responds
aggressively by attempting to diminish Sam and finally ends by threatening that the White House needs him. (He is popular and a guaranteed nomination). While the audience is now positioned to dislike the judge, Sorkin
uses Sam's speech to seal his fate. The viewer is asked for an emotional
reaction rather than a cognitive one. The issue is not debated beyond Sam's
passionate speech, which is meant to elicit feelings about what it means
to be free in America. The president and Toby are immediately convinced
and decide to nominate a new candidate.

If the audience is still in doubt over their feelings toward the nominee, Sorkin directs them again with a brief scene between the nominee and
Charlie, the president's young African American personal aide. While the
judge is waiting in an anteroom during Sam's speech, he thinks he recognizes Charlie, who confirms that he was a caddy at a golf club where the
judge is a member. The audience then learns that a Hispanic nominee will
replace the judge, who is white. The subtle implication is that his race and
privilege also make him a villain. In turn, Sam's aggressiveness toward the
judge is all the more affective because he is depicted as a freedom-loving
citizen, rallying the viewer with patriotic rhetoric. Against his political
goodness, the nominee's political badness becomes starkly vivid. The effect

is to reduce any complexity his position may have had into a simple equation of good versus evil.

In an episode from the second season, Sorkin again uses Sam to generate an emotional response from the viewer with a passionate argument that reflects the character's vision of America and privileges the affective over the cognitive. When Leo's daughter Mallory suggests that the money spent to develop and launch Galileo, a Mars lander, should be directed to more important areas such as food, housing and education, Sam argues that exploration is vital to national identity. It is America's duty to go to Mars:

> 'Cause we came out of a cave and we looked over the hill and we saw fire and we crossed the ocean and we pioneered the West and we took to the sky. The history of Man is hung on a timeline of exploration. And this is what's next ["Galileo"].

In Sam's vision, it is the Bartlet administration's obligation to support and fulfill the country's destiny, which embraces a spirit of achievement and adventure. The tone again relies on a feeling about the country rather than a cognitive argument about the issues. The presidency is not only connected to feelings of pride in the nation's past but also entrusted with maintaining confidence in its future.

In addition to using speeches that rely on emotive language rather than cognitive reasoning, Sorkin characterizes Sam as a public servant who exists outside the normative view of the political world. Sam's passionate arguments become associated with the good side of politics because other political characters in the series, defined against Sam, maintain the conventional role of disingenuous, self-serving operatives. This allows Sam to represent an ideal of politics that plays on the viewer's earliest affective understanding of government and the presidency as forces for good. Sorkin uses Sam's status as an outsider to great effect in two episodes from the series. In one, the character's idealistic belief leads to a clash with a colleague, while in the other, an impulsive choice damages the president's reelection campaign. Both episodes frame Sam as a victim of harsh politics.

In "The Drop-In," Sam convinces the president to use a cancelled overseas trip as an opportunity to address an environmental lobby group and announce an important clean-air initiative. The speech becomes an all-consuming project as Sam begins work on draft number twelve, desperate to convey his passion and literally bring the audience to their feet. While he is lost in the excitement of promoting an issue he strongly supports, Toby sees the negative political implications and urges the president to use a drop-in line admonishing the environmental group for not condemning acts of ecoterrorism. He purposely excludes Sam from the decision.

Watching the speech, Sam hears the line for the first time and later discovers that it was prearranged. Furious at being excluded, he is also outraged over the political maneuver and confronts Toby demanding an explanation:

> TOBY: I didn't want the discussion.
>
> SAM: Then what are you doing here talking to me?! Now you want the discussion. You and the president may think they deserved it, but the cynicism of attacking your friends for political protection offends them. And it offends me. And it offends you. And there's really nothing I can do to make you feel better about that.
>
> TOBY: We can't govern if we can't win.

A political decision is evaluated on affective terms—cynicism versus optimism, honesty versus manipulation.

Sam's appeal to Toby fails when it is countered by an obvious political truth, but this does not weaken the affective power of the scene. Sorkin's depiction of Sam as the political innocent facing the harsh side of politics maintains sympathy for the character as a friend and colleague betrayed. The viewer is not encouraged to separate Sam's political argument from his hurt feelings. While Sam loses the argument on political terms, he wins it on emotional ones by placing himself and his vision for the presidency above deceit and manipulation. This characterization shifts Sam to the role of righteous political outsider and is repeated in an episode where his trust in a friend leads to a bad choice.

As the senior staff strategize for Bartlet's reelection campaign, Sam anonymously receives a videotape of an advertisement that attacks the president's integrity. After some debate, the staff and Bruno Gianelli (a campaign consultant) agree to ignore the tape. Sam, however, suggests that he meet with his friend Kevin, who works for the Republican presidential candidate, Rob Ritchie, to discuss the situation. In what Sam believes is a fortunate coincidence, Kevin calls and invites him to lunch. Suggesting that they meet regularly to "keep things under control if they get bad" Kevin sincerely wonders if the pair could be "emissaries" to engage in "genuine dialogue" between the two parties during the campaign ("The Black Vera Wang"). Sam, convinced of Kevin's honorable intentions, decides to discuss the attack ad, despite receiving no instructions from Bruno or Leo to do so. He warns his friend that the Republican campaign has a leak and gives him the tape. Kevin expresses surprise and promises to investigate.

The audience learns of Kevin's disingenuous nature before Sam does when Bruno is informed that Sam's meeting was leaked to the media, along

with the tape. Bruno confronts Sam, dramatically turning on every television outside his office to a different news channel. The attack ad is the
story on each one. The Ritchie campaign has successfully aired the tape
while claiming no responsibility for its creation. Sam is shocked and
horrified at his mistake, as Bruno confronts him with the now obvious
truth: "You got played Sam and you forgot that all warfare is based on
deception..." ("The Black Vera Wang"). Still reeling from the betrayal,
Sam angrily confronts Kevin on the street later that night. It is a physical
and emotional moment for Sam as he grabs his friend from behind and
screams, "I can't believe you did that!" Kevin harshly dismisses him and
reveals his actions were in revenge for a gaffe that Bartlet made to a reporter,
joking about Ritchie's intelligence.

In this scene, Sorkin contextualizes Sam's powerless state and outsider
status by having him confront Kevin outside of a work environment, which
strips Sam of the protection and force of the White House. Sam must face
his political disillusionment alone. When Kevin suggests that he is certain
there will be more sly attacks on his candidate from the Bartlet camp, Sam
assures him there will be. It is here that Sorkin temporarily disrupts the
political innocent characterization of Sam by having him commit to a
course of action he has previously shunned. In his threat to Kevin, Sam
loses a significant part of his political naiveté. Yet, the viewer is encouraged
to sympathize with the character's feelings of anger and betrayal, which
undermine the image of Sam's initiation into political warfare. Sam is foremost a friend betrayed. This makes it easy to accept that he may be less
trusting in the future but hard to believe that he will be transformed by
the experience.

Sorkin confirms this in the last two episodes of the third season. After
the mistake, Sam is quiet and disengaged from his work, even prompting
several colleagues to ask him how he is feeling. Leo expresses concern by
requesting that Toby give him "an encouraging word," and an old acquain-
tance relays a message that it is time to "get up off the dirt" ("We Killed
Yamamoto"). The clear impression is that Sam has the full support of his
colleagues and his mistake is easily forgiven. Leo's comment that he loves
the way Sam went about it—"full speed, bam, like there's a Sam Seaborn
shaped hole in the wall"—also undermines any perception the viewer may
have that the mistake has changed the fundamental nature of the character. He is admired for employing the same passion in failure as he does in
success. Sam is punishing himself rather than being punished, yet by the
end of the episode, he quickly recovers by expressing his usual enthusiasm
for a proposal to expose Ritchie's support for special interest groups, claiming that "it's the right thing to do" ("We Killed Yamamoto"). In the final

episode of the third season, his political maneuvering consists of a calculated plan to make Ritchie late to an event that the president is also attending by using the official motorcade to block traffic. His action is more akin
to a juvenile prank than a malicious political move, proving that his fundamental nature has not changed.

Sam's noble vision of politics is most fully realized in the fourth season, when he runs for a congressional seat. Sent to deal with a congressional
campaign being fought in a Republican stronghold whose candidate has
suddenly died, Sam meets dedicated campaign manager Will Bailey (Joshua
Malina), who refuses to concede the race. Will's strong conviction persuades
Sam to be the replacement nominee in the unlikely event that the Democrats win the election. Will achieves a surprise victory, and Sam leaves the
White House to honor his commitment. While Sam's choice reflects the
character's fundamental belief in the value of civic duty, it also allows
Sorkin to repeat his emotional construction of Bartlet.[23]

With Sam's campaign struggling, the senior staff arrange for Bartlet
to attend several events in Sam's district. The weekend visit coincides with
the Republican's announcement of a tax plan. The White House's tax plan,
if announced before the visit, would damage Sam's race in the mostly
Republican district. Bartlet's choice to delay the announcement (thereby
making the White House look weak) allows Sorkin to frame the president
as one who chooses family over politics. Sam's reaction to the decision is
equally personal. Realizing what his friends have done, he responds: "The
hell with the election! There's a guy in St. Louis making $55,000 a year
trying to send his kid to Notre Dame" ("The California 47th"). Later he
tells Toby: "If I'm going to lose, I'd like to lose doing something" ("The
California 47th"). In this characterization, Sam (like Bartlet) is both a
loyal member of the presidential family and a self-sacrificing public servant.

Throughout the series, Sorkin uses Sam's simple, straightforward
approach to politics (relying on his belief in the right thing) to form the
cornerstone of the character's conception of the presidency. Sam's function
is to narrate the presidency as a mandate to faithfully serve the electorate
by ensuring a prosperous and safe future for all. To do anything less would
be considered wrong. With the character's dialogue, Sorkin suggests that
the president should be a leader who challenges the status quo and is unafraid
to pursue ambitious dreams.[24] Sam's story lines express a clear understanding of Bartlet's role within this dynamic. Yet Sorkin does not use Sam to
challenge Bartlet's shortcomings as president because in this representation, Bartlet is inseparable from the sanctity of the office. Sam claims that
Bartlet is "the real thing" ("In the Shadow of Two Gunmen, Part I"). He

represents a man who is pure enough to keep Sam's vision of the presidency and politics safe. While this purity is momentarily challenged when Bartlet is forced to reveal he has multiple sclerosis, it is ultimately restored by Sam's reaction.[25]

Through the character of Sam, Sorkin makes government a symbol for something larger: "This country is an idea and one that's lit the world for two centuries" ("Somebody's Going to Emergency, Somebody's Going to Jail"). Sam's narrative also recalls a fundamental precept of early political learning, wherein the president cares for and protects the citizen. Sorkin also uses Sam to articulate a textbook version of government, wherein the president's staff diligently works to make the country more prosperous without manipulation or questionable ethics. He attempts to counter any cynicism the audience may feel toward politics through Sam's honorable behavior. Coupling this with dialogue that consists of highly affective rhetoric, Sorkin asks the viewer to recognize Sam's goodness. In this recognition the presidency is good by association.

> *I put no organization to the writing process. The writing is done on the fly.*
> *When I finish one script I have no idea what's going to happen in the next.*
> (Aaron Sorkin, 2002a, 151)

Sorkin's lack of an organized writing process for *The West Wing* is a key factor in understanding the power of his characters to create a feeling about government and the American president. De Jonge argues that this method of writing limits the series dramatically but has value commercially because the lack of sequence allows the viewer to "stumble onto the show at any point ... and get hooked" (2001). Issues are debated but rarely resolved. The senior staff participates in numerous policy discussions that remain open-ended so the audience may engage with the text and the characters on their own terms without having detailed knowledge of the narrative arc. Chambers suggests that this narrative structure is valuable because it creates a new way of understanding the nature of democracy. He argues that the "process proves dramatically more significant than the endpoints" because the ideal of democratic debate is still valid when based on struggle rather than automatic consensus (2001). In terms of the methodology of this book, the process becomes significant for an additional reason. Its importance lies in the emotional resonance it leaves behind. The main characters not only engage in debate that remains unresolved but also saturate that debate with their passions and emotions. With discussions that rarely reach conclusions, the audience is left with little substance beyond the feelings of the characters.

For Sorkin, argument is the cornerstone of drama. He suggests that his goal is "to create great arguments" so that his characters capture the audience through their "strong positions" (quoted in Barclay 2001). The implication is that an argument is only captivating dramatically when the participants express themselves with feeling. By leaving his characters' positions unresolved, Sorkin is privileging an affective response over a cognitive one. In his work on the series, Chambers analyzes an exchange from "Six Meetings Before Lunch" to support his thesis that the show provides a new dynamic for the concept of democratic debate (Chambers 2001). However, the scene is significant for another reason. The inability to reach a consensus, while it may inform the audience's understanding of democracy, also reduces the substance of the debate to affective rhetoric.

In the scene, Josh is meeting with Jeff Breckinridge (Carl Lumbly), an African American nominee to the Department of Justice, who has praised a book supporting slavery reparations. Josh is responding to the concerns of the Republican members of the Senate Judiciary Committee who have the power to block Jeff's confirmation. He attempts to resolve the problem by discussing it in the abstract, but Jeff is unwavering in his strong commitment to the issue. The dialogue grows increasingly heated as the two cover issues from the Civil War to the Holocaust. In the end, they fail to reach a consensus, and the viewer is left with no clear resolution. Josh tells Jeff that "there's going to be a lot more of these meetings before your confirmation," suggesting to the viewer that the debate will continue regardless of Jeff's appearance in any future story line. The impression that this dialogue leaves the audience is important because it forms the basis for a theme that runs throughout the series. It is not just an obvious understanding that Josh and Jeff will have future meetings to work out their differences; rather, it is an impression about government and the Bartlet White House.

The substance of this impression is found in Jeff's closing remarks to Josh. He ends the exchange with an impassioned speech on the idea of democracy as epitomized by the illustrations on the dollar bill:

> Take it out. Look at the back. The seal, the pyramid is unfinished with the eye of God looking over it and the words "annuit coeptis," "He (God) favors our undertaking." The seal is meant to be unfinished because this country is meant to be unfinished. We're meant to keep doing better, we're meant to keep discussing and debating, and we're meant to read books by great historical scholars and then talk about them—which is why I lent my name to a dust cover.

Jeff's use of this example frames his actions in a historic context. He is connecting his stance to an overall national ideal that supports debate.

He advocates dialogue over consensus. Chambers argues that, rather than analyzing this concept as a rejection of democracy, it is, in fact, the process of debate that forms "the very idea of democracy as incomplete, provisional and always agonistic" (2001). For Chambers, the process is paramount and fundamental to the idea of democracy. He suggests that this reading of the text reveals the "political potential" of the show that goes beyond analysis of its liberal discourse (*ibid.*). I would suggest that this speech serves an additional purpose outside of politics. It reveals an important tone of the series, which supports Sorkin's position that his first obligation is to create captivating drama.

Jeff's closing comments reduce a complex issue to basic principles that play to the audience's sense of patriotism. An intense debate that covered topics from race relations to the Holocaust ends with an affective reading of the founding father's vision for the country. Reducing issues to simple metaphors leaves the audience with an emotional residue that outlasts the cognitive complexity a debate may have offered. Jeff's impassioned reading generates a vision of the future that is connected to history and based on sentiment. Because the narrative focuses on the process of their debate and their failure to reach a conclusion, the audience is unable to take sides with either Jeff or Josh. The viewer is left with an impression of the process of argument. It is an impression that is ultimately sanctified by a grand vision of American democratic destiny. (Dialogue and debate is desirable; our founding fathers meant for it to be so).

The affective frame for political debates is so firmly established in the series that it exists in episodes where a political issue is only raised and not discussed. In "In Excelsis Deo," the plot focuses on Toby's efforts to organize a military burial for a homeless Vietnam veteran found dead on a park bench wearing a coat Toby had given to charity. The policy implications of this event are never discussed in the episode. No debate takes place between any characters. Instead, the story is framed as Toby's touching crusade. The audience later listens to the president's secretary tell Toby a sad story about her sons' deaths in Vietnam. They attend the funeral as the episode ends. It is a powerful scene that is saturated with patriotism and pathos. The complexity of the issue is sacrificed for an emotional, dramatic moment that does more to develop Toby's character than it does to stir political debate.

Indeed, this seems to be a response somewhat encouraged by the audience. An NBC network vice president notes that audience research "shows that viewers find the complex plots and jargon-heavy political topics difficult to follow but worth the effort" (quoted in Miller 2000). It is not necessary to understand the politics of the series because the viewers' efforts are rewarded with the emotional elements that contribute to satisfying drama. In *The West Wing*, satisfying drama is created with appealing, attractive characters engaged in intelligent, fast-paced and often humorous debate infused with strong personal ideals. The politics of an issue often serves as the backdrop to the characters' values and beliefs.

For those working on the show, the characters tap into a specific audience need. In his interview for *NewsHour with Jim Lehrer*, Sorkin sees them as satisfying a subconscious desire for the heroic rather than the "Machiavellian" image most often associated with public service officials (September 27, 2000). Wells suggests that the popularity of the show lies in the public's desire to believe in the noble motives of politicians: "The public wants to believe in the political process ... that the people who are leading us are doing so ... to make the country better" (quoted in Waxman 2000). This belief is a fundamental component of early political learning. *The West Wing* recalls it through its characterizations of the president's senior staff. They believe in a leader who wants to do the right thing. Their open-ended political debate leaves the audience with a feeling about issues, policy and the presidency. The characters take *The West Wing* viewer into a world where the president becomes an emotional association. The fictional president is saturated with feeling, as is the real American president. The boundary between the two, as the next chapter will show, is distinctly blurred.

CHAPTER FOUR

True Fiction

Look, I'm a fiction writer. I don't feel any responsibility to truth, to fairness, only to the elements of storytelling.

(Aaron Sorkin quoted in Spitz, 2001)

In the *NewsHour with Jim Lehrer* interview, Aaron Sorkin tells Terence Smith that *The West Wing*'s sole obligation is to produce interesting drama:

It's important to remember that, first and foremost, if not only, this is entertainment. We're not telling anyone to eat their vegetables.... Our responsibility is to captivate you for however long we've asked for your attention [September 27, 2000].

Sorkin's claims, often repeated throughout the show's first four seasons, appeared disingenuous to some critics, who saw the series as striving for more ambitious goals. Writing for the *Atlantic Monthly* in 2001, Chris Lehman argued that the show "has an overt agenda" (np). In his view:

The West Wing sets out, week after week, to restore public faith in the institutions of our government, to shore up the bulwarks of American patriotism, and to supply a vision of executive liberalism—at once principled and pragmatic; mandating both estimable political vision and serious personal sacrifice; plying an understanding of the nation's common good that is heroically heedless of focus groups, opposition research, small-bore compromise, and re-election prospects—that exists nowhere else in our recent history.

The contrast between Sorkin's comments and those of Lehman provides an interesting starting point from which to investigate a significant element of *The West Wing* narrative. While Sorkin clearly positions the series in fiction, structured according to the rules of effective drama, Lehman reads

107

it as "an exercise in wish-fulfillment fantasy" for liberal viewers (*ibid.*). Sorkin resists this description, suggesting that the Bartlet White House is not an idealized Clinton administration and any similarity to real events is purely coincidental (Deggans 2001). Responding to a suggestion that *The West Wing* functions as the "voice of the loyal opposition," Sorkin agrees but adds this perspective:

> I like thinking of it as loyal opposition even when there was a Democrat in the White House.... The Democrats have been the enemy just as much as the Republicans have been the enemy on this show. If there's an enemy on this show, it's a lack of conviction, a lack of compassion [quoted in Barclay 2001].

Again, Sorkin removes the argument from a real reference to politics and frames it around a narrative issue. The plots are only about opposition in a dramatic rather than political sense while lacking conviction or compassion is a character trait that may be an element of any narrative, not just a politically focussed one. *The West Wing*, however, clearly follows the liberal ideology of a Democratic presidential administration. For Bradley Whitford (Josh Lyman) the choice is simply pragmatic: "People respond to progressive Democrats. It's more heroic to fight for civil rights legislation than a tax cut" (Waxman 2000). A self-described "white-bread pinko liberal" (*ibid.*) who campaigned for Al Gore in several states during the 2002 presidential race, Whitford clearly brings his politics to his performance.[26] While his reasoning is based on his liberal ideology, Whitford makes an important point about the show's narrative. The power of the story lines comes from the emotions behind the political issue, whether they are classified as "heroic" or not. Where Whitford is probably wrong is that Sorkin would view the dramatic potential of a fight over tax cuts as equally compelling as a fight over civil rights because argument supercedes the issue. As Sorkin explains in the *NewsHour* interview with Smith:

> There's also drama to be gotten from issues that most people would consider very dry and wouldn't want to pay any attention to. Those are the fields you're going to plant.... Any time you get two people in a room who disagree about anything, the time of day, there is a scene to be written. That's what I look for.

Sorkin does not deny that he is politically liberal. In an often-repeated anecdote, he claims that part of him is still trying to pay back an old lady who hit him over the head with his "McGovern for president" sign as Nixon's motorcade drove by on their way to a rally (Waxman 2000). Yet, in his interview with Smith, he stresses that art is beyond political categorization: "I don't think that television shows or, for that matter, movies or plays or paintings or songs can be liberal or conservative. I think that they can only be good or bad" (*ibid.*). However, the press continues to discuss the show in terms of liberal versus conservative ideology, a discussion that was intensified before and shortly after the 2000 presidential election. During this period, the subtitle of an article covering the show for *George* magazine read:

> No matter who wins on November 7, *The West Wing* will still rule. But impresario Aaron Sorkin isn't taking any chances. He's putting some Republican spin on his liberal pitch [Waxman, 2000].

The "Republican spin" came in the form of second season consultants: Marlin Fitzwater, former press secretary to Presidents Reagan and Bush, and Peggy Noonan, former speechwriter to President Reagan.[27] Sorkin argued that the decision to hire Republican consultants was not made to deflect conservative criticism; rather, they were "very smart people" who were hired "not so much for their Republicanness as much as for their wisdom" (quoted in Waxman 2000). The arrangement was short-lived. Fitzwater, Noonan and Frank Luntz, a former Republican pollster, were fired from the series in summer 2002. Commenting on the termination, Luntz said: "There really wasn't much for us to do in the fictional White House of President Josiah Bartlet" (2002). While Sorkin did not comment on the issue, it seems reasonable to suggest that the consultants were, in fact, hired to counteract claims that the show lacked political balance, and their wisdom was not easily separated from their political ideology.[28]

In addition to the commentary that debated the show's political merits, several critics saw the series as a contribution to civic education. Television critics called the show "didactic" (Poniewozik 2001), while scholars commented that it had value as a "pedagogical tool" (Beavers 2003, 176). Consultants on the show made similar claims. Frank Luntz noted that "for better or worse, Americans by the millions get their information about politics from *The West Wing*" (2002) while Dee Dee Myers suggested that

> there's a great opportunity ... to explain issues that are sometimes too complex or too obscure feeling for the press to make interesting and accessible [quoted in Miller 2000, 95].

For Myers, the series not only assumes the role of the news media, but also succeeds where it fails. Her comments are less important as a criticism of the news and more important as testimony to the nature of *The West Wing*'s didactic power. By emphasising that it is the characters' personal engagement in the political process that makes issues "accessible" rather than the process itself, Myers suggests that the show's didactic quality is not necessarily intellectually based. Executive Producer and Director

Thomas Schlamme offers a similar understanding of the show's textual affect. He suggests that many scenes are successful because they teach emotional rather than political lessons. As evidence, he describes a scene from "Mr. Willis of Ohio" with C. J. and Sam in which Sam has to explain the complexities of the census:

> The essence of the scene is not about teaching us about the census; it's about how are these two people going to end up being closer to one another by the end of this episode. So if you start from that, then you can lay on ... any dialogue you want and it's fascinating [quoted in Miller 2000, 95].

The emotions behind the characters' relationship are so significant as to make the dialogue, political or otherwise, a secondary consideration. Sorkin, who admits to a lack of confidence in writing about the complexities of the political process, confesses that the series should distance itself from issues such as war because "I'm in way over my depth" (*ibid.*). His comments confirm Schlamme's viewpoint that in *The West Wing* affective drama takes precedence over political fact and the only lessons the audience should expect to be taught are emotional ones. As *The West Wing*'s portrait of the presidency seeps from political fiction into political fact and back again, both the audience and politicians appear to be learning these lessons. This chapter will explore the didactic qualities of the show's presidential representation as it enters public discourse. Rather than creating a new form of presidential education, its instruction is firmly rooted in the affective lessons of early political socialization.

Representing the White House

For those who produce *The West Wing*, the Bartlet White House is more about the essence of a presidency than the reality of one. This approach is taken from set design to script development. Series cinematographer Thomas Del Ruth suggests that the fictional White House of *The West Wing* is a matter of pride because it aesthetically exceeds the reality of the actual space: "I've been told that our White House looks a lot nicer than the real one!" (quoted in Oppenheimer 2000). Del Ruth calls his set design "a Camelot for the masses" (*ibid.*), a reference to the Kennedy presidency and the home of the legendary King Arthur.[29] The description suggests an interaction between the presidency and myth that is indicative of the show's complicated relationship with reality and fiction. A signifier for specific cultural values that guide the conduct of both leaders and followers, the myth of Camelot promotes ideas about fairness, justice and equality within a framework of government. To offer a "Camelot for the masses," Del Ruth is reclaiming for the series the collective consciousness that the Kennedy/ Camelot association has created. Implicit in his desire is to offer something that has been lost, to recreate a reality of the presidency that has been dormant. In this way, the White House set is a representation of the real and the mythic, the physical and the emotional. The visual cues from the title sequence to the subtly lit picture of President Roosevelt in the "Roosevelt Room" encourage the audience to locate Del Ruth's representation of the White House in a patriotic vision. In this context, his White House is more than a physical space of recreated rooms. It is a mythic vision of a presidency experienced through layers of fiction and fact.

For Thomas Schlamme, the series tries to portray an atmosphere, a sense of the workplace of the president. He argues:

> We are absolute fiction, so what we care about getting right is the emotion of what it's like to be part of the West Wing.... It's not a history lesson or civics lesson or accuracy of government [Elber 2002].

Schlamme's comments suggest that the reality of the series is found in its ability to reach an emotional truth, a perception he shares with those who have experienced the real West Wing. In separate interviews for *News-Hour with Jim Lehrer*, former Clinton press secretary Joe Lockhart comments that the show "captures some of the essence ... the tension, the pace" (September 13, 2000), while Marlin Fitzwater suggests that it gives the audience "a feel for the frenzy and the hectic activity" (September 8, 2000). Katharine Seelye, a former White House correspondent, agrees. While the set design is "much glossier than reality" and the Mural Room does not exist, "people really do carry on intense conversations, if not while barreling from office to office, at least as they lurch from crisis to crisis, although few speak in such well-considered sentences" (quoted in Creswell 2001, 44). For these former presidential staff, the series is a successful representation of an inner, emotional reality. Yet the commentary about the show suggests a desire for a deeper level of authenticity. While critics and commentators do not regularly discuss the verisimilitude of programs featuring lawyers and doctors, they do consistently address the issue of how Sorkin's *West Wing* compares to the real West Wing. Despite Sorkin's claims that he is only committed to a dramatic truth rather than a political one, he courts these comparisons because he addresses real political issues and uses the contributions of former White House staff members to write his scripts.[30] While this structure lends credibility to the show's representation of politics, the viewers and critics who negotiate the series as an alternative to the real presidency are also responding to Sorkin's recreation of the symbolic meaning system that signifies the White House.

In his work on forms of television representation, Barker argues that the process of meaning production for television is an engagement between the text and the viewers whose "own histories as discursive subjects" allow them to "negotiate the degree of verisimilitude" (1988, 51). For viewers of *The West Wing*, signs of the presidency are implicit in the White House and Oval Office setting. The visible artifacts of the president's workspace and public areas of the White House are culturally recognizable as connoting the presidency. In negotiating these artifacts' relationship to the real, viewers are influenced by their personal histories as socialized citizens as well as by former White House staff who discuss the show's physical and psychological authenticity or recreation of the real. Their direct experience is accepted as truth. Following this, their claims of the show's authentic recreation of emotional reality are also accepted as valid, despite being entirely subjective. This subtle transfer from an objective description of the president's physical space to a subjective confirmation of feelings about that space perpetuates the affective understanding of the presidency. The White House, already a symbolic space for the viewer, is given additional meaning through the feelings of former staff. Their claim on the truth of the space gives Sorkin's White House an additional and significant layer of reality. This interaction between reality, fiction and feelings is further complicated by the public's fascination with the most powerful workplace in the nation.

Within the series, a vital component of the verisimilitude of the presidency is the naturalized code of the White House. According to Stuart Hall, naturalized codes are

> processes of signification so widely distributed throughout a culture and assimilated by its members at such an early age that their artificiality dissipates [quoted in Barker 1988, 44].

The processes of signification for the White House, assimilated by most Americans in early political learning, invest the building with cultural authority. The White House is national icon and historic artifact. It is also the president's home and workplace. The familiar senses produced by these meanings of home, work and nation converge to become a naturalized code of the presidency. While these discourses have varied connotations, the demands of drama and narrative that *The West Wing* must meet reduce much of their complexity. In turn, Sorkin uses basic imagery to communicate the White House's identities. As workplace, the White House is limited to the offices of its West Wing, where the dominant symbols of work are easy to identify. It is a space for meetings, discussion and negotiations. The president is often shown behind his desk, reading documents, signing paperwork and making telephone calls. In addition, each week's plot focuses on the work of the senior staff members, who are variously framed as negotiators, facilitators and mediators of numerous policy issues.

Sorkin signifies the White House as home with recognizable scenes of domesticity. The president is shown watching a film with his daughter in the White House theater ("Ellie") and arguing with his wife in the bedroom of the building's residence section ("The White House Pro Am," "The War at Home"). For the senior staff characters, the White House is framed as home in similar if less obvious ways. Visually, the lack of scenes depicting the characters' actual homes creates the impression of the White House as their literal home.[31] On a narrative level, information about their personal histories is revealed almost exclusively within the space of the White House where it competes with the work plots of the show. This merging of private life with work life is an important device for framing the White House as a complex representation of personal and public space. While the dynamic is found in the majority of Sorkin's scripts, an episode from the first season illustrates its relationship to the audience's understanding of both the White House and the presidency as primarily affective texts. The following brief analysis of the episode "Mandatory Minimums" illustrates how Sorkin frames a policy issue around competing personal narratives. Ultimately, the representations of the White House as home and work are united by a domestic and emotional vision of the presidency.

In "Mandatory Minimums," a leaked memo surfaces that questions the tenacity of Bartlet's legislative vision. This prompts the character to abandon the president's traditional role of accepting congressional nominees to the Federal Election Commission (FEC) and to assert his right to nominate two appointments. The decision angers powerful members of Congress, who warn Bartlet that they will deliberately derail his future policy agendas. One of these policies is a mandatory minimum sentence for drug offenders, an issue the administration believes is racist and privileges incarceration over treatment. As the title implies, this issue is the focus of the episode.

However, rather than encouraging a substantive debate on drug policy, Sorkin uses "Mandatory Minimums" to emphasize the emotional states of several characters. He begins the episode with a black screen and Bartlet saying: "I get nervous around laws that fundamentally assume that Americans can't be trusted." With no visual context, the provocative statement demands the viewers' attention. The screen then reveals the president giving a speech to an enthusiastic and supportive crowd. As he makes his announcement regarding the FEC decision, the scene changes to the office of a member of Congress who is sharing a drink and an anecdote with his aides. The camera's attention shifts to one of the aides who has turned to watch the president's speech on television. Enjoying his conversation, the congressman tells his aide to join the group, dismissing the president's speech as uneventful. The aide, sensing the impending FEC announcement, becomes visibly distressed and urges his boss to listen. The congressman's mood dramatically shifts when he hears Bartlet's plan. He becomes furious, makes a threatening and derogatory remark about Josh and demands to be put through to him immediately. The scene shifts to Josh listening to the president's speech. Anticipating the harsh phone call, Sam attempts to bolster a disinterested Josh, who is calm and focused on the president. Taking the call from his assistant, Josh delivers the line, "You can shove your legislative agenda up your ass," and hangs up the phone. The main title sequence begins.

With this teaser scene, Sorkin introduces an emotional tone that will continue throughout the episode. The affective context that he creates through the responses of Josh and the congressman prepares the viewer for the various personal narratives of the president's senior staff that will form the crux of the episode. The message from Sorkin's opening scene is simple and clear: This episode is going to pack an emotional punch. As the plot develops, Sorkin's emphasis on the feelings of the staff not only overshadows any debate on drug policy but also frames the president as the father of the White House home.

As the episode unfolds, Sorkin continues the opening scene's emphasis on Josh's emotional state by developing the character's romantic feelings for a coworker. Throughout the episode, Josh repeatedly interrupts his work duties to discuss his fascination with an attractive female pollster. When she purposely embarrasses him by publicly announcing in the corridor that she is no longer "sleeping with" a man Josh dislikes, his attempts to articulate appropriate behavior in the White House are comedic and ineffective. After several false starts where he confronts her with stuttered phrases, he finishes with "This is a place where work is done and nothing else." Clearly, the narrative says otherwise, and Sorkin derails any substantial cognitive debate on policy with romantic banter.

Sorkin continues to undermine the drug issue with the character of Toby. While he has Toby directly discuss mandatory minimums, it is written as an exchange between the character and his ex-wife, who is a member of Congress. Their personal relationship leads to more banter, and their argument over mandatory minimums is unintelligible as they talk over one another until the viewer only clearly hears the congresswoman proclaim that "mandatory minimums are racist." Again, a policy issue is reduced to an emotionally provocative statement and the intimacies of a personal relationship interrupt work.

Sorkin's positioning of C. J. and Leo also contributes to this episode's reliance on personal narrative over policy debate. C. J. has an angry confrontation with the senior White House reporter, who accuses her of being an amateur after she refuses him access to information. The conflict evokes their history and is more satisfying to the viewer, who is aware that the two characters share a flirtation and that C. J. feels betrayed by Danny's choice (in a previous episode) to report on a damaging memo. For Leo, Sorkin also uses a story line that is personal to the character. In order to encourage their employers' professionalism in the upcoming drug debate, Leo assembles various congressional aides in the pressroom. He reveals the details of lenient sentences for drug offenses given to many of their bosses' relatives and compares these to the harsher punishments demanded by law. In return for "lively debate" he will not release the information to the press. Sorkin then tempers Leo's tactics by framing the Bartlet administration as fair and reasonable. Leo informs the group that the president "wants to hear opposition" but will not "stomach hypocrisy." Later, when Leo confesses to the president that as a recovering addict he is not comfortable with his public role in the debate, Bartlet responds:

> If there's anyone qualified to talk about the benefits of treatment versus criminal action, it's you. Is there anyone whose life would be better right now if you'd gone to jail instead of rehab?

By narrowing the drug-sentencing issue to focus on the circumstances of one character who is depicted as an honorable man, Sorkin encourages the audience to feel something about the debate. As a result, the policy of mandatory minimum sentences is never explored in the episode outside of emotionally charged statements that are integrated with the personal narratives of the senior staff.

As the episode concludes, the merging of work and home occurs with the staff each filing next to the president's bedside. (He has retired early for the night). They individually express their feelings about the events of the day, and Bartlet comments on their emotional commitment: "Everybody calm down. Leo's got your engines firing like you're running Daytona." He offers advice and encouragement: "You all had a good day.... If we do this right, people are going to respond." Questioned about his thoughts on the drug debate, the president responds with no clear commitment, only offering that, after a day of meetings, he is "a day closer" to a position. While this remark hints at the complexity of the drug sentencing issue, his closing words to Leo reveal that his only true commitment is to the inspiration that he feels:

> I'm sleeping better. And when I sleep I dream about a great discussion with

experts and ideas, diction and energy and honesty. And when I wake up I think "I can sell that."

The result is an episode that leaves the viewer with a feeling about the issues surrounding drug policy instead of an idea about its inherent political, economic and social complexities. The narrative moves between various personal encounters of the senior staff that serve to further distract the viewer from the policy issue and ultimately ends with an emotional speech from the president. Three of the characters deal with domestic, relationship issues, while Leo struggles with his personal demons.[32] The social interactions of work are combined with the behavior of the personal, and the president becomes the traditional paternal figure. When the staff enters the domestic space of the presidency to discuss work concerns, Bartlet is framed as both the wise patriarch to a loyal and loving family and the commanding boss to an earnest staff. The White House meanings of *work* and *residence* merge until the presidency is defined through its private space.

In her work on the mythic dimension of the presidency, Patricia Misciagno argues that the presidential private sphere is one of the essential elements of the institution's mythic power (1996, 329).[33] In this sphere, a president's "fictional image, with corresponding qualities, [can] be formulated, maintained, and protected" (332). Cultural scholar Joshua Meyrowitz argues that media exposure has disrupted this process and "demystified" leaders by "destroying the distance and mystery that once enhanced their aura and prestige" (1985, 303). As the public has been given more information regarding the president's personal scandals or misconduct, the resulting skepticism has challenged the president's power to appeal to the electorate. In short, the public has grown increasingly cynical about the motivations of presidents who are caught in dishonorable situations. When the show's first season coincided with the Clinton presidency, this argument often appeared to inform the commentary surrounding the series. Ezell argues that the timing of the series played a large role in its reception. Because it aired during "the moral disappointments of the Clinton presidency" it "seemed the perfect antidote for a nation weary of human frailty in its ultimate leader" (2003, 160). The comments of one critic repeat the sentiment. The show was a welcome retreat from the Clinton administration's scandals:

> The West Wing is more than a great show. For me, an aging baby boomer, as for many others, the show is a yearning cry and a fantasy of desire fulfilled. Its President Bartlet is more than a great character ... he is the President Clinton could have been—the full expression of the intelligent, perceptive, good-hearted visionary agenda-setter and change agent that Clinton can be, but without Monica Lewinsky [Joseph 2000].

For many viewers, Sorkin's fictional representation provided a soothing alternative to the real president's disappointing behavior. However, the comfort they found in Sorkin's version is more complicated than what is suggested by simple comparisons between an ideal fictional president and a flawed real president.[34] The viewer who takes solace in a fictional representation of the presidency is not only expressing a desire for their perception of an admirable man but also for the myth that shapes the presidential institution. The myth is damaged when the men who occupy the office are perceived to have failed it. Sorkin's representation works most successfully for those viewers who want to believe that it is possible for a president to meet the expectations of the myth.

I'm Not a Politician But I Play One on TV

The window into Bartlet's private space appears more authentic through the association with the real, yet the conventions of staging a compelling drama create a romanticized vision. The audience is attracted by comparisons with the real and seduced by the fictional drama. When George Stephanopoulos commented in the *Boston Globe* that his *West Wing* visit was "as close [to reality] as you could possibly get" and it "was easy to just be transported" (quoted in Jurkowitz 2001), the series' credibility was strengthened. When the cast was in Washington, D.C., to attend the White House Correspondents' Association annual dinner and aides from the Bush administration gave them a White House tour complete with photos (Lindlaw 2001), the relationship between reality and fiction was blurred further.

Similar mergers of real and fictional politics continued to occur as the show moved into its second, third and fourth seasons. In early May of 2001, San Francisco Democrat Kevin Shelley adjourned a session of the California Assembly in memory of Mrs. Landingham, President Bartlet's secretary. (Late in the second season, the character died in a car accident when a drunk driver hit her.) Prior to closing the legislative session, Shelley called Mrs. Landingham a "great American" whose "contributions to the nation were too numerous to count" (*California Assembly* 2001). Shelley, who, the article notes, lives in Sacramento during the week but calls his wife during commercial breaks to discuss *The West Wing*, commented on his colleagues' reactions: "At first everyone was stunned but then they were rolling in the aisles. Several said that they really appreciated that" (*ibid.*). In addition, Shelley has reportedly told aides that he wants his office to resemble the White House as featured in the series. While Assemblyman Shelley's display was humorous, if not a little peculiar, the connection between real politics and *The West Wing*'s version is not confined to American politicians.

In late June of 2002, John Spencer was invited to the British Prime Minister Tony Blair's residence to meet privately with Jonathan Powell, Blair's chief of staff. The two had a photograph taken, which an article notes will "take pride of place on the press office wall, alongside a picture of C. J. Cregg" (Ahmed 2002). Spencer was invited to London to launch the third season of the show for Channel 4. A week earlier, Gene Spurling, the former head of President Clinton's national economic council and a series consultant, attended a private dinner with Prime Minister Blair, where the two reportedly discussed education and benefits policy (*ibid.*). As the article suggests, Spurling has a level of credibility that permits him to advise political leaders. Yet, the connection between political fact and political fiction is tempting to parody, as the title of the article is: "Blair Seeks *West Wing*'s Help: Downing Street courts stars of hit American TV show as politics imitates art." The report quotes an MP who offers that his colleagues (many of whom are attending the launch) are drawn to the series because "they think it shows politics in a good light, people with their hearts in the right place battling to make the world a better place" (*ibid.*). The idea that politicians are using a fictional drama to authenticate their identities and their work not only reflects the impact of *The West Wing* on popular culture but reveals the show's role in supporting and perpetuating an ideology wherein politics is associated with noble motivations and pure intentions. More important, *The West Wing* supports the belief, strengthened by early political learning, that the American presidency is a sacred mantel that is safe even from those who fail to uphold the responsibilities. In this conception, political work in general, and the American presidency in particular, are innately good and endure despite being corrupted by unworthy people. *The West Wing* recalls this understanding, and politicians are embracing the message.

Reel Politics

When commentators discuss *The West Wing* in terms of its success or failure in reflecting political reality, they clearly attempt to validate the show by judging the authenticity of its fictional representation against real politics. Many also celebrate Sorkin's representation for offering a truer picture of the presidency than nonfiction media does. This type of commentary establishes a level of credibility for a fictional representation of political staff that often serves as a platform from which to describe the deficiencies of the news media's representation of public servants. In turn, this perpetuates the elements of early political learning that promote an affective portrait of noble public servants that serve an equally noble president. An article by Matthew Miller, a former aide in the White House budget office, offers one example.

Miller begins his article by describing a scene in which President Clinton is hard at work on his final State of the Union address. Blending fact with fiction, he juxtaposes the scene with another in which President Bartlet, as written by Sorkin, is hard at work on his State of the Union address. He ends the comparisons by establishing the article's central argument. In his view, the series "presents a truer, more human picture of the people behind the headlines than most of today's Washington journalists" (2000, 88, 90). Miller articulates a theme expressed by many who write about the series. He implicates a real media representation in the creation of a fictitious view of politics and celebrates a fictitious media representation for its creation of the real. In his view, the Washington press fails by not giving the audience an authentic picture of politicians because the group focuses on scandal. Miller's complaint is not over journalists' attempts to personalize politicians; rather, it is with their negative portrait of them. By hailing *The West Wing* as capable of a "truer" picture of politicians, Miller assigns the fictional series a level of reality equal to that of nonfiction media forms. He frames this theme with examples meant to give validity to the show's representation of the real. He notes that Sorkin looks to consultant Dee Dee Myers for "reality checks" (93). While it may be important to Miller that Sorkin turns to a former West Wing staffer for real experience, Sorkin's comments suggest that his concern lies with the dramatic potential of a scene and the consultants' contributions merely save him research time and allow him to make it "the difference between C-SPAN and watching television" (93). While Sorkin acknowledges the dramatic difference between the news and series television, Miller does not. Rather than recognize the fictional qualities of news broadcasts, he positions them as a misrepresentation of politicians that *The West Wing* corrects.

For Miller, the show's didactic potential lies not only in its contribution to the education of political journalists but in its instruction of the public as well. While his argument is limited by his preference for positive portrayals of politicians over negative ones and his failure to recognize the fictional qualities of the news, it relies on the central idea that the show achieves a level of reality through its depiction of the characters' emotions.

In his *NewsHour* interview, Joe Lockhart makes a similar argument.

Discussing his impressions of *The West Wing*, Lockhart suggests that one of the program's most important contributions is its portrait of public servants:

> There are thousands of people who work in this government who are either Democrats or Republicans, who come to work every day because they care.... And this show, while not real, it gives you a flavor of some of these people [September 13, 2000].

For Lockhart, fictional media has succeeded where real media has failed. In his view, *The West Wing*'s depiction of public servants is commendable not only because it is a positive representation but also because it exists. The series validates political work by narrating it on a television screen through well-meaning and hard-working characters. Lockhart's frustration is with media coverage that neglects to focus on the people behind the president. Lockhart, of course, is one of these people, and he is expressing a desire for recognition. More important, he is promoting the idea that the screen legitimizes his work. The image of a public servant with integrity and just ideals validates his identity as one. The assumption is that the audience accepts these representations as real, a position reinforced by the questions that Lockhart is asked during the interview. Smith's entire interview, in fact, is based on questions of reality. He moves from specific questions about the character of the president, "They have the president doing things that I wonder if the president really does," to a general overall query, "How close to reality is it?" Lockhart, however, is careful to note that the show is not real. Rather, he offers that it gives the audience a "flavor" of the people who work for the president. He stresses that the characters "oversimplify every issue" but this process is not a "disservice to reality" just a "condensed version of reality that's more entertaining."

For Lockhart, the press calls attention to the work of public servants when their actions fail and scandal, controversy or disaster occurs. In his view, *The West Wing*'s value lies in its depiction of the good intentions, dedication and commitment behind the failures. Lockhart's comments may be understood in the context of his role as a press secretary who was under pressure to defend a scandal-ridden Clinton administration. Clearly, a depiction of the difficulties and various nuances of his work is a welcome characterization. However, other former White House staff members, who were not faced with the same level of intensity, make similar comments. Marlin Fitzwater, in his interview with Terrence Smith, discusses the show's relationship with the news and suggests that "one of the great lessons" of the series is its ability to "teach people how politics works" by showing the stories that the news fails to cover:

SMITH: Are you saying then that they, in certain ways, get at the truth better or more successfully than the conventional news approach?

FITZWATER: Well, I think in some ways they can dramatize things that happen that you'll never see any other way [September 8, 2000].

Sorkin's drama, then, is capable of reaching political truths that the news is unable or unwilling to report. Yet this outcome is reliant on a dramatic relationship between fact and fiction. Pompper argues that in "enabling the spheres of fact and fiction to overlap" the series gives audiences "a means for democratic engagement that journalism alone cannot" (2003, 31). Both journalism and drama are about storytelling. For Fitzwater and Lockhart, journalists do not fail in reporting the reality of politics. Rather, they fail in the version of the story they choose to tell.

According to Niklas Luhman, encouraging the audience to find reality in fiction is the goal of entertainment products. In his discussion of the reality of the media, Luhman argues that "entertainment performances always have a subtext which invites the participants to relate what they have seen or heard to themselves" (2000, 60). *The West Wing*'s narrative structure allows many viewers to relate to the reality of the show through what Luhman calls inclusion "as excluded third parties" (*ibid.*). The viewer is excluded through his lack of access to the president and the White House but included through the show's connection to real issues, people and emotions. The episodes offer recognizable political debate (drug policy, gun control) dramatized by engaging characters. When former presidential staff members such as Lockhart and Fitzwater comment on its authentic reproduction of their emotional experiences, fact and fiction is blurred once more. Attempting to capitalize on this relationship between political fact and political fiction is the *"The West Wing" Documentary Special*. In it, the viewer finds Luhman's genre of "highly personalized experiential accounts" (60) used to maximum affect, inviting them to accept *The West Wing*'s fictional reality.

Documentary Special

In his work on documentary theory, John Corner notes that *documentary* is a "loose and often highly contested label" used to define types of film and television that "reflect and report on 'the real' through the use of the recorded images and sounds of actuality" (1996, 2). He goes on to classify documentary forms into several modes of image and speech that include "proactive observationalism" and "testimony," respectively (28-9). While a critical analysis of documentary theory is beyond the scope of this book, Corner's categorical distinctions are useful for an examination of *"The West Wing" Documentary Special*. Broadcast during the third season in the show's regular 9 P.M. timeslot, the documentary juxtaposes interviews of former presidents and their aides with scenes from the series.[35] The program's status as both drama and documentary raises significant questions about the relationship between reality and representation as it is found on *The West Wing*.

Corner suggests that "proactive observationalism" is an evidential mode of documentary image that "when pushed further, can be transformed into that of dramatised reconstruction" (28). In this mode, conventional documentary practices connect with narrative fictional styles so that actuality merges with entertainment (32).[36] Corner argues that the narrative of drama may be applied to documentary material in two ways. Of these distinctions, "documentary-drama" comes closest to defining *"The West Wing" Documentary Special*. In this category, the documentary is

> essentially a form of a play, but a form which is seen to develop a documentary character either as a result of its referentiality to specific real events (private or public or both), *or* because of its manner of depiction [*ibid.*].

The special broadcast of *The West Wing* develops a documentary character by using fictional drama to refer to the private, real events that the non-actors describe through interview speech. In the broadcast, the recollections of the real staffers are used to confirm the truth of the series' ability to faithfully represent their experiences. The non-actors' narratives are tied to the actors' narratives in a way that suggests a seamless match between real and fictional West Wing experiences. After Ken Duberstein, President Reagan's Chief of Staff, tells the camera, "Almost everyone walks into the Oval Office and gets cotton in their mouth. Their tongue gets tied," the picture cuts to a scene from "Lies, Damn Lies and Statistics" in which a nervous member of the FEC is struck speechless when introduced to President Bartlet and several other high-profile government officials in the Oval Office. President Carter then shares a similar sentiment, lending the story more validity. When Duberstein discusses the precautions staff members must take to keep their comments from being leaked to the press, a scene plays wherein Toby is admonished by Leo for letting his guard down and inadvertently providing a quote that helps the opposition ("The Leadership Breakfast"). Not only does the scene seem to bring Duberstein's comments to life but it is also briefly narrated by him when his voice is edited over a few seconds of the action.

The matching narratives of the recalled stories and the scenes from the series suggest a level of self-conscious performance by the non-actors that problematizes the nature of their recollections. During the program, the non-actors appear to be unprompted, giving the impression that they are freely choosing which meaningful moments to share from their work in the White House. The viewer does not hear the questions asked by the director and the two assistants who are credited with conducting the interviews. In addition, several of the participants, including Dee Dee Myers, Peggy Noonan and Marlin Fitzwater, are paid consultants for the show. The deliberate structure of the special and the choice to include several people directly involved with *The West Wing*, calls into question the level of performance given by those being interviewed.

By using eyewitness or first person experiential accounts as the central feature of exposition, the broadcast may also be categorized as testimony. A traditional convention of documentary, testimony depends upon the "resonance" produced between the "individual and particular case and the social and civic body" (Dovey 2002, 16). This resonance "can be either enhanced or restricted by the narrative system which produces it" (*ibid.*). If the participants' memories successfully produce a resonance with the audience, it is because they capitalize on the affective power of the presidency. The comments of David Gergen, White House advisor for the Nixon, Ford, Reagan and Clinton administrations, offer a typical example:

> There are glamorous days too where you look back and say: "Wow. I can't believe that really happened." I had the privilege of going with President Reagan to a summit conference in Versailles. When the meeting was over (we spent the first night in the palace) we walked out to helicopters, went over and got on Air Force One and flew to see the Pope for lunch.... We got back on helicopters, went out to Air Force One and flew to London and had dinner at Windsor Palace with the Queen.... How can one have a more interesting, richer experience than that? ... The White House does that sometimes. It's a place where things can happen and you say: "This is magical."

Gergen's recollections create a fantasy scene in which the power and majesty of the presidency transports a regular man to extraordinary events otherwise impossible to experience. All the interviewees contribute to this idea with a similar expression of feelings. The presidency is a noble calling, as described by Michelle Crisci Meyercord, Special Assistant to the Clinton administration: "I remember the first paycheck. Of course you need to cash it and pay rent but there's a small part of me that thought, I could frame it." It is worth the sacrifices, according to Gene Sperling, White House Chief Economic Advisor during the Clinton administration: "To have an office in the West Wing, I would take half of a windowless closet ... and that's pretty much what they gave me." The staffers' recollections resonate with the ideal spirit of early political education. Because the fictional scenes from the series also invoke this spirit, the documentary's narrative structure enhances the affective power of their testimony.

Thomas Schlamme, who served as the program's executive producer, notes that the project's goal was to capture the feelings of presidential work:

> We went out and interviewed quite a broad spectrum of people.... We approached all these people by saying, "We just want to do an interview with you that is much more of a memory piece, recollections and feelings about what it was like working in the West Wing." ... We wanted to dig out what the emotional feelings of those times were [quoted in Cohn 2002].

For Schlamme, the interviews were a way to authenticate the reality of the series' presidential representation. Upon completion of the documentary, he recalls feeling that "hey, we're kind of getting this thing right" (quoted in Elber 2002). What *The West Wing* is "getting right" however, is the emotions behind the work. Schlamme offers that "what we found out ... is the absolute commitment and passion [the interviewees] have for the public service of politics. It's that passion that *West Wing* tries to replicate..." (quoted in Godmilow 1997). If, as Shapiro suggests, documentary "straddles the categories of fact and fiction, art and document, entertainment and knowledge" (1997, 80), then the *Documentary Special* offers a valid investigation of *The West Wing*'s contributions to political reality. What is evident from the participants' comments is that this reality may also be understood as a presidential narrative written by Aaron Sorkin and learned in early political education.

Performing the President

> *"He strikes me as a character who could be the president," said Wendy Shaw, a West Wing viewer in Los Angeles. "He's strong, he's got a smart-aleck side to him, he's got some chinks in his armor—he's a real person."*
> (Quoted in Nissen 2000)

While television did not create the idea of the president as performer, it brought the performance to the national stage. For Bruzzi, the emphasis on the performative nature of politics constructs the citizen as a "spectator" who may recognize that the president's media image is not necessarily "a direct correlative of his off-screen personality" (2000, 129). To counter the negative effects this distinction often causes, presidents attempt to bring intimacy to their public performances. The first President Bush demonstrated this in the third debate during the presidential election of 1988.

Responding to a reporter's question on what his opponent has taught him, Bush got personal:

> Barbara and I were sitting there before the Democratic convention, and we saw the governor and his son on television the night before, and his family and his mother who was there. And I'm saying to Barbara, "You know, we've always kept family as a bit of an oasis for us." You all know me, and we've held it back a little. But we use that as a role model, the way he took under-standable pride in his heritage ... and we said "Hey, we've got to unleash the Bush kids." And so you saw 10 grandchildren there jumping all over their grandfather at the [Republican] convention [quoted in Hart 1994, 31].

As an example of what Hart terms the "language of intimacy" (*ibid.*), Bush's scenes of domestic tranquility attempt to blur the separation between a public and private president so that the performance appears to be a genuine representation of the real man. Almost a decade later, another President Bush would promote a similar image. When George W. Bush's various gaffes during the 2000 election campaign exposed his public performance as constructed (in the sense that his mistakes were "off-script"), his consultants used it as an opportunity to claim that the electorate was witnessing the real Bush. The goal was to make Bush's appearances lose their status as performance. However, the relationship between the president and performance is not so easily dismissed.

In her work on documentary practices, Bruzzi examines the relationship between presidential performance and the reality it refers to by analyzing the media images of presidents Kennedy, Nixon and Clinton. She suggests that the Kennedy presidency's close relationship with image and performance resulted in its idealization, accrediting it a mythic status "made more significant by such idealisation being the result of real rather than fictional representations" (2000, 128). This belief in the recorded image of the presidency allowed Kennedy's performance to surpass representation and reach truth. While Kennedy's media performance enhanced the idea of presidential reality on-screen, Nixon's screen performance eroded it. Bruzzi argues that it was Nixon's failed relationship with the media in general, rather than the Watergate affair in particular, that ignited a crisis in the national consciousness. With Nixon, the presidential myth begins to lose power because he

> represents the moment at which a belief in such a myth became untenable.... This negativity is not simply the result of Watergate, it was innately linked to Nixon's own public persona, his inability to convincingly mask the cracks between who he was and what he sought to represent [135].

Nixon's media performances, characterized by "discernible tension in his face, gestures, words," lacked the naturalness of Kennedy's interactions; his "ease and affinity with the observational camera ... repressed knowledge of falsification and media manipulation" (152). Consequently, Nixon's unnatural performances "proclaimed their untruthfulness" and exposed the presidency as artifice (*ibid.*). The relationship between presidential reality and presidential performance, while indistinguishable with Kennedy, became obvious with Nixon. When Nixon was exposed as a liar, the relationship between the media and presidential reality changed. As Bruzzi explains:

> Kennedy was venerated at a time when his ease in front of the camera, his accessibility still signified his realness—and the realness of an idealized, glamorous presidential institution. Post-Nixon, the straightforward belief in the realness of the factual image has been replaced by cynicism about politics and a disillusioned knowingness about the infinite corruptibility of the real [148].

As Nixon's criminal activity eroded the sanctity of the presidency and his performance was exposed, the public's attitude toward politics shifted and the reality of the presidential image became suspect. For Bruzzi, Clinton's "varied and contradictory" televised performances ushered in a new dynamic that made the distinction inconsequential (*ibid.*). In her view, Clinton's broadcasts, particularly during the Lewinsky scandal "serve as reminders that to try to enforce the distinction between the 'real' person and the performance is futile, the politician is necessarily performative" (*ibid.*). While Nixon's transparent media appearances enforced the distinction between president and performance, Clinton's screen image dissolved the distinction until president became equal to performance.

Bruzzi argues that the shift in presidential performance on-screen can be traced through presidential documentaries, suggesting that the legacy left by Nixon's public deceits has not only changed the documentary filmmaker's approach to the president but altered the reception of these films as well. Using the example of *Primary* (Drew Associates, 1960), a documentary covering Kennedy's campaign for the presidency, Bruzzi notes that it was "elegant and evocative, suggesting that there was still a mystique surrounding the presidential fight" (144). The documentary also gave the impression that the filmmakers had been given "privileged, unprecedented access" to the presidential candidates (*ibid.*). As contrast, she points to two documentaries that examined the 1992 presidential campaign, *Feed* (Kevin Rafferty and James Ridgeway, 1992) and *The War Room* (Chris Hegedus and Donn Pennebaker, 1993). While *Feed* illustrates how the candidates are "mere cogs in a system that comprises dull, trivial, ugly television images," *The War Room* focuses on the manufacturing of Clinton's public image (144,

147). Both films, Bruzzi argues, show "the assembly of the performance" and the "purely artificial construct" that is the modern candidate (147–48). Meyrowitz suggests that once this knowledge is given to the public, "once the techniques of establishing awe and mystification are opened ... the mystification is undermined" (1985, 303). The result is an acceptance on the part of Americans that "the president himself must be a skilled actor and that he must *perform* the role of president rather than simply *be* president" (*ibid.*). This idea, traceable through the documentaries covering both Kennedy's and Clinton's campaigns, is indicative of a shift in the public's notion of the presidential image that has significant implications for the reception of fictional representations of the president. The shift is a move from believing in a reality behind the presidential performance to believing that the "performance is the reality" (Bruzzi 2000, 150). The most significant result of this, as Bruzzi suggests, is that the public now acknowledges the politician as an artificial construction and the "desire for idealized presidential images can only be satisfied by the creation of fantasy characters" (*ibid.*). Often, the media's role in this process is to retell the myth through fictional representations. Citing the various nondocumentary, president-centered films of the 1990s, Bruzzi suggests that their "cinematic archetypes" are a means to "fill the gap between reality and the fantasy figure of our imagination with ideals made familiar by escapist fiction" (*ibid.*). Meyrowitz contextualizes this idea in terms of television, arguing that

> Win or lose, today's presidents and presidential hopefuls are judged by the same standards, those of "good television": are they lively and humorous; do they look friendly and alert; are their facial expressions pleasant to watch ... [304].

Presidential performance is presidential reality. Within this reality, the idealized, mythic figure of early political learning is reborn in representation.

Screening the President

When the screen was used as evidence of Nixon's duplicitous nature, the truth it gave to presidential performance was not lost. While political cynicism may have increased as a result of Nixon's performance, the audience became a knowing participant in the constructed president. Documentaries such as *The War Room* and *Feed* are a response to this awareness. Yet, the awareness of presidential performance does not lead to a rejection of it because the audience/citizen wants to believe in both the fiction of the performance and the truth the screen assigns to this fiction. When the performance fails, it is not because the public sees its falseness. Rather, it is because the public is confronted with the mythic nature of the presidency and the man behind the performance inevitably fails the myth. When the myth is shaken, it is revealed, and in this revelation, the presidency is exposed as a fiction.

Nixon's performance failed the myth, but in his separation from the ideal, the presidency was saved from the man who soiled it. As Clinton's presidency was perceived as "one extended performance" (Bruzzi 2000, 148), the president, the man and his performance became inseparable. With Clinton, the performance itself failed the myth. The presidency, in turn, is constructed in numerous fictional cinematic representations in which the ideal is often realized in heroic, fearless and honest screen images. The public turns to the screen to support a myth that can only be realized in fictional presidents. Television's contribution to these screen images has often been equally ideal, but its nonfiction formats have added an important dimension to presidential performance. Hart's work on television and politics suggests that the intimacy between presidents and the public generated by the news media has consequences because intimate associations often lead to high expectations. The president's actions will inevitably bring criticism and disappointment because the public's demand for intimacy eventually undermines their faith in the man behind the institution. When the public's expectations are not met, disillusionment sets in (30). The process is about performance with both television and the president playing specific roles:

> We come to know politicians, not necessarily to like them.... So political intimacy is almost always a case of bait-and-switch. The politician opens up his or her heart. We are drawn in. The politician then does something craven or stupid—an inevitability in politics. We jump back, scorned, again. We declare the lot of them toxic waste. Then television brings us a new, more vulnerable soul to probe. The soap opera continues [29].

Hart suggests that this is "intellectual intimacy not affection based" because "we come to *know* politicians, not necessarily to like them" (28). Yet, the public can only get to know a politician through his or her media performance. As that performance becomes more deliberately constructed as intimate, the public is encouraged to focus on their feelings about a politician's image. If the public's reaction is to "jump back, scorned" when they perceive a politician to be acting badly, then they experience hurt feelings that go beyond an intellectual reaction to disappointing behavior. The lure of television is that it promises to bring a new opportunity that is as much about "intellectual intimacy" as it is about emotional closeness. Intellectually, the public may recognize the players of the familiar presidential performance but what allows them to repeatedly watch the "soap opera" is, in part, the hope that the next politician will make them feel better.

One important part of the presidential "soap opera" is the context into which it places the nation's leader. Hart argues that the political training made possible through television "homogenizes" voters and leads them to "evaluate candidates just as they evaluate all other television personalities" (68). That is, people "come to think of their leaders as intimates simply because they spend so much time with them" (*ibid.*). Quantity of time, however, should not be privileged over the quality of the experience. Thomas and Pika suggest that, as a central player on the "nightly dramas" of television news, the president's significance as an "object of psychological feelings may be greater today than ever before" (1997, 98). The president may be mediated as news, but news narratives allow him to perform intimacy. As the lines between news and entertainment become increasingly blurred, the role of president as performer is made familiar. With personality politics, the president becomes another player on the television screen, subject to similar affective evaluations. Similar to Meyrowitz, Hart sees this privatization as a failure that only initiates cynicism. However, the process forms an important foundation for the public reaction to the fictional President Bartlet. Primed for an intimate relationship with their real president, the viewer of *The West Wing* is encouraged to accept Sorkin's intimate depiction of a fictional president. While the success of the series speaks to the popularity of this depiction, the level at which President Bartlet enters public debate deserves more scrutiny.

In October 2002, the National Education Association, the largest teachers' union in the United States, issued the following written statement:

> We agree with President Bartlet that we must come together as a country and "do better" on behalf of America's children and America's public schools. The president can be sure that the members of the NEA will do our share to make public schools great for every child [Cardman 2002, 1].

The statement followed an episode of the series that showed President Bartlet speaking before fictional members of the union. On the banner behind Bartlet was the union's official slogan and logo, used by the producers with permission (*ibid.*). In a similar merger of fiction and reality, Rock the Vote, a nonprofit organization focused on youth civic involvement, appeared in the story line for the fourth season episode "College Kids," in which C. J. speaks to a crowd during one of the organization's fundraising events. A spokesperson for Rock the Vote commented on zap2it.com that the group's mission to "connect with youth and engage them in the political process will surely be helped by such prominent placement in America's hottest and smartest political drama" (October 2, 2002).[37] While this level of engagement may be dismissed as a marketing ploy, many viewers of the series have a similar interaction with the fictional president. In an article for the *Detroit Free Press*, published during the 2000 presidential race, a reporter not only claims that Bartlet is "the closest thing we have to an inspiring leader at the moment" but also writes the piece as a list of favorable qualities to which the presidential candidates should aspire. She extols Bartlet as "fun," "decisive," "human" and "larger than life," while suggesting that Gore and Bush "would be wise to copy" these traits (Hinds 2000a). The journalist's comments were echoed by a Detroit viewer who claimed that she would vote for Bartlet for president because "I really know him better than Bush or Gore" (Hinds 2000b). During the same period, other viewers were expressing similar sentiments in print reports and Internet chat rooms. One commented: "I have a couple of friends and we wish that when we go to vote, we could just write in 'Josiah Bartlet' for president" (quoted in Nissen 2000). Another wrote on a CNN message board that she would vote for Bartlet because "he seems to have developed the courage of his convictions, to do what he sees as right..." (*ibid.*). Bartlet also received support from high-profile Democrats who preferred him to Al Gore. Donna Shalala, the former secretary of Health and Human Services during the Clinton administration, commented that Bartlet made real-life presidential candidates Gore and Bush seem "plastic" because he "seems more human" (*ibid.*).[38] The sentiment even crossed party lines. Writing a December 28, 2002, editorial piece for the *New York Times* entitled "President Bartlet, Please Take Me Back," former Republican consultant to the show Frank Luntz outlined his reasons for wanting to return to work on the series:

> I wish "The West Wing" would take me back, even though I wasn't an essential cog in the wheel of production.... I love the characters, particularly President Bartlet. I don't ever agree with anything Martin Sheen the actor says politically. But when Martin Sheen as President Bartlet says the same kind of things, it's just so, well, presidential.

For Luntz, the emotional power of the fictional president surpasses his feelings for the liberal actor who plays him. While he separates the actor from the character, his reaction implies that he is placing an emotional value on the fictional representation. Luntz's response underlines an essential component of the presidential mythos. That is, his interpretation of the meaning of *presidential* is based on emotions rather than intellect. President Bartlet seems presidential because Sheen embodies the character with those qualities that Luntz believes represent the president. Because those qualities are not based on Luntz's political ideology, he is responding to an affective performance rather than a cognitive confirmation of his values.

The comments from viewers like Luntz who claim that a fictional president seems more real than actual presidential candidates suggests that the public would be satisfied with more intimate knowledge of their national leader. Bartlet only seems more human than his real life counterparts because the viewer is allowed access to his identities outside that of president. (He is a father, son and friend.) While real presidents offer similar access to these roles, it is often perceived as constructed and artificial. Sorkin offers the fantasy that the presidency can be unscripted—that the president can be a flawed but admirable man. He empowers the audience by putting faith in their ability to reconcile the humanity of the man with the myth of the institution. Sorkin makes Bartlet's performance appealing because his narrative seduces the viewer into thinking that a president can be an intimate figure and a mythic figure simultaneously.

While Sorkin can tell presidential stories that the news cannot,[39] nonfiction television forms do construct the president as a character in a narrative. In television news, the president plays the title role in the story of the nation. Watching the performance, the audience is often encouraged to have an affective response. For Hart, the power to make the television audience feel something about politics rather than think something about it is creating a dangerous trend that "distracts us from traditional political knowledge" (1994, 73). He argues that television's obsession with political power undermines its depiction of political authority. While the television camera captures political power with selective shots of the right reaction to a politician, "that same camera is mute about political authority" which is "too mystical, too opaque" for the camera (75). The viewer, he urges must "feel less and think more" if they are to succeed in "recapturing a sense of political authority" (*ibid.*). Underlying this argument is Hart's definition of political authority as "that which authorizes the state" (*ibid.*). This ignores its synonymous relationship to power, instead relying on its meaning as knowledge or experience that ensures reliability. For Hart, the television camera is able to capture the feelings that illustrate power but not those that illustrate authority because authority assumes a level of thinking that a television image cannot relay to an audience. Yet television images do capture political authority. Images of political protest, even in the absence of sound, signify the existence of political authority by representing a challenge to it. Hart quotes anthropologist Clifford Geertz, who suggests that a prosperous society needs the "inherent sacredness of central authority," but Hart argues that "in an age of television, Geertz's claim sounds like monarchial sentimentality" (75). Central to Geertz's argument is emotion. To recognize the "sacredness of central authority," a society must first believe in it. They must feel that it deserves their allegiance. For Hart, television fails because it "does not know how to reverence authority" (*ibid.*). Yet if television is to succeed in this goal it must generate an emotional reaction from the audience because to revere is to feel—respect, awe, fear—rather than to think. What Hart suggests that television achieves most successfully, inspiring feelings is the key to "recapturing" the political authority he seeks.

Hart concludes his argument on television's role in political authority by turning back to Geertz's words:

> Thrones may be out of fashion, and pageantry too; but political authority still requires a cultural frame in which to define itself.... A world wholly demystified is a world wholly depoliticized [76].

For Geertz, political authority must be found within a specific framework that is partially inaccessible; a level of fiction ensures that political influence survives. Geertz's comments recognize the role of narrative in politics as necessary to maintaining a unified national vision. A system of government defines a nation both for its citizens and the world. The narrative of that institution is the narrative of the nation. Hart uses Geertz's comments to suggest that television's reliance on intimacy or the personalization of politicians is demystifying and therefore depoliticizing. This leads to his caution that the public can continue to learn from television but must "choose more carefully from among its dazzling pictures and invasive biographies" (75). The implication is that the images of television distract the audience by generating feelings rather than thoughts about politics. Hart's argument is not only totalizing, but it also underestimates the power of television's images to provide a necessary affective context for politics and the presidency. The acceptance of political authority requires an underlying narrative that allows the public to believe in that authority, and a powerful narrative must contain elements to which the listener can have an affective response. Television has replaced Geertz's "pageantry" to become the cultural framework through which the narrative of political authority is told.

For Hart, factual television has failed as a framework because its images encourage the audience to excessively rely on their emotions at the expense of their ability to think. In his words: "television serves its own needs" while "we must learn to better serve our own" (76). Yet the comments of *West Wing* viewers quoted throughout this chapter suggest that television is serving a need. The audience of the series is using a fictional narrative to reclaim a cultural frame in which to contextualize their president. Rather than signaling a dangerous trend, as Hart would suggest, their responses reveal a recapturing of political authority. In their feelings toward the fictional President Bartlet, they are reclaiming the narrative that is necessary to support a belief in political authority. The narrative of the presidency is a complex interaction of fiction, myth and facts. The series satisfies the audience's desire for the personal president, as he is depicted in factual media, by contributing to the "language of intimacy." Yet this demystification does not lead to depoliticization as Hart and Geertz would suggest because the president is made accessible within the familiar confines of the fictional. The narrative of the presidency is safely maintained within the cultural framework of fictional television's conventions.

On October 3, 2001, NBC screened a very special episode of *The West Wing* entitled "Isaac and Ishmael." Contrary to Sorkin's usual writing aims, the episode was a direct response to the terrorist attacks of September 11.[40] The plot revolves around the senior staff giving an impromptu lesson on terrorism to a group of high school students, who are prevented from leaving their tour of the White House by a security breach. The security breach is a White House employee who shares the same name as a suspected terrorist. While it was poorly received for its overly preachy setup, it was praised for generally attempting to address the issues. The comments of one television critic offer a typical example:

> Whatever the deficiencies of the script, the very idea of interrupting a serial drama and using its characters in a one-time only "play"—for this cause or even a lesser one—is the kind of fresh, quick-response thinking most of TV could use [Poniewozik 2001].

Poniewozik's comments suggest that the fiction of *The West Wing* is not only an appropriate vehicle for the reality of political discourse but a valuable one as well. As this chapter has demonstrated, the reaction of both critics and viewers underscores the complicated relationship that the series has formed with politics and culture and reality and fiction. This complexity is not limited to positive responses, an idea suggested by this review of "Isaac and Ishmael" for Salon.com:

> I figured out that these folks took themselves way too seriously, and were a little confused about their actual role in this country, when they were

omnipresent at the Democratic Convention in Los Angeles last summer, as
though anyone cared about what these actors who played political leaders
and staffers on TV had to say about politics. (Of course, the most horrifying
thing was, people did care. The cast's little workshops were packed with star-
struck delegates, while panels on policy and the Democratic platform were
empty) [Walsh quoted in Chambers and Finn 2001].

Walsh's contempt for the series' relationship to politics is clear, yet
her contradictory evidence undermines her insistence that culture and politics are distinct. Her failure to see the connection while giving an example of it suggests the limitations of a narrow analysis.

A month after the air date of "Isaac and Ishmael" (and Walsh's review)
the Canadian Foreign Affairs Minister, John Manley, used the episode in
a speech he gave in New York City. While Manley's comments pointed
out the episode's factual mistakes (Quebec borders Vermont, Ontario does
not), his reference to the show suggested a deeper connection among Sorkin's narrative, politics and culture. Responding to the episode's contention
that terrorists were crossing the border between Canada and the United
States, Manley noted that no evidence exists to support these claims and
the resulting misconceptions were hindering cross-border trade relations.
Chambers and Finn note that national news broadcasts played clips of the
episode's mistake juxtaposed with Manely's speech, giving "proof of Sorkin's
reach" (2001). The attention given to the "terrorism" episode by the media
(Chambers and Finn describe the pre-show hype and post-show reviews as
"frenzy") is important because it assigned political power to a fictional representation. A television show attempted to bring closure to a national
tragedy. While both the critics and the audience may have found that the
narrative failed their expectations, they accepted it for the attempt. As
Chambers and Finn suggest, in September 2001, audiences turned to the
drama for more than entertainment, and the transition to "public soapbox"
was complete (2001). With "Isaac and Ishmael," *The West Wing* secured its
place in the complex interaction between the reality and the performance
of politics.

A year later, *The West Wing*'s relationship to political discourse was
still powerful when Sorkin's comments in an interview for the *New Yorker*
sparked controversy. Commenting on the news media's representation of
the president, Sorkin criticized Tom Brokaw, the host of an NBC broadcast entitled "The Bush White House: Inside the Real West Wing," for
allowing the program to become "a valentine to Bush" (quoted in Friend
2002). Sorkin accused the White House of misrepresenting the president
by showing him "much busier and more engaged than he is" and suggested
that the media was failing in their responsibility to report objectively:

I also think it's absolutely right that at this time we're all laying off the bubblehead jokes. But that's a far cry from what the *Times* and CNN and others on whom we rely for unvarnished objectivity are telling us which is that "My God! On September 12 he woke up as Teddy Roosevelt! He became the Rough Rider!" ... That illusion may be what we need right now, but the truth is we're simply pretending to believe that Bush exhibited unspeakable courage at the World Series by throwing out the first pitch at Yankee Stadium.... The media is waving pom-poms, and the entire country is being polite [*ibid.*].

Sorkin criticizes the news media for fictionalizing the presidency by creating an emotional "illusion" that fails to serve the public interest. While he insists that the news media have a responsibility to keep political reality and political fiction separate, he fails to make the same demands of *The West Wing*. As the interview continues, he repeats the familiar claim that *The West Wing* is "completely fiction" and "nonpolitical" but then reveals that one of the early story lines for the series' fourth season will focus on President Bartlet running against a Republican governor "who's not the sharpest tool in the shed" (*ibid.*). More directly, he tells the interviewer that "it was frustrating watching Gore try so hard not to appear smart in the debates ... to an extent we're going to rerun the last election" (*ibid.*).[41] If Sorkin's insistence on the "nonpolitical" nature of the series is taken at face value, then his reenactment of some of the issues surrounding the American presidential election of 2000 is indicative of his belief in the show's powerful place in public discourse. His confidence in dramatizing a fictional political narrative that so closely resembles real life events makes it hard to believe that he is not responding to the impact.

The affect of the "terrorism" episode was to cement *The West Wing*'s place as a force in political and cultural debate. The controversy over Sorkin's comments criticizing the news media for being uncritical of the Bush administration further suggests the power and influence of the show's narrative (and its creator) on political discourse.[42] This influence, however, is not separate from the program's existence as a television product. Its fiction gives it the means to affect reality. Wolff suggests:

To be sure, *The West Wing* does not in the least rise above the limitations of its genre. It's a television set piece, something entirely formulaic, earnest, goody-goody, proud of itself, overproduced. And exactly for these reasons, it may be on its way to being the most important political document of its age. Like a lawyer show or cop show or doctor show, it begins to create an entertainment distortion field that not only changes the way we view reality, but changes the behavior, affect, and self-image of the people who work in these jobs [2000].

The result is a cultural product that is not easily separated from the reality of its fictional representation. The link between the two is found in the nature of presidential performance.

As the real president is judged on how successfully his performance portrays a visual truth (how real his performance is in its fiction), so the fictional president is celebrated when the performance comes close to meeting those same expectations. Both the real and fictional president must satisfy the expectations of the myth, a fictional construct learned early in the process of political socialization. As the real president inevitably fails to realize the myth, his fictional counterpart is free to embody it. The result is, as Barker suggests, a different measure for what constitutes the real:

> It is a curious and perhaps insidious dimension of contemporary culture and society that many people now measure the reality of the original against the bench mark of the mediated experience ("Gee, this is just like on TV!") [1988].

For Barker, television's screen images are now used to negotiate the meaning of the real, as the mediated experience becomes the truth against which the original is understood. For the *West Wing* viewers cited in this chapter, the meaning of the American presidency is measured against Sorkin's televisual representation.[43] However, this negotiation, rather than taking place between an "original" and a "mediated experience," as Barker suggests, occurs between two mediated experiences. The reality of the presidency, as experienced by the majority of Americans, is a mediated one. The president, as a system of meaning, is a complex construction of media images and political learning. The viewers who define *president* by the attributes of Jed Bartlet are using one mediated experience to measure another. Their response is a longing for a presidential ideal that only a fictional character is capable of satisfying.[44]

In an interview with National Public Radio, Martin Sheen expressed his thoughts on the role of *The West Wing* in American culture:

> We call ourselves a parallel universe to the real world. We know we're a fantasy. But at the same time, there are sometimes periods of history where fantasy is not a bad idea to focus on every now and then [quoted in Edwards 2003].

More than expressions of his desire for a different political climate, Sheen's remarks directly compare a fictional representation with reality. As a "parallel universe," the series exists in its own sphere of realism. In Sheen's view, the series is not only worthy of this designation, but its qualities also surpass those of real world politics. As this chapter has shown, viewers, critics and politicians publicly express a similar desire for *The West Wing* fantasy that Sheen advocates. Yet this fantasy of a noble president and idealistic staff is not merely a yearning for wish fulfillment on the part of a disillusioned citizenry. Rather, it is a response to a media environment that privileges an affective view of the president over a cognitive one and works as a reaffirmation of the lessons learned in political socialization. When Meyrowitz first wrote of the electronic media's impact on social behavior in 1985, he discussed the primacy given by journalists to political image over political issues. He argued that electronic media, as the stage for performance of political ritual, had changed the requirements necessary for success (279). Television, he suggested "does not foster the formal, front region behavior traditionally associated with the presidency" (283). Almost two decades later, electronic media's exposure of the intimate "backstage" behavior of presidential performance is commonplace. The sexual indiscretions and other misadventures of American presidents and candidates for the office are reported on regularly. Rather than undermining the mystique necessary for authoritative rule, as Meyrowitz has suggested, this chapter has argued that television's intimate exposure has strengthened the presidential myth by making it more powerful, even as it seems more unattainable. The disillusionment that the public may feel for the actual president lies in their assessment of his personal failure to fulfill the myth rather than a failure of the myth itself.

The president of *The West Wing* serves the myth because he embodies the character traits that support a collective understanding of the ideal. More than that, the reality of *The West Wing*'s presidency is found in the idea of presidential performance. As Nixon's failures led to the deconstruction of the president's factual image and revealed the transparency of performance, the public lost faith in the man behind the institution. However, the resulting cynicism did not lead to a rejection of the truth that the screen provided. The truth became an understanding that the president is performance. The fact that the public is a knowing (and willing) participant in the performance allows the reality and fiction of the presidency to merge until they are indistinct. The presidency is a fiction that requires a fiction to maintain it. The next chapter explores the role of Sorkin's President Bartlet in this maintenance.

CHAPTER FIVE

The Making of a President

According to a poll conducted during the first season of *The West Wing*, Jed Bartlet would have won the 2000 presidential election with 75 percent of the vote (Berens 2001). The "win" is impressive for a fictional president, particularly one who was originally conceived as an occasional, minor character. The decision to expand the role is attributed to the enthusiasm of both Sheen for the character and Sorkin for Sheen's performance in the "Pilot" (*Official Companion* 2002, 260). Other sources suggest that focus groups, having viewed the first episode in which Sheen appears briefly at the end, wanted to see the president as more than a minor character (Lowry 2003). The NBC network soon revised Sheen's original contractual obligation to appear in only six of the first season's thirteen episodes, making him a full-time cast member. The decision altered Sorkin's original narrative focus on the ensemble cast and led to the development of a character who has become the show's defining force.

While the poll's voters embraced Sorkin's fictional president, the critics were less enthusiastic. Commenting on the first episode, Joyce Millman, a television critic for online journal *Salon*, claimed that Sheen's performance was "wheezy, overexuberant" and "canned ham" (1999). Yet her overall reaction to the show and its representation of the presidency was that it "sucks you in" with "swiftly paced multiple story lines" and a president who is "all principle, compassion and New England vigor" (1999). A year later, Millman had tempered her reaction to Sheen's President Bartlet, claiming that it is "hard not to get all stirred up by him" (2000). While admitting that Sorkin's presidential vision is a passion that is "as charming as it is corny," Millman goes on to embrace the character as a president who "puts the greater good above special interests" and "remains true to his convictions" (*ibid.*). Echoing Millman's earlier sentiments, television critic Caryn James of the *New York Times* suggested that the first episode "falls apart" with the entrance of Sheen. The character is written and played, she noted, for "maximum hokiness and cracker-barrel wisdom" (1999). While James saw no merit in Sheen's performance or Sorkin's characterization, a fellow critic at the *New York Times* suggested that Bartlet's commitment to his principles was, in fact, so desirable that the character had increased the public's "dissatisfaction with flesh-and-blood candidates" (Lippman 2000). Still, others argued that the series was a "sunny weekly fable" with a president who is merely a "two-dimensional glyph of implausible virtue" (Lehmann 2001).

Embraced as an inspiration to politics or dismissed as a political fantasy, Sorkin's presidential representation achieved a degree of power in public discourse that continued past the show's first season. In 2003, as the series was midway through its fourth season, controversy over Sheen's antiwar activities, including addressing rallies and leading a virtual march on Washington to protest the war in Iraq, reportedly resulted in pressure on the NBC network to fire him from the series or face advertiser and viewer boycott (Campbell 2003, 4).[45] A political activist for many years, Sheen has been arrested over sixty times (Stuttaford 2003), although none of these arrests caused as much controversy as his antiwar activities in 2003. While the public outrage over Sheen reflects the complex relationship between patriotic feelings and the ideological environment of a country still coming to terms with the effects of September 11, it also suggests that Sheen is somehow misrepresenting the character he plays on the series. Discussing Sheen's political activism in *National Review*, Andrew Stuttaford argues that the actor's authority is "reinforced by the fact that he portrays a president on an upscale soap opera" but acknowledges that this power is "our fault, not his, if we take an actor seriously for the roles he plays" (*ibid.*). Considering Sheen's activist history, it's unclear how he would credit his role as President Bartlet with strengthening his antiwar message, although he has used the identity directly since portraying the character. Working with the environmental organization Defenders of Wildlife, Sheen sent an email message urging people to preserve the Arctic refuge. He begins by saying "in my TV role as President Bartlet" and ends with "now in the real world" (De Vries 2002). Including this comparison suggests that Sheen (and the organization) feel that the identity of President Bartlet lends credibility (or at the very least recognition) to the actor and his message.

The public outcry over Sheen's antiwar activities suggests a similar connection. Although Sheen did not refer to President Bartlet in his antiwar campaign, the other actors involved in the movement were not targeted to the same degree. The public demands for his termination from the series imply that his perceived lack of patriotism reflected poorly on his presidential alter ego. It is a position that reflects the underlying power of Sorkin's presidential representation. The character of Bartlet is admired and dismissed for the same basic reason. He is either a shining example of noble ideals or an overly idealized fantasy. In both cases, the reactions are based on deep-seated notions of what the president means. This meaning system is both a cognitive and affective process. Sorkin, however, consistently reinforces the affective by constructing simple, easily recognizable frames for his president. His construction of Bartlet recognizes the various characters that are inherent to the identity of the president as it is defined in early political socialization. Throughout the series, Sorkin positions Bartlet as paternal, intellectual and moral; the character is father, scholar and moral leader. These identities recall the most basic understanding of the president as the concept is taught to most Americans. While these roles have clear cognitive components—the viewer of the series intellectually understands the idea of father, scholar and moral leader—the emotional association is stronger because Sorkin's narrative ensures it takes precedence over an intellectual response. Within each characterization, the emotional element of the role is either the sole emphasis or used to justify actions that may otherwise be subject to cognitive evaluation. For example, Sorkin consistently encourages the audience to view Bartlet's intellect through the emotional reactions of his staff or the character's own insecure feelings about his intelligence. The subject, in fact, becomes a recurring story line throughout the series. If Bartlet is portrayed as a distant father, it is a result of his feelings rather than a carefully considered intellectual choice. Sorkin also ensures that Bartlet's morality, while often the subject of cognitive debate, is ultimately reduced to choices that feel right. These subtleties are important because they give the character an affective power that simplifies the viewer's experience of the president. Where some critics such as Millman and Lippman see virtue in the character's simple construction (he is straightforwardly noble), others such as Lehmann and James respond to this same framing as simplistic fantasy (he is too good to be true). All are reactions to the basic affective identities that Sorkin employs to construct the character.

However, Sorkin's construction of Bartlet has a more complex component because the character is also the president. While the various dimensions of Bartlet are not unique to fictional television characters, the complexity of the president as both a real-life character mediated through the news and a larger than life character created by political socialization processes means that the fictional president and the real president are not so easily separated. To understand the power of Sorkin's fictional representation of the president is to understand the power of the fictional complexities of the real president. The president's roles, as they are learned in early political education, are basic, unambiguous and emphasize the most ideal traits attached to each identity. As a concept, the president represents the best version of a father, an intellect and a moral leader. Despite the complex understanding of the president that accompanies adulthood, these roles retain their basic, emotional resonance. They have an emotional power that is not entirely lost in adult conceptions of the office. For Edelman this affective understanding of leadership works to simplify a complex social world:

> If the subtle effects of economic conjunctures, historical change, and ideologies daunt the general public as well as historians and social scientists, belief in the beneficent or malevolent power of leaders offers a satisfying resolution.... Leaders are ready symbols of good or evil ... objectifications of whatever worries or pleases observers of the political scene because it is easy to identify with them, support or oppose them, love or hate them [1988, 39].

Edelman's argument suggests that it is easier to understand political leadership by attaching feelings to the individual who holds the office rather than the complex social, economic and historic forces that shape their decisions. Connected to this argument regarding the psychological uses of leadership is his claim that the public "assuages personal guilt and anxiety by transferring responsibility to another" (*ibid.*). This is a transference that implies emotion. Mediated political communication ensures that the public is able to connect with their leaders through their feelings for them. The "easy" identification that Edelman refers to ultimately relies on emotions.

With simple frames or ideal identities, Sorkin constructs a fictional president who both recalls and satisfies the American viewer's most basic conceptions of the real president. Yet Sorkin's president, like the real president, does not always meet the expectations of his assigned roles. Bartlet does not represent a president who is always an ideal father, scholar or moral leader. Yet as previous sections of this book have noted, much of the commentary surrounding the show suggests that the character has become a signifier for the ideal political leader. The inconsistency is possible because Sorkin positions the viewer to experience Bartlet's flaws through the emotional filter of the show's senior staff. This filter often reduces the character's flaws to eccentricities or constructs them as sympathetic because they originate from deep-seated emotional pain. In some cases, Bartlet's suspect actions are justified as serving a greater good. The result is a representation of a political leader who the audience is encouraged to understand as a flawed man first and a flawed president second. The distinction is subtle but important because it allows Sorkin to explore the flaws of the president without damaging the ideal. This chapter will examine the three main identities that Sorkin uses to construct Bartlet. It will argue that the paternal, the moral and the intellectual roles of the character promote an affective presidential representation. The framework, however, does not create a new meaning system for the president. Rather, it succeeds by reinforcing the emotional template of early political education.

The Paternal President

A lot of the inspiration for Bartlet comes from my father, who is very much of another world.... At times I'm writing my father, at times I'm simply writing a character I think my father would like.
(Aaron Sorkin in *Official Companion* 2002, 261)

Perhaps the most fundamental framework used to communicate the idea of the president in early learning is that of authority figure. As noted previously, political socialization studies suggest that many American children learn to conceptualize the president as an authority figure like their parents. Often, parental authority is "transferred" to political figures, making them "parents writ large" (Easton and Hess 1962, 242; see also Greenstein 1960). Clearly, the president as a male takes on the traits of father in this dynamic. While the complexities of the patriarchal nature of the American political system are beyond the scope of this book, it is useful to note that the presidency has a long history of paternal associations.

Kann suggests that the "language of political fatherhood pervaded the entire founding era" (1996). Citing the work of Gordon Wood, Kann notes that while the American Revolution destroyed the idea of paternal authority, many of the founders of the fledgling nation believed that restoring the image of political leaders as "trustworthy civic father[s]" was necessary in order to revitalize public confidence (*ibid.*). Writings throughout this time offer numerous examples of paternal references to politics. Citing various texts, Kann notes that public officials were often addressed as "honored fathers" while the authors of the Articles of Confederation were described as "fathers of their country" filled with "parental tenderness" (*ibid.*).

As a tool for legitimizing their power, America's new political leaders hoped that the public would use the fatherly identification to embrace the idea of authority without tyranny. Kann suggests that it was a natural assumption because "American males were accustomed to paternal authority. They honored their own fathers and expected their sons to honor them" (*ibid.*). The transfer of fatherly attributes to political leaders followed accordingly, as those leaders who "successfully donned the mantle of fatherhood elicited considerable citizen respect and deference" (*ibid.*). The comforting and familiar image soothed the anxieties of a nation recently freed from monarchial rule. Yet, as Kann suggests, this image also signified (benign) authority, creating an environment where dissent was discouraged. A balance was struck between obedience and independence where "a man could obey a biological or civic father without feeling that he forfeited his manly independence or citizenship" (*ibid.*). For a fledgling nation fearful of despotic rule, the balance ensured stability by allowing both admiration and controlled dissent.

In the early days of the American Republic, the patriarchal language used to describe civic leaders was quickly transferred to the national political debate. Kann notes that federalists used paternal imagery to ensure the smooth ratification of the U.S. Constitution. He writes:

> Early in the debates, James Wilson trumpeted the prospect that the new president would not be a tyrant but a father-figure who would "watch over the whole with paternal care and affection." Federalists felt fortunate that America's greatest father figure, George Washington, was apt to be the first president. Ministers, writers, and citizens considered him "the father of the country" [*ibid.*].

By associating Washington's leadership with the benign connotations of patriarchal authority, the founders of the new republic created an institution that was understood to embody a natural human relationship, that of parent and child. Implicit in this paternal representation was the discourse of masculinity. The traits inherent in the conceptions of masculinity during this time—power, control and mastery—were easily transposed to presidential leadership.

While demonstrations of masculinity may shift as particular cultural contexts change (so that there are masculinities rather than one singular masculinity), the presidential office has remained a distinctly masculine one. That is, specific qualities inherent to masculine discourse are in turn inherent to presidential leadership.[46] The role of the president, conceived as the masculine father/leader, enters a citizen's consciousness from an early age. It is an association he is encouraged to recall throughout his life by those who seek and hold the office as well as by those who mediate its image.

Campaign Discourse and the Power of the Paternal

Images of the president as father/leader are powerful symbols that embed the idea of family into the discourse of the presidency. While a detailed examination of these images is beyond the scope of this book, pictures of recent American presidents, from Bill Clinton walking the grounds of the White House holding his wife and daughter's hands to George W. Bush being told about September 11 as he reads to schoolchildren, offer compelling evidence of the relationship between the presidency and the discourse of family. Perhaps one of the most enduring images of this association is that of three-year-old John F. Kennedy, Jr., saluting his father's casket three days after President Kennedy's assassination. The image became an iconic symbol of the Kennedy mythology as well as a signifier for the presidency as the eternal father/leader. These images underscore the broader argument that general campaign discourse has often depicted the paternal nature of presidential candidates (Fisher 1982; Schram 1991).

In their study of presidential image construction, Parry-Giles and Parry-Giles explore the move in United States political campaigning toward an increasingly intimate style of self-disclosure. Basing their work on the idea that "explorations of a candidate's family life provide an easy crossover to the paternalistic role presidents are expected to play while in office" (1996), the authors analyze the campaign films of presidents Reagan, Bush and Clinton. They suggest that a significant component of the shift towards intimacy, as it is depicted in these films, directly connects the candidates' roles in their family life to their leadership capabilities. Their research argues that Reagan's intimacy, while not specifically related to his family, set a trend for the future campaign films of Bush and Clinton, who would expand the emotive tone to construct their leadership success as directly related to their status as family men. While Reagan's campaign film stressed an intimacy with the voter, it was contained within a construction of Reagan as private president rather than Reagan as private individual (*ibid.*). Bush, however, relied on his family to construct his image. His use of intimacy, the authors note, derived from the image of him as patriarch of the large Bush family rather than affective speeches on policy issues or a focus on the institution of the presidency (*ibid.*). The format of the untitled film involved Bush, his wife Barbara and President Reagan speaking directly to the camera. The authors note that the direct address, particularly when the Bushes recount their history together, is reminiscent of "the way children are told of the lives of their parents and grandparents" (*ibid.*). The result is a film "less institutional in its focus and more disclosive of the Bush persona as a 'fatherly' or paternal candidate" (*ibid.*). The image of Bush as the fatherly presidential contender served a greater point, as the family meta-phor used in the film connected the Bush family to the family of Ameri-cans, "suggesting that Bush function as the patriarch of both" (*ibid.*). This metaphor is most evident in the closing image of the film, in which the viewer watches a young girl running through a grassy meadow. It is a repeat of the opening image, except this time the camera follows her as she runs into the arms of George Bush, her grandfather, who lifts her up and kisses her. The image of Bush's granddaughter cements the "metaphoric link between family and country" that is the film's narrative goal and "activates a powerful ideological structure of meaning deeply embedded within American culture" (*ibid.*). The structure of meaning not only recalls the ideology of fatherhood but its basic relationship to political leadership as it is constructed in the processes of political socialization. Viewers of Bush's campaign film are able to accept his portrait of leadership as akin to pater-nal benevolence because it is an ideology that is fundamentally accepted as part of the discourse of the presidency.

In his 1992 campaign film, *The Man from Hope*, Bill Clinton employs similar techniques to Bush's by framing his intimate narrative through the recollections and testimonials of family members. Unlike Bush, Clinton intensifies the private, family discourse. In the course of the film, he recalls his teenage confrontations with an alcoholic stepfather, his feelings over the birth of his daughter Chelsea and the pain and pride he felt when Chelsea, having just watched the television interview where Clinton and his wife discuss their marital problems, responded simply: "I'm glad you're my parents" (*ibid.*). Clinton's emphasis on his image as father and leader of a family reaches its climax at the end of the film. The visual montage of home videos that include scenes of Chelsea in a party dress, the family fishing and Clinton and his wife sharing a private conversation while danc-ing are played with a voiceover by Clinton discussing his goals for the country (*ibid.*). Parry-Giles and Parry-Giles argue that *The Man from Hope* is a departure from the Reagan and Bush films because the Clinton intimacy comes from the "character and persona" of the candidate (*ibid.*). Yet, the personal revelations that allow the viewer to experience Clinton's charac-ter are intimately connected to his identity as a father and husband, a con-cept that is demonstrated by the film's montage images.

In concluding their study, Parry-Giles and Parry-Giles refer to the work of Jasinski (1993) who suggests that a politics of intimacy "shifts away from the 'what' of human interaction ... and refocuses attention on the topic 'who' (embodied in the quests for the 'essence' or ultimate motive of the person)" (*ibid.*). However, as the beginning of this chapter has shown, the who of politics has a long history of taking precedence over the what.

The earliest figures of the American political system were conceptualized as much for their ability to fulfill the image of father as they were for their ability to articulate issues. The two ideas were codependent; a successful father figure was understood to embody the qualities of a successful leader and vice-versa. The idea, as the campaign films of recent presidents demonstrate, has not lost its influence.

Bartlet as Father Figure

Clearly, the idea of the president as father provides an accessible means by which young American children are able to conceptualize their national leader. This goal is not dissimilar from that of the nation's founders, who used the familiar concept to ensure that the presidency was both easy to relate to and easy to respect. While the average American adult may not associate the president with the concept of father, many of the mediated images (that play a prominent part in shaping their understanding of him) often emphasize a paternal role. Campaign films that depict the president hugging his granddaughter or news footage that shows the president reading to a classroom full of children suggest that the paternal image forms an intricate part of the overall meaning of the president. These visual cues elicit understandings of father. Combined with the meaning of the president as leader, they offer a shared cultural knowledge that assigns the presidency one of its most fundamental roles. As one of the shared cultural meanings of president, the father/leader concept is often transferred from the reality of news images to fictional depictions. The performative nature of the candidates in the campaign films examined previously suggest that the boundary is, in fact, often blurred. The result is a representation of constructed intimacy that connects presidential leadership character to paternal character. In the narrative of *The West Wing*, Sorkin employs a similar method by constructing an intimacy around Bartlet that positions the character as the presidential father.

One of the ways that Sorkin's narrative gives the viewer access to the private, intimate Bartlet is through the various levels of his paternal character. Bartlet is the father of three daughters, the father figure to his senior staff and, as president, the father of the nation. Within each relationship, Bartlet assumes the primary role while simultaneously embodying paternal signifiers. The character is depicted as nurturing, supportive, protective, loving and authoritative. More importantly, all of these qualities are firmly planted within the character's presidential identity. That is, Bartlet is never characterized as father outside his identity as president, except when he fails in the role. This is an important narrative construct because it both contributes to political socialization processes and protects those processes from losing their affective power. Because Sorkin makes the separation between president and father difficult, the viewer is encouraged to understand the president as a figure who inherently embodies the qualities associated with the paternal. This connection recalls one of the basic identities that political socialization uses to construct an understanding of the president, which allows Sorkin's character to achieve a resonance with the viewer. Alternatively, Sorkin's protection of the ideal role of the president (as ideal father and leader) is achieved by isolating Bartlet's failures as a father. When Bartlet behaves like a bad father, it is attributed to his failings as a man rather than his role as national leader.

As this chapter's opening quote suggests, Sorkin's conception of the paternal and the presidential are not so easily separated. Writing Bartlet as a direct embodiment of his father or someone his father "would like," Sorkin clearly conceives Bartlet on personal terms. The writer's discussion of his father's traits, then, provides a useful starting point from which to begin an examination of Bartlet as the paternal president. Sorkin describes his father this way:

> He's a lawyer, a terribly wise and gentle man with a kind of "Aw, Dad" sense of humor. He's devoted to his family and filled with emotion about great men and women and events gone by [*Official Companion* 2002, 261].

A character modeled on his father, a man "filled with emotion," Sorkin's construction of Bartlet rests on the same affective foundation. The traits that Sorkin ascribes to his father—wisdom, gentleness, familial devotion, an eccentric sense of humor and an emotive relationship with history—manifest themselves throughout his general construction of Bartlet.

In the pilot episode of *The West Wing*, the character of President Bartlet is experienced emotionally before he is experienced visually. Before physically introducing the character, Sorkin emotionally constructs Bartlet through the reactions of the senior staff. As the episode begins, the viewer watches each member of Bartlet's staff receive the message that he has been in a bicycle accident. Their reactions are a mixture of concern and urgency, as they each move quickly to respond to their pages. The viewer, then, is encouraged to feel this concern as well as understand Bartlet as a president who engages in informal, leisure activities such as riding a bike. Sorkin's choice is significant because it establishes an underlying tone for the character that is carried throughout the series. Rather than introduce the president engaging in formal, political duties or activities that signify president, Sorkin reveals a personal side to the character. As the episode concludes, the private side of Bartlet is quickly connected to the paternal. Addressing the staff in the Oval Office, he interrupts their boisterous teasing of one another (interactions that recall sibling relationships) and says:

> Seems to me we've all been taking a little break, thinking about our personal lives or thinking about keeping our jobs. Breaks are good. It's not a bad idea to take a break every now and then. I know how hard you all work.

After acknowledging their contributions and offering support for their occasional loss of focus, Bartlet continues with another short story about his granddaughter and then begins to list the number of Cuban asylum seekers that the Navy has recently intercepted or declared missing and presumed dead. He ends the speech this way:

> With the clothes on their back they came through a storm and the ones that didn't die want a better life and they want it here. Talk about impressive. My point is this break's over.

In this scene, Sorkin positions Bartlet as the gentle but firm father of his staff family who wisely guides them back to their responsibilities. By juxtaposing this idea with the image of desperate Cuban refugees who have endured tremendous hardship to join the family of Americans, Sorkin affectively connects Bartlet's paternal leadership of his staff with his paternal leadership as president.

The visual direction of the concluding scene also contributes to Sorkin's construction of an affective presidency. Bartlet's speech occurs in the Oval Office, the one room in the White House that most strongly signifies the presidency. He speaks from behind and in front of his desk, an angle the audience experiences through the staff's point-of-view shots. As the scene and the episode ends, Bartlet takes a seat behind his desk and the camera moves from facing him to an overhead shot that positions the viewer behind and above him. The audience is positioned to survey the room, a viewpoint that now includes the clearly visible seal of the president on the carpet of the office. The dialogue between Bartlet and his secretary discussing his schedule fades as the camera and the viewer leave the president to run the country. The power and patriotism of the office and Bartlet's role within it are now firmly established both visually and aurally.

As previous sections have discussed, Sorkin often develops the story lines of the senior staff characters to frame Bartlet as a father figure. The characters, particularly C. J. and Toby, are consistently depicted as seeking his approval in a way that suggests a paternal relationship. Sorkin contributes to this characterization by portraying Bartlet in scenes that emphasize informal family moments with the staff. While a general camaraderie between the president and his senior aides is evident throughout the show's narrative, some scenes are more clearly familial than others are. In various episodes, the viewer sees Bartlet playing poker with his staff ("Mr. Willis of Ohio"), taking them Christmas shopping ("In Excelsis Deo"), making them chili and playing basketball ("The Crackpots and These Women"). These interactions move beyond a simple characterization of Bartlet as a friendly and personable employer because the underlying tone of the series makes the paternal connection more explicit. Early in the first season, Sorkin has Bartlet describe his feelings for the senior staff:

> You guys are like family. You've always been there for me, always been loyal, honest, hardworking, good people and I love you very much. I don't say that often enough ["Five Votes Down"].

While the scene is intended for laughs (Bartlet has taken too much pain medication and appears intoxicated), the president is also depicted as sincere, a tone that is suggested by the bemused but touched reaction of the other characters. In a more direct reference to the president as father, Sorkin has Bartlet refer to Josh as his son in "Two Cathedrals." This theme is reiterated in the relationship between the president and his personal aide Charlie Young (Dulé Hill), a character who Sorkin claims is also "a son to Bartlet" (*Official Companion* 2002, 70). A young African-American, Charlie is introduced in the third episode of the series and eventually begins to date Bartlet's youngest daughter Zoey. Sorkin uses the interracial relationship to both articulate Bartlet's trust and affection for Charlie and as the impetus for the attempted assassination story line that concludes the first season.[47] However, Sorkin most clearly demonstrates the paternal nature of Bartlet and Charlie's relationship in a scene from the second season in which the president gives Charlie a carving knife that has been in the Bartlet family for generations and traditionally passed from father to son ("Shibboleth").

While Sorkin engages Bartlet in paternal interactions with the senior staff, he contains the role within the character's identity as president. Despite the familiar, personal and often humorous interactions that suggest Bartlet's characterization as father, Sorkin prevents the role from overshadowing the larger identity of president. This is achieved through a narrative that rarely shows the character of Bartlet not performing presidential activities, as well as a repetition of the words "Mr. President," spoken continually by the senior staff in their interactions with the character. These visual and aural signifiers of the presidency in turn encourage the audience to relate the two identities but not to completely merge them. Father and president become emotionally bound together but not indistinct.

The relationship between Sorkin's conceptions of the paternal and the presidential is also found in his characterization of Bartlet as the father of three children. In perhaps the most direct connection between the ideas surrounding the president as a father figure, Sorkin incorporates Bartlet's relationships with his daughters into the show's narrative. Similar to his depiction of Bartlet as the father of his staff, Sorkin writes the character's interactions with his children within the confines of the presidency. That is, Bartlet's relationships with his daughters are only realized within a political context. This allows Sorkin to connect the paternal to the presidential. However, Sorkin only maintains the connection between the personal and the political until Bartlet fails in his role as a father. When this occurs, Sorkin temporarily positions Bartlet as a fallible man rather than an imperfect president.

Sorkin introduces two of Bartlet's three daughters during the show's first and second season. The third and eldest daughter, Elizabeth is briefly mentioned as the mother of his granddaughter Annie in the "Pilot." The viewer first meets Zoey (Elisabeth Moss), Bartlet's youngest daughter, in a scene in which Bartlet is conducting a meeting with economists. He receives a note that she will be in town to look at university housing and announces that he will cook a batch of his famous chili for the staff to celebrate the occasion ("The Crackpots and These Women"). The scene is short but establishes Bartlet as a loving and engaged father. It also allows Sorkin to inject a scene that typifies the president's working day with a personal view of the president as a father.

At the conclusion of the episode, Bartlet makes a short speech to the assembled party guests. After commenting on his delight that Zoey is there, Bartlet tells the group that she will be starting university in the spring. He walks to her, puts his arm around her and says:

> It's an incredible adventure you're starting on sweetheart. An amazing four years full of people and experiences you haven't yet dreamed of and if you will allow me just one minute of business please. (He addresses the group). I hope that by the time we're done with our four years here, we'll have seen to it that every young person who chooses can go to college and beyond regardless of their economic status.

The scene directly combines the paternal with the presidential. As Bartlet is the father and provider for his daughter Zoey, so too should his administration be the father and provider for the children of the nation, ensuring that each has the opportunity for a successful future. Sorkin cements the inspirational tone with Bartlet's concluding remarks to the group. The character urges them to collectively strive for grand achievements "as we did in a time when our eyes looked toward the heavens and with outstretched fingers we touched the face of God." The overall effect of the scene is to connect the pride of a father with dreams for his child to the pride of a leader with dreams for his people.

Sorkin revisits Bartlet's relationship with Zoey in "Mr. Willis of Ohio." In a heated scene between the two, Bartlet expresses his feelings over being both the president and a father. Again, the dialogue suggests that the two roles are not easily separated within Sorkin's conception of the presidency. Informing Zoey that he will be increasing her secret service protection after a confrontation with some male university students in a bar, Bartlet angrily responds when she begins to protest the idea. He describes a kidnapping scenario in detail that would result in his dual roles as president and father being compromised:

> So now we got a new problem because this country no longer has a commander-in-chief. It has a father who is out of his mind because his little girl is in a shack somewhere ... with a gun to her head. You get it?!

Stunned, Zoey quietly agrees. Bartlet apologizes for raising his voice and says that her position is "a privilege" and an "experience that must be cherished beyond measure." In this highly emotional scene, the viewer watches Bartlet grow increasingly animated and angry while telling his "nightmare scenario." The scenario is affective because it paints a stark picture of the president's political and personal responsibilities. Sorkin forces the viewer to confront his understanding of the president as both leader and father with a situation that places both roles under unthinkable stress. However, while he positions the viewer to see the president as literal father, Sorkin frees the audience from having to make a choice between the two roles. He leaves the "nightmare" unresolved. Bartlet does not finish the story by telling the viewer his choice. This lack of closure allows the narrative to maintain Bartlet as both president and father. Yet Sorkin does not create an equal balance between the two roles. Bartlet's closing remarks to Zoey suggest that Sorkin privileges the presidential role. By having Bartlet urge Zoey to embrace her role as a president's daughter as something to be "cherished beyond measure," Sorkin encourages the audience to feel a sense of awe for the presidency. The underlying tone of the dialogue is that the presidency is more important than the personal demands it may place on those who experience it. The scene allows Sorkin to articulate a personal, fatherly side to Bartlet within the context of his role as president. It is a theme he will repeat in an episode from the second season when he introduces Bartlet's middle daughter, Eleanor (Ellie) (Nina Siemaszko).

Sorkin's introduction of Ellie adds a new element to his construction of Bartlet as president/father. For the first time, the viewer is positioned to see Bartlet as a failed father. Before the introduction of Bartlet's middle daughter, Sorkin gave the audience, through Zoey, a portrait of Bartlet as a concerned, loving and supportive parent. With Ellie, Sorkin disrupts this frame, yet he does so in a way that isolates Bartlet's failings from the office of the presidency. This, in turn, allows the viewer to see Bartlet as an imperfect father rather than an imperfect president.

The plot that introduces Ellie is structured around her comments to a newspaper reporter. After the Surgeon General, her godmother, makes some controversial statements regarding marijuana's status as a "schedule one narcotic," Ellie phones a reporter and tells him: "My father won't fire the Surgeon General. He would never do that" ("Ellie"). Under intense political pressure to dismiss the Surgeon General, Bartlet is furious that his daughter would put him in an embarrassing position. The scene between them quickly moves from the political to the personal:

BARTLET: There's politics involved in this, Ellie, and you know it would make me unhappy and that's why you did it and that's cheap!

ELLIE: I didn't do it to make you unhappy, Dad.

BARTLET: Well, you sure didn't do it to make me happy.

ELLIE: I don't know how to make you happy, Dad. For that you gotta talk to Zoey or Liz.

The confrontation allows Sorkin to expose a darker side to Bartlet's paternal identity by making it clear that he shares a damaged relationship with Ellie. The character is not an ideal father, a fact Sorkin expands upon in a later scene between Bartlet and the Surgeon General. Because the scene is a strong example of the complexities of Sorkin's paternal characterization of the presidency, it will be examined in some detail.

Like the emotional meeting with Ellie, the confrontation between Bartlet and the Surgeon General (Mary Kay Place), also takes place in the Oval Office. This is important because it allows Sorkin to maintain the image of presidential authority while depicting a domestic scene. The scene's combination of formal and informal elements is established by the tone of the characters' conversation as well as the contrast between Bartlet's dress and the Surgeon General's clothes. He is dressed in jeans and a sweatshirt while she wears the military uniform of her office.

Still hoping that his daughter did not purposely embarrass him, Bartlet asks the Surgeon General, or Millie as she is referred to, if she pressured Ellie into speaking to the reporter. She denies it, and Bartlet bluntly asks her, "Why haven't I ever been able to get her to like me?" Millie is uncomfortable and hesitates, suggesting that it is inappropriate for her to speak to him about this. Bartlet replies, "I'm asking you," and repeats the phrase to emphasize his sincerity. They have the following conversation:

MILLIE: She worships you Mr. President.

BARTLET: She's mad at me.

MILLIE: Well, you're mad at her.

BARTLET: Yes, I am.

MILLIE: Sir—

BARTLET: I was running for president. Where was she?

MILLIE: She was with us.

BARTLET: Not like Zoey and Liz.

MILLIE: Sir—

BARTLET: She's always belonged to Abbey.

MILLIE: You frightened her.

BARTLET: No, I didn't.

MILLIE: Sir—

BARTLET: How did I frighten her?

MILLIE: Jed! Look where you're standing!

Bartlet protests that he was elected two years ago and Ellie is old enough not to be intimidated. Millie responds: "You've been the king of whatever room you've walked into her entire life." When he suggests that his other daughters do not feel threatened by him, Millie comments that all children are different. She ends by saying, "You'd be amazed. You'd be stunned at how soon they understand they're not their father's favorite." Bartlet is shocked and offended. He responds that he "will bear with the nonsense" of various political groups but he will not permit someone to tell him that he loves one of his children "less than the others." Despite his anger over Ellie's comment, Bartlet eventually admits: "it's the nicest thing she's ever said about me." He ends by refusing Millie's resignation. When she protests that his administration needs to focus on the "bigger things," he replies, "These are the bigger things."

Sorkin's construction of this scene makes Bartlet a distant and defensive father, dismissive of his daughter's feelings and unable to take any responsibility for their damaged relationship. This characterization, however, does not damage Sorkin's portrait of the presidency because he ensures that Bartlet is positioned outside of it. He achieves this both visually and aurally. Despite the Oval Office setting, Bartlet is visually framed as unpresidential. That is, his attire suggests an informality that separates him from the usual formality that signifies the office. In jeans and a sweatshirt, he visually represents less of a president and more of an upset Dad. In addition, Sorkin chooses to have Bartlet discuss his feelings with a personal friend who is not a member of his immediate staff. He takes Bartlet outside the White House family and places him with his actual family, the godmother of his child. Millie's failure to maintain a formal dialogue with Bartlet as president is permitted because Sorkin temporarily removes Bartlet from the role. When Bartlet repeats "I'm asking you," Sorkin frees the character to become Jed, a father seeking answers. With Bartlet now speaking as a man, a father in pain rather than the president, Sorkin positions the audience to accept the character's failings as personal mistakes. The viewer sees Bartlet as a father who wants to be loved by his daughter. The narrative, however, reunites the two identities because Bartlet uses the presidency for redemption. His refusal to accept Millie's resignation is due to his belief in "the bigger things," a desire to repair his damaged relationship with his daughter. When Josh comments that everyone will think Bartlet refused the resignation because his daughter asked him to, he replies that if Josh ever has a daughter, he will find that there are worse reasons to do something. By engaging Bartlet in a presidential activity, Sorkin returns the character to his formal role. Because Bartlet's actions are intended to repair his relationship with Ellie, who has led him to understand larger truths about himself as a father and as a man, his presidential actions become the context for his paternal identity. This protects the presidency from being tarnished by the character's imperfections as a father. In fact, the presidency has become the vehicle through which he has sought to perfect his paternal role. The scene's careful visual and aural construction allows Sorkin to articulate a presidential father who ultimately upholds the ideals of both identities by containing them within a larger conception of the power of the presidency.

In his work on the assessment of presidential character, Buchanan suggests that "Americans' collective sense of what it is to be presidential is strongly affected by history's lessons about the great presidents..." (1987, 33). The images and events that surround the administrations of Washington, Jefferson, Lincoln, Kennedy and others form "shared understandings" and "subliminal definitions" of the presidency that the American public uses to conceptualize presidential greatness (Buchanan, 32). The man who takes office, then, is partially understood as the inheritor of a sacred mantel. More than that, his personality and achievements are often judged against those of his presidential predecessors. Buchanan refers to this as "paired comparisons of presidential qualities," for example, "'Nixon lacked

Eisenhower's integrity,' or 'Carter lacked Kennedy's charisma'" (33). However, this method for measuring presidential qualities serves a larger purpose because it contributes to a sense of collective American identity. Baldwin argues that "what passes for identity in America is a series of myths about one's heroic ancestors" (quoted in Loewen 1995, 18). A large number of these "heroic ancestors" are presidents, who undergo a "heroification" process (Loewen, 19). In the pages of history textbooks, Loewen argues, the great presidents are often promoted as "wartless stereotypes" (33). The result is the creation of iconic presidential figures whose legendary status and achievements become the measure for those men who follow. The strength of the measure lies in the public's belief in the greatness of the presidential heritage. While individual presidents are elevated above others, their status is ultimately "forged in emotionally significant national experience" (Buchanan 1987, 32). The presidential legacy then becomes a discourse of feelings for both the men who hold the office and the events over which they preside.

Sorkin's construction of Bartlet as the nation's father relies on this sense of a shared, affective understanding of heroic ancestors. As the first season ends, Sorkin expands on Bartlet's family history. Addressing a town hall meeting, Bartlet ends the event by responding to being called a liberal populist and a socialist during the course of the night:

> I'm an economics professor. My great-grandfather's great-grandfather was Dr. Josiah Bartlet who was the New Hampshire delegate representative to the Second Continental Congress. The one that sat in session in Philadelphia in the summer of 1776 and announced to the world that we were no longer subjects of King George III but rather a self-governing people. "We hold these truths to be self-evident"—They said that "all men are created equal." Strange as it may seem that was the first time in history that anyone had ever bothered to write that down. Decisions are made by those who show up. Class dismissed ["What Kind of Day Has it Been"].

Sorkin constructs Bartlet as the direct descendent of a founding father; he is positioned as a legitimate heir to the presidency. This status connects the character to the notion of heroic ancestors but is tempered by his initial identification as an economics professor. Bartlet is framed as humble in the face of his ancestry. Yet, as the speech continues, the affective tone succeeds in assigning Bartlet's personal history to the broader notion of the national family. He tells a story of men and events that shaped the most treasured principles of the nation and concludes the lesson by reminding the fictional audience (and the viewer) of their role in ensuring that the legacy endures. With this speech, Sorkin confirms Bartlet's status as the nation's father by connecting the character's history with the wider symbolism of real historical events.

In his article on the politics of America's founding era, Mark Kann suggests that the American Revolution weakened patriarchal authority (1996). The idea that political leadership signified the benevolence and strength of the paternal was rejected in the struggle for independence. The power of the metaphor, however, was only temporarily disrupted. The connection between civic leadership and the paternal was reestablished after the Revolution in the hope that reviving it would restore the legitimacy of public authority (*ibid.*). The result was a discourse of "political fatherhood" that "persisted many decades after the Revolution" (*ibid.*). As this section has demonstrated, the language of civic fatherhood has, in fact, persisted well into the twenty-first century. Presidential campaign discourse encourages a strong association between the candidates' leadership abilities and their roles as family patriarchs. It is an association that is repeated in *The West Wing*'s fictional representation of the presidency. Through a narrative that consistently frames Bartlet as the patriarch of his family, his staff and his country, Sorkin encourages the viewer to connect the presidency to the language and imagery of fatherhood. He achieves this by engaging the character in situations where political ideas are contextualized in the discourse of fatherhood. A scene that begins with Bartlet depicted as a proud father celebrating his daughter's future ends with a depiction of President Bartlet delivering a stirring speech on his hopes for the future of the nation's children. An episode that focuses on the character's troubled relationship with his middle daughter uses his revelation about fatherhood to frame a political decision he makes as president. In addition, Sorkin's use of the fatherhood frame strengthens the symbolic meanings of the paternal president without damaging the overall ideal. While Bartlet often represents the ideal presidential father, in all its identities, Sorkin does depict occasional failures. Yet he carefully confines these failures to his characterization of Bartlet as an imperfect man rather than a damaged leader.

The Moral President

The presidency is preeminently a place of moral leadership.
(Franklin Roosevelt quoted in Pious 2000)

In her rhetorical study of the presidency as a symbolic institution, Barbara Hinckley argues that symbolic meaning does not have to be factually true "but will tap ideas already in the public philosophy..." (1990, 15). One of the most prominent ideas in American public philosophy is that of morality. Shapiro and Jacobs comment that the evidence to support the morality of the American public is "overwhelming" (2000). They suggest that public opinion, in addition to other sources, indicate that Americans rank among the most religious people worldwide "in terms of belief in a supreme being, membership in religious organisations and attendance at religious services" (*ibid.*). For Shapiro and Jacobs, this sense of morality, rather than remaining isolated in the personal expression of religion, seeps into political discourse. As proof, they offer the public response to President Clinton's scandals in office:

> The fact that the Clinton scandal captured the nation's attention and that polls showed a sharp jump in the percentage responding that morality and values were most important speaks for itself. The public has a strong sense of morality that is readily primed and evoked [*ibid.*].

Polls conducted during this time also indicate that the majority of the American public, while finding Clinton untrustworthy and dishonest, approved of his presidential performance (Miroff 1999). This suggests that, for many, a clear separation can be made between a president's private morality and his public morality. A detailed examination of the public response to Clinton's moral behavior is beyond the scope of this book, but it is significant that the debates did not disconnect morality from the presidency.[48] Rather, the standards of moral judgement had shifted to allow many people to confine the morality of their president to the misconduct of the man in office rather than the institution. Miroff argues that "the moral codes that shape public expectations of presidential conduct are changeable" and that standards for presidential morality in the 1990s differ from those that existed during the establishment of the presidency (*ibid.*). While these moral codes are not static, they remain a significant component of the public's understanding of the presidency.

Standards of morality for the presidency may change over time, but they are strongly rooted in the history of American democracy. Traveling the country in the 1830s, Alexis de Tocqueville noted the connection between religion and government:

> I do not know whether all the Americans have a sincere faith in their religion ... but I am certain that they hold it to be indispensable to the maintenance of republican institutions. This opinion is not peculiar to a class of citizen or to a party, but it belongs to the whole nation, and to every rank of society [quoted in Hutcheson 1988, 27].

De Tocqueville's observation is the foundation for the later concept of "civil religion," a phrase attributed to Rousseau in *The Social Contract* and later developed by the sociologist Robert Bellah in his 1967 essay *Civil Religion in America*. For Bellah, America's founding fathers used identifiable religious symbolism and belief in their written and oral construction of the nation (Hutcheson, 28). The themes and rituals of this civil religion are observable during national holidays such as Thanksgiving and Memorial Day, as well as the inaugural address of many presidents (*ibid.*). While Bellah's conception of civil religion has been vigorously debated, the relationship between American democracy and religion is not easily dismissed. Hutcheson offers the perspective that civil religion has integrated the institutional separation of church and state with a cultural integration of religion and society "to produce a workable consensus undergirding 'public virtue'" (31). In their work on the presidency and civil religion, Pierard and Linder suggest that while the First Amendment to the United State's Constitution guarantees that church and state are separate, it does not guarantee a similar division between religion and politics (1988, 19). They argue that Americans are fundamentally religious, a characteristic that "extends to every level of life, including politics" (*ibid.*). Accordingly, the president becomes the representative of the nation's civil religion:

> He affirms that God exists and that America's destiny and the nation's policies must be interpreted in the light of the Almighty's will. The rituals that the president celebrates and the speeches he makes reflect the basic themes of American civil religion [20].

Hutcheson recognizes a similar role for the president in civil religion, suggesting that presidents have "created and maintained" it through their "verbal expressions" (1988, 32). Citing the work of Bellah and others, Hutcheson notes that, in addition to the "founding documents," the oral construction of civil religion is "almost entirely from the public statements of presidents" with inaugural addresses being the most clear example (*ibid.*). These addresses form a large part of Barbara Hinckley's rhetorical study of the presidency. Her work suggests that the language of inaugurations is so removed from politics as to make those events "religious celebrations" (1990, 74). While Hinckley makes a distinction between religious references (defined to include bible quotes, religious imagery and references to faith and prayer) and morality (words like moral, values, good), she combines the two when discussing her results. Examining the inaugural speeches of presidents Truman through Reagan, Hinckley argues that aside from explicitly religious language, the speeches rely on the ambiguity of moral words for their power. As she explains:

> The ambiguity is often achieved by the repetition of a word in several senses. Thus *courage* in a moral sense shifts to a fighting courage and shifts again to

the courage of economic entrepreneurs. *Principle* links moral tenets, political practices, and foreign policy positions [77].

The result, Hinckley suggests, is that the "nation's history, goals, and economic system are painted with a common moral brush" (*ibid.*). The idea that the painter who wields this brush is the president allows for his ascension to the head of the nation's civil religion. It is a role that Hinckley recognizes as both moral and religious:

Clearly, they engage in moral—and explicitly religious—activity. Literally they preach, reminding the American people of religious and moral principles and urging them to conduct themselves in accord with these principles. They lead prayers, quote from the Bible, and make theological statements about the Deity and His desires for the nation.... They are the moral leaders and high priests of the American society [73].

The role of presidents as "moral leaders" and "high priests" forms a fundamental component of presidential identity. It is an identity created through the historical processes of political socialization and perpetuated by presidents, who Hinckley argues, "believe in their role of moral leadership and take it seriously" (78). Presidents attempt to fill this role because it is part of a larger tradition that reflects an accepted public philosophy, one that Dante Germino calls "theocentric" (quoted in Hinckley, 79). In a nation where the public pledges allegiance to "one nation under God," the president is fulfilling a role that history and society demands.

If the president is the head of the nation's civil religion, then television is his church. Gregor Goethals, in his work on the representation of rituals in secular life, suggests that television's images represent more than pictures; they are "ways of mediating faith" (1986). Contextualizing religion in sociological practice, Goethals argues that sacramental images, once the property of religious institutions, have been appropriated by secular institutions. He uses television as a primary example, suggesting that its visual narratives are the nation's "moral tales of success, failure, sin and salvation (*ibid.*). As he explains, American television's secular communication constructs faith for the nation:

From soap operas to news to sports, commercial telecasting performs a fundamentally sacramental function: it mediates and legitimates a belief in the American way of life. It assists in an important way in shaping our loyalty to the American socio-political-economic system. Witnessing to sentiments and aspirations that transcend denominational beliefs, television provides a common vision [*ibid.*]

Presidential communication contributes to this sacramental function in specific, if subtle ways. Describing the presidential press conference,

Goethals argues that its visual message may frame the president as a religious figure. Viewers "may be dimly conscious of the image of a Protestant minister standing behind a central pulpit, framed by two flags, delivering a sermon to inspire faith and conviction" (*ibid.*). Alternatively, the president's words may ensure the nonsecular association as he "confronts his adversaries, calls us to look at the 'facts,' returns us to time-honored values, articulates the differences between good and evil and then makes the right choice" (*ibid.*). The television audience becomes a congregation, gathered to listen to the words of their national preacher. The president, then, is cast as "the moral leader for a moral nation" (Hinckley 1990, 79). It is a role created by history, endorsed by presidents (and scholars) and communicated, in large part, by television's images.

Communicating this aspect of the presidency is, for Sorkin, a matter of bolstering general attitudes toward religion. Commenting on his depiction of morality in *The West Wing*, he claims that his purpose is to counteract the "insidious" tendency of people to use religion as "an instrument of hypocrisy or, worse yet, of bullying" (quoted in Haught 2001). In turn, he wants to demonstrate that "faith can be magnificent, an enormous comfort and an incredible road map" (*ibid.*). Sorkin's depiction of faith is often found in story lines where the characters confront politics from the perspective of personal morality. The result, as this book has previously argued, is a narrative where the characters consistently choose to do the right thing when faced with morally suspect political situations. Yet Sorkin ensures that the characters do not act in isolation by making Bartlet the center of *The West Wing*'s moral universe. Not only does Sorkin insert explicit religious references into Bartlet's narrative, but he also uses the character's moral convictions to frame his political decisions. The president, then, leads by his own righteous example, a characterization that recalls the discourse of the president as moral guardian.

However, as he does with his construction of the paternal president, Sorkin disrupts the ideal by having Bartlet engage in morally ambiguous behavior. In the course of the narrative, Bartlet makes a series of decisions that question the nature of his moral character. Sorkin claims his goal in this portrayal is to increase the dramatic tension by positioning Bartlet in "the hard places between personal faith and public duty" (quoted in Haught 2001). This choice is significant because it allows Sorkin to frame Bartlet as an ethical, virtuous man who is often forced by institutional forces to act against his nature. In this way, Bartlet's choices are sacrifices, and he is sympathetic. This sympathy frame is also applied when Bartlet admits to having multiple sclerosis, a fact he kept from the public and his staff. Carried through several episodes, the story line is based on the affective reactions of Bartlet, his wife, the staff and even a Republican lawyer who is involved in the president's eventual censure hearing. Alternatively, Sorkin uses morality to recast political issues until a dubious moral choice, such as Bartlet's decision to order an assassination, is positioned as the only right course of action.

The Oval Office as Sacred Space

Before examining Sorkin's construction of Bartlet as a moral president, it is useful to analyze how he creates the Oval Office as a nonsecular space. While the opening scene of Leo's walk-through in the "Pilot" establishes the overall visual and aural style of the series, it also foreshadows the narrative's moral undertones by defining the Oval Office in specific terms. When Leo enters the room, he has the following exchange with Mrs. Landingham in response to her concern over the president's bicycle accident:

LEO: He's a klutz, Mrs. Landingham, your president's a geek.

MRS. LANDINGHAM: Mr. McGarry, you know how I feel about that kind of talk in the Oval Office.

LEO: I apologize.

MRS. LANDINGHAM: Just in this room, Mr. McGarry, is all I'm asking.

Mrs. Landingham chastises Leo for what she feels is disrespectful language by defining his transgression as strictly related to the space he occupies. The distinction is significant because it connects the space of the Oval Office with the space of the sacred. Her comments suggest that once outside this space, Leo is free to speak about the presidency as he chooses. Within this space, however, the presidency is embodied and his comments are elevated to the level of blasphemy. Martin Sheen's interpretation of the scene echoes this religious tone: "We see it (the Oval Office) and it's stunning. It's like walking into a church and seeing the main altar" (*Official Companion* 2002, 8). From the opening episode, the presidency is positioned as an institution that deserves more than the audience's respect. It requires nothing short of their faith.

To analyze the show's depiction of the Oval Office and the presidency as a sacred space, it is useful to briefly summarize the work of Belden Lane. In his examination of what constitutes a sacred place, Lane draws on the distinction between Aristotle's conception of place as *topos* and Plato's understanding of place as *chora*. While *topos* represents "a mere location, a measurable, quantifiable point, neutral and indifferent," *chora* is "an energizing force, suggestive to the imagination" (2001, 53). The transition from an experience of neutrality to one of active engagement, Lane argues, lies in "one's participation in deliberate ritual activity" (*ibid.*). As he explains it:

> For most people in the United States, for instance, a McDonald's restaurant offers a classic example of topos, a place without any distinctive sense of presence. "If you've seen one of them, you've seen them all." But, if you have proposed to someone you love in a particular McDonald's restaurant or experienced a life-changing conversation in another, that topos suddenly becomes a chora, intimately a part of your life [54].

For the American audience of *The West Wing*, the Oval Office, the inner sanctum of the White House, becomes a *chora* with every viewing experience. It no longer exists as an indistinct place but rather becomes a clearly identifiable space, with a specific rhythm and energy. An American audience, already steeped in the historical and political symbolism of the building, shares a specific intellectual meaning when visually presented with its image. In addition, the inside view that the television representation affords this audience turns the culturally formed terrain of the building into a personal and privatized experience of it. It is no longer merely a cognitive experience but one saturated in feelings about the energy and power of the presidency as it is expressed through each weekly story line.

Lane argues that the ontological perspective of sacred space conceptualizes it as a site "radically set apart from everything profane, a site recognized as manifesting its own inherent, chthonic power and numinosity" (54). Following this framework, Mrs. Landingham's exchange with Leo in the Oval Office suggests that the space exists as distinct from the White House. The character's reverence is a response to her belief in the space's mysteries, its power to contain the sacred from within itself. She is positioned as a believer, participating in the mystery of the office (and urging others to do the same). The ontological perspective also understands sacred spaces as those where "supernatural forces have invaded the ordinary" (*ibid.*). Sorkin's Oval Office achieves this status in an episode from the first season in which President Bartlet, a practicing Roman Catholic, kneels in the office and makes a formal confession to his priest ("Take This Sabbath Day"). Bartlet's actions directly link the Oval Office space with the divine in the ritual of confession. The space of an office transforms into the space of a sacred ritual. As with more overtly religious places, the Oval Office, through Bartlet's actions, becomes associated with healing properties. The divine enters the ordinary.

While the conception of the Oval Office in the series shares properties of sacred space from the ontological perspective, the approach is limited because the space is not by its nature religious. It is the secular seat of national government. However, Lane argues that some sacred sites are "able to function wholly apart from an institutionalized religious structure" and may be understood as sacred through the presence of "symbolic meaning" (62). The Oval Office of the series is steeped in symbolic meaning for the characters and the audience. The atmosphere of the space embodies a mood to which the characters react and respond. Mrs. Landingham's impatience with Leo's verbal disrespect of the space is echoed in a scene from the third season in which President Bartlet refuses to engage in disingenuous behavior while physically occupying the office. In "Posse Comitatus," he declines to shake hands with the foreign minister of Qumar, who he knows ordered a terrorist bombing against Americans. The president whispers to himself, "not in this office." His refusal is entirely premised on his belief in the sanctity of the space. While the Oval Office is a nonreligious, culturally mediated site, Sorkin's choice to routinely treat his version as a sacred space contributes to Bartlet's moral role. If the space that the fictional president occupies is imbued with moral significance then so too is the presidency itself.

The President as Preacher

As noted earlier, when Sorkin introduces Bartlet in the premiere episode, the president interrupts a tense meeting between senior staff and members of the religious right by quoting the First Commandment. The scene continues with Bartlet telling a story about his granddaughter and the effects of religious extremism:

> Now Annie, all of 12, has always been precocious, but she's got a good head on her shoulders and I like it when she uses it, so I couldn't understand it when her mother called me in tears yesterday. I said "Elizabeth, what's wrong?" She said, "It's Annie." Now I love my family and I've read my Bible from cover to cover so I want you to tell me: From what part of Holy Scripture do you suppose the Lambs of God drew their divine inspiration when they sent my 12 year-old granddaughter a Raggedy Ann doll with a knife stuck through its throat?

When the story begins, Sam, Leo and a secretary appear in a doorway and move into the room. Not only do Bartlet's words have the assembled group at full attention, but they are powerful enough to gather outsiders to his presence as well. The scene quickly takes on the qualities of a religious ceremony as the crowd becomes witness to the president as preacher.

Delivering his sermon to a captivated crowd, he instructs an influential member of the group on his penance, "You'll denounce these people, Al. You'll do it publicly." Then he casts the group from the presidency until they redeem themselves: "And until you do, you can all get your fat asses out of my White House." Sorkin's script directions for the end of this exchange read: "Everyone is frozen" (2002a, 73). The implication is clear—the power and sanctity of the Bartlet presidency has silenced those who would sin against its values. Yet the Bartlet administration also exercises the power to forgive. The emotional impact of this scene allows the Bartlet presidency to share this power with the audience. As the president is horrified by the story, so too should the viewer be. Bartlet's response is a display of his presidency's authority but also of its goodness. The offenders may be redeemed through their penance to the administration and the public.

This characterization makes Bartlet's moral leadership acceptable and accessible because it taps into the viewer's feelings about childhood innocence and the dangers of religious extremism. Sorkin often relies on this type of affective depiction when he constructs Bartlet's spirituality. He inserts Bartlet's morality, a code that is not easily separated from the character's feelings, into various political issues, creating an ethical tone that underlies many episodes. Bartlet's morality is most often a simple set of principles based on the idea of the right thing. This is evident in "The Short List," an episode that sees the senior staff celebrating over their nominee for the supreme court only to find out his position on the right to privacy is controversial. Bartlet's response to the new nominee comes at the conclusion of the episode, but Sorkin uses its simplicity to form the story's central moral message. Bartlet tells the nominee: "You are not the first choice but you are the last one and the right one." Then he finishes with: "Let the good fight begin" ("The Short List"). The fight is a "good" one because the nominee is constructed as the right, moral choice, a frame made more explicit by Sorkin's characterization of the failed nominee as an elitist. In "The Midterms," Sorkin again reduces Bartlet's morality to a simple theme of the right thing. One of this episode's story lines has Bartlet enormously frustrated that he cannot speak out against a candidate running in a local New Hampshire school board race. The man is someone Bartlet knows from his early days in politics. The audience, however, only hears Bartlet describe him this way before trailing off in disgust:

> I've known men of faith in my life, towering men, men of wisdom and compassion, men of all faiths, of healing and of peace: pro-choice, pro-life, Republican, Democrat, men and women of God—Elliot Roush ["The Midterms"].

With no information outside Bartlet's perspective, Sorkin establishes Roush as a failure in moral terms. Specifically, he fails to meet Bartlet's moral standards. In the end, Bartlet chooses not to interfere with the race, instead putting his faith in the democratic system. It is a subtle shift but an important one because it allows Sorkin to connect secular faith in democracy with spiritual faith.

When the moral situations are not easily reduced to basic ideas of right and wrong, Sorkin uses Bartlet's feelings to drive the narrative. The result, while often compelling drama, is that moral lessons are felt rather than learned. In "A Proportional Response," Bartlet's demands for retribution over a downed American plane carrying his personal physician, Captain Morris Tolliver (Reuben Santiago-Hudson), are wildly disproportional. Upon hearing the news of his doctor's death, he declares that he will "blow 'em off the face of the earth with the fury of God's own thunder" ("Post Hoc, Ergo Propter Hoc"). The following episode continues the theme when he demands a response that will bring "total disaster" ("A Proportional Response"). To make Bartlet's feelings seem justified, Sorkin establishes an emotional connection between the president and the physician. The scene moves from friendly banter to personal revelations to heartfelt advice. Bartlet admits feeling uneasy around his military advisors. He claims to have no violent feelings toward the nation's enemies and fears that if they knew, they would consider him weak. Rather than having Bartlet take the senior role in the exchange, Sorkin uses Tolliver to comfort the president over his vulnerable feelings. To complete the effect, the scene ends with Tolliver, a new father, showing Bartlet a picture of his baby girl.

Because Sorkin sets up this brief history, Bartlet's demand for vengeance and his frustration with the military response is easily attributed to his feelings. While the episode offers the potential for a debate on the merits of a proportional response, it reduces the president to both victim and mourner. Bartlet is a leader who must accept proportional response as "what there is" and a man suffering the loss of a friend. The moral situation is not simple but the episode is effective because Bartlet's initial immoral response (disregard for large civilian casualties) is easily dismissed and he maintains his status as a good leader.

Similar to "A Proportional Response," the narrative of the two-part season four episode "Inauguration Day" depicts a complex moral situation where Bartlet's initial response is atypical but easily excused. Both episodes focus on Bartlet's approach to foreign policy, as genocide rages in the fictional African nation of Kundu. Sorkin uses both verbal and visual cues to establish the horror. C. J. tells a press briefing that 20,000 people have been killed, while Josh explains to Charlie that people in the same family are being forced to rape one another. At the conclusion of the episode, Josh turns to watch the television in his office. The camera follows his gaze and pictures of dead bodies fill the screen ("Inauguration Part I"). The emotional construction of the conflict intensifies Bartlet's inaction. He is conflicted over the idea of sacrificing American lives to save Kundunese lives and reluctant to intervene. While some senior staff view intervention as a straightforward moral imperative, others recognize the political implications. Toby suggests that "this one haunts him," and Josh argues that though Bartlet's Catholicism does not distinguish between American and African lives, "the voters do" ("Inauguration Part II"). The comments confirm Bartlet's status as a good man who often has to sacrifice his personal values for his public duty. Once this characterization is firmly established, Sorkin changes Bartlet's position. Hesitant and anxious throughout the early part of the narrative, Bartlet is suddenly transformed into a commanding and decisive leader who declares a bold new direction for U.S. foreign policy:

> We're for freedom everywhere. We're for freedom to worship everywhere. We're for freedom to learn for everybody. And because in our time you can build a bomb in your country and bring it to my country what goes on in your country is very much my business. And so we are for freedom from tyranny everywhere.... No country has ever had a doctrine of intervention when only humanitarian interests were at stake. That streak's gonna end Sunday at noon ["Inauguration Part II"].

The speech connects Kundunese suffering to American values and strengthens the emotional impact of the narrative without sacrificing Bartlet's status as a moral leader, despite his earlier inaction. The next scene completes this subtext as Bartlet quotes scripture to Leo while standing in the Oval Office.

In constructing Bartlet's morality, Sorkin often encourages a direct connection between the role of president and the role of preacher. In several episodes, Bartlet quotes scripture and gives short sermons that combine religious values and patriotic lessons. The result is a presidential character who is both spiritual and secular, faithful to both God and the constitution. Again, this allows Sorkin to create a generic spirituality for the president that safely locates faith in both moral principles and patriotic values. While Sorkin's introduction of Bartlet in the "Pilot" emphasizes the character's dual role as spiritual and secular leader, he repeats the theme in both "Shibboleth" and "The Midterms." In "Shibboleth," Bartlet must decide if a group of Chinese refugees seeking asylum from religious persecution are telling the truth. If they are truly faithful, he reasons, they would be able to demonstrate an innate understanding of the word *shibboleth*, an ancient password found in the Bible that helped the Israelites discover enemies from allies. To emphasize the significance of the word, Bartlet quotes the scripture passage from which it originates. In a meeting with Bartlet, the Chinese refugee not only passes the test but also quotes a bible verse on the power of faith and names eleven of the twelve apostles.

The scene illustrates Bartlet's role as religious guardian of American values. Faith becomes the key to both spiritual and secular America. While Sorkin could have made the issue a legal or diplomatic one, he chooses to contextualize it in religious terms and gives the president the lead moral role. In an earlier episode, "The Midterms," Sorkin frames Bartlet as preacher and president more explicitly. Greeting a group of radio talk show hosts during a reception in the White House, Bartlet addresses a woman who has publicly called homosexuals an "abomination," a designation she argues is found in the Bible. Bartlet counters with a string of biblical references, wondering how much he might be paid for selling his daughter into slavery as suggested in Exodus 21:7 or if he should kill Leo for working on the Sabbath as Exodus 35:2 instructs. Having exposed the weakness and danger of using a strict interpretation of the Bible to justify bigotry, Bartlet's final words to the woman emphasize the power of the presidency:

> Think about those questions would you? One last thing: While you may be mistaking this for your monthly meeting of the ignorant tight-ass club, in this building, when the president stands, nobody sits.

In this scene, Sorkin constructs a clear moral position for Bartlet while maintaining the character's status as civic leader. In addition, the radio talk show host is characterized as both morally misguided and politically foolish.

In both "The Midterms" and "Shibboleth," Sorkin ensures that Bartlet's morality is not alienating because it is generic; it emphasizes basic ideas of right and wrong that are easily accepted. In "Shibboleth," the Chinese refugees are depicted as true believers because their representative demonstrates that faith is a feeling, not a recitation of facts. This simplicity is made more sympathetic when Sorkin blends their plight with patriotic rhetoric. When Josh asks Bartlet if the refugee "passed the test," the president replies:

> You think I would send him back if he failed catechism? Let me tell you something: we can be the world's policeman, we can be the world's bank, the world's factory, the world's farm—what does it mean if we're not also—They

made it to the New World, Josh. And do you know what I get to do now? I get to proclaim a national day of Thanksgiving ["Shibboleth"].

The faith of the refugees is rewarded with entry into Bartlet's faithful America. In "The Midterms," Bartlet's faithful America is a place where a moral presidency ensures that all people deserve respect.

One of Sorkin's most transparent constructions of Bartlet as moral leader occurs in the two-part opening episode of the second season. At the conclusion of the series' first season, gunmen shoot at the president and his entourage as they leave a town hall meeting. As the second series begins, the audience learns that both Bartlet and Josh have been wounded. The action surrounding this discovery and its aftermath is cut with a series of flashback scenes that portray how each senior staff member joined Bartlet's campaign for the presidency. In this flashback narrative, Sorkin establishes the Bartlet presidency as a sacred calling—a mission that will fulfill the spiritually empty lives of the central characters. He achieves this affect by framing each character's pre–Bartlet career as unfulfilling. Despite holding a senior position in John Hoynes' (Tim Matheson) campaign, (a front-runner for the Democratic presidential nomination), Josh is characterized as frustrated and disillusioned over the campaign's lack of focus, telling his boss: "I don't know what we stand for" ("In the Shadow of Two Gunmen, Part I"). This theme is continued when Josh meets with Sam, who declines his friend's offer to work for Hoynes because he is not "the real thing." As with Josh, Sorkin depicts Sam's career life as spiritually empty. Despite his impending promotion to partner at his law firm, Sam chooses to derail an important meeting by reprimanding his clients for their greed. Sorkin writes a similar situation for C. J. Working in a public relations firm in Los Angeles, she is fired after refusing to meet the demands of an unreasonable client. For Leo, Sorkin expresses the character's frustration over the lack of meaning in politics:

BARTLET: Why you doing this? You're a player. You're bigger in the party than I am. Hoynes will make you national chairman.

LEO: Because I'm tired of it. Year after year after year after year having to choose between the lesser of who cares. Of trying to get myself excited about a candidate who can speak in complete sentences. Of setting the bar so low I can hardly look at it. They say a good man can't get elected president. I don't believe that. Do you?

When Bartlet admits that he has doubts, Leo responds: "Act as if ye have faith and faith shall be given to you. Put another way, fake it till you make it." Sorkin alludes to the religious tone of Leo's speech in an earlier scene in which Bartlet is speaking to a local crowd. Answering a question from an angry dairy farmer who was hurt by his legislative choices as governor of New Hampshire, Bartlet admits, "Yeah, I screwed you on that one," and then continues:

> Today, for the first time in history, the largest group of Americans living in poverty are children. One in five children live in the most abject, dangerous, hopeless, backbreaking, gut-wrenching poverty anybody could imagine. If fidelity to freedom and democracy is the code to our civic religion then surely the code of our humanity is faithful service to that unwritten commandment that says we should give our children better than we ourselves receive.

To complete the lesson, Bartlet finishes:

> Let me put it this way. I voted against the bill because I didn't want to make it hard for people to buy milk. I stopped some money from flowing into your pocket. If that angers you, if you resent me, I completely respect that. If you expect anything different from the president of the United States, you should vote for someone else.

Sorkin's mix of secular and spiritual language connects the mission of government with the mission of faith. He frames Bartlet as the head of this mission, a role that easily shifts to that of moral leader guiding and instructing his followers. In addition, Sorkin makes the message of the scene simple. Bartlet's choice was good, the farmer's desires, while understandable, were not. Sorkin's religious framing of Bartlet is complete with the conversion of Josh. It is both a physical and mental transformation. Throughout the scene, when Bartlet is speaking, Josh is doing a crossword puzzle. When Bartlet addresses the dairy farmer, Josh physically changes. He sits up and pays attention with a look of respect and admiration. Sorkin then uses Josh to convert Sam, who leaves his law firm to work for Bartlet, despite never having met him. While C. J.'s conversion is less spontaneous, Sorkin maintains the moral theme by having her ask Toby if Bartlet is "a good man."[49]

With this two-part episode, Sorkin elevates Bartlet's moral role by framing the character as inherently good, an idea he suggests through the narrative's clear leader/disciple imagery. One by one, the characters choose to follow Bartlet on the strength of his character. Sorkin's history, then, does more than expand the back stories of the show's characters. It establishes Bartlet as the source of their moral commitment. The power of this morality is, in fact, so strong that it converts a nonbeliever. In the second season, Sorkin introduces the character of Ainsley Hayes (Emily Procter), a Republican lawyer who is aggressively opposed to many of the administration's policies. Leo offers her a job, on Bartlet's request, because the president "likes smart people who disagree with him" ("In This White House"). Sorkin uses Ainsley's interaction with several of the characters to guide her transformation, but it is complete when she watches Bartlet plead with an African leader not to return to his country after a coup attempt. In the scene, she is quietly watching unnoticed from outside the Oval Office. The framing positions Ainsley as witness to Bartlet's true nature. In a conversation with friends later that night, the extent of Ainsley's conversion is clear. As her friends relish her rejection of the job, they wonder if she met anyone who "wasn't worthless." She responds:

> Say they're smug and superior. Say their approach to public policy makes you want to tear your hair out ... but don't call them worthless. The people that I have met have been extraordinarily qualified. Their intent is good. Their commitment is true. They are righteous and they are patriots. And I'm their lawyer.

While Sorkin claims that the introduction of Ainsley was "to attract more younger females" (*Official Companion* 2002, 195), he also acknowledges a political motivation by suggesting that he created the character to counter what he saw lacking on television news. He says:

> There was a period of time where you couldn't flip through cable news without finding a young, blond Republican. It turns out most of them didn't know anything and got the reputation for not knowing anything and not really being much more than young, blond and leggy. I thought it would be fun if we had a character who they assume was that and turned out to have more going on [*ibid.*].

Aside from Sorkin's desire to use fiction to balance an image of women and politics on the news, the character of Ainsley contributes to his narrative construction of Bartlet as a compelling and persuasive moral leader. The character is transformed by her experience of Bartlet, ultimately testifying to her devotion in the faith he represents.

While Sorkin's narrative consistently generalizes Bartlet's morality, reducing it to simple constructions of right versus wrong, as Haught suggests, Bartlet is "not just generically Christian" (2001). Rather, he is a practicing Catholic who chose to attend Notre Dame because he was thinking about entering the priesthood ("The Portland Trip"). Sorkin uses Bartlet's Catholicism as a point of reference for the character's spirituality. By showing Bartlet in activities associated with the Catholic faith (in various episodes, the character is shown holding a rosary, returning from mass and confessing to his priest), Sorkin avoids the generic Christian label. This anchors his construction of morality in a recognizable framework of religious tradition, allowing him to create a more convincing representation of the moral leader. Yet Sorkin tempers his characterization of the Catholic Bartlet. In episodes in which Bartlet's faith plays a central role, Sorkin often distracts from it so that the viewer is left with a theme of spirituality rather than a strict Catholic discourse. When Bartlet angrily confronts God in "Two Cathedrals," the scene is less about a specific religious faith and more about a general spiritual crisis. When he launches into a speech about the weaknesses of a homily he recently heard in mass, it quickly digresses into a passionate appeal for the power of words ("War Crimes"). In the episode in which Bartlet's Catholicism is most obvious, "Take This Sabbath Day," Sorkin uses the narrative to explore the question of capital punishment from the perspective of several different religions rather than focus exclusively on the Catholic position. All these choices allow Sorkin to achieve a balance between a generic and a specific spirituality. The result is a presidential representation of the moral leader that is validated by one faith but not easily dismissed for serving it exclusively.

While Sorkin only claims to be concerned with the conflicts that arise when personal faith confronts public duty, some critics suggest that his characterization of Bartlet's faith is more significant. Thompson argues that Bartlet's Catholicism "creates a powerful sense of the earnest leader" (quoted in Haught 2001) while Feuerherd sees the show's depiction of religious faith as an important demonstration of how morality affects political work (2000). Sorkin's concern with the stories that happen when faith clashes with duty is evident in many of the senior staff narratives that this book has previously discussed. However, these struggles are not easily separated from Sorkin's representation of the presidency. In fact, as this book has argued, the faith of the characters is often based on their secular devotion to the presidency as civil religion empowered by their belief in Bartlet's moral vision. Sorkin characterizes Bartlet in a similar manner. He constructs him as both a true believer in the presidency and its symbol of morality.

Sorkin's first detailed examination of the relationship between Bartlet's religious faith and the character's political choices, while briefly mentioned in the "Pilot," occurs late in the first season.[50] In "Take This Sabbath Day," Bartlet struggles with his power to stay the execution of a federal prisoner. The episode's theme, the struggle between political duty and personal faith, is first established visually. Sorkin opens the episode with a secular scene, as the camera pans across a solemn panel of Supreme Court judges in a dimly lit courtroom. The viewer hears that the final legal appeal of federal prisoner Simon Cruz has been denied and he will be executed in forty-eight hours. Shortly after this, Sorkin depicts a religious scene. Toby is attending a temple service where the rabbi's sermon stresses the immoral nature of vengeance. The two themes unite when Toby is interrupted by Sam's urgent call to return to the White House to deal with the fallout from Cruz's impending death. Sorkin continues this combination of the secular and nonsecular in two later scenes that feature Catholic imagery in the Oval Office. In one shot, Bartlet is peering solemnly through an Oval Office window. The perspective is from outside the window, it is snowing and Bartlet is clutching a rosary, his fingers moving back and forth over the beads. The scene is cut with black and white grainy images of Simon Cruz lying on a table as his lethal injection is prepared. It shifts to an old woman with her head covered, grieving. At the conclusion of the episode, Bartlet kneels on the floor of the Oval Office to make his confession to his childhood priest. These visual choices are clearly dramatic and emotive, goals Sorkin could have achieved without religious overtones. Yet he chooses to tie religious sensibility to a secular issue. The result is a narrative that visually establishes a relationship between the presidency and Bartlet's religious faith.

In terms of dialogue, Sorkin makes Bartlet's first reaction to the pending execution a specifically Catholic one. The president requests his boyhood parish priest and calls the Pope. Yet Sorkin also softens this approach by having Bartlet seek advice from various characters. The discussions are both secular and religious. For the secular perspective, Sorkin uses the characters of Charlie and C. J., but only Charlie speaks to the president. While both characters represent a secular point of view on capital punishment, their responses also reveal feelings of guilt and anger. The result is an affective reaction to the death penalty issue that undermines the potential for secular debate.

Previously established as a likeable and thoughtful character, Charlie's view regarding capital punishment is dramatic and confronting but not unexpected in light of the character's back story. When Charlie is introduced, the viewer learns that he is a high school student seeking work because his mother, a local police officer, was shot and killed in the line of duty and he must now support his young sister. His answer to Bartlet's question on the appropriate punishment for his mother's killer—he would personally execute the man rather than have the state do it—seems atypical of the character, and Sorkin uses it to unsettle the viewer. However, Charlie's response is also easily anticipated as the highly emotional reaction of a young man who has had to struggle without his mother.

Sorkin reveals C. J.'s position to be apathetic. She bluntly states that she has no feelings over Cruz's death, yet Sorkin also has the character read aloud the White House's official response to the execution, which includes the details of exactly how Cruz's body will respond as he is dying. As the scene unfolds, C. J. grows uneasy, finally stating that her responsibility to announce Cruz's death to the president and the press would be easier if she did not know his mother's name was Sophia.

Charlie and C. J.'s secular take on the death penalty appears straightforward. They do not face a moral dilemma. Yet Sorkin disrupts this characterization by giving both Charlie's and C. J.'s responses a moral context. While the aggressive nature of Charlie's feelings seem emotionally justified by the unjust circumstances of a boy forced to live without his mother, his thirst for vengeance implies a deeper moral dilemma. C. J.'s seemingly unfeeling response is juxtaposed with the vivid details of Cruz's death, details that Sorkin uses to cloud the character's neutral position. C. J.'s emotional reaction to knowing Cruz's mother's name personalizes him as a victim and forces the audience to do the same.

To balance the secular argument, Sorkin uses Toby to present the Jewish perspective and introduces a new character to represent the Christian side. Sorkin makes Toby's initial response to Cruz's death a political rather than moral one. Toby is concerned that Bartlet's Catholicism will be seen as unduly influencing his presidency if he chooses to commute the sentence, particularly after consulting the Pope. In this context, Sorkin constructs Bartlet's Catholicism as a political problem rather than a moral strength. Politicizing Bartlet's religious status allows Sorkin to dilute the character's Catholic morality in favour of a generalized moral belief. In turn, the president's anti–death penalty stance becomes less of a Catholic law and more of a personal moral principle. Toby is eventually persuaded by his rabbi to acknowledge his feelings against capital punishment and speak to the president. The conversation, designed to present a Jewish view on capital punishment, remains grounded in political rather than religious rhetoric. Toby simply suggests that the state should not kill people, and the discussion focuses on the idea that Jewish leaders made it virtually impossible for the state to kill someone, despite the fact that it is not prohibited in the Torah.

Maintaining a similar tone but in a weaker conceit, Sorkin offers a Quaker perspective when Bartlet meets a Democratic campaign manager as she is wandering the halls of the West Wing. Inviting the woman into the Oval Office, Bartlet engages in small talk, and the audience learns that she is from a Quaker background. He then abruptly asks her opinion on capital punishment. She replies that the state should not kill people. He quotes from Thomas Aquinas and St. Augustine, Catholic philosophers who both advocated a life for a life. She counters with a quote from Kant. Bartlet offers that 71 percent of the American people support the death penalty. When she bluntly suggests "that's a political problem," he replies, "I'm a politician." While the scene clearly establishes Bartlet's preoccupation with the issue to the point that he is willing to discuss it with a stranger, it also serves a larger purpose by expressing Bartlet's central conflict of moral conviction versus political expediency. By having Bartlet engage in the struggle, Sorkin suggests that presidential decision-making is not unaffected by the personal feelings of the man who holds the office. The institution and the man are not easily separated.

Hayton offers this point in her examination of the series as a representation of the metaphor of the king's two bodies. As she explains, the phrase:

> refers to a time when people understood political sovereignty more explicitly as the notion of having a dynamic, individual ruler who can impose his will upon a land and, at the same time, the notion that he was simply a placeholder in a timeless office. The king's two bodies were both individual or local, and universal or timeless ... [2003, 63].

The complex notion of the king's two bodies, or a ruler's separate yet unified identities, is one that Sorkin's narrative continually confronts in his representation of the president. Hayton argues that, despite the American public's desire to understand the president as the man separated from the office, Sorkin's narrative frustrates this notion by "refusing at almost every level, to allow us to divorce the character of Josiah 'Jed' Bartlet from his job as president of the United States of America" (67). Hayton uses the scene in "Take This Sabbath Day" between Bartlet and his priest to support her argument, suggesting that the characters' conversation offers a clear example of Sorkin's refusal to separate Bartlet's two identities.

In the scene, the priest from Bartlet's boyhood parish arrives moments before Cruz is executed, having been unintentionally delayed. Slightly overwhelmed by his surroundings, the priest asks whether Bartlet would prefer to be called "Jed" or "Mr. President." Bartlet answers that he would prefer "Mr. President" because

> There are certain decisions I have to make while I'm in this room. Do I send troops into harm's way? Which fatal disease gets the most research money? It's helpful in those situations not to think of yourself as the man but as the office.

The priest, however, quickly reminds Bartlet that the separation he seeks is an illusion, a point he makes clear by wondering how Bartlet, a "boy from his parish," has the authority to call the Pope for comfort. Soon after that, C. J. enters with a note confirming Cruz's death, and Bartlet kneels to make his confession. Hayton argues that Bartlet's confession at the conclusion of the episode "undoes any attempt (even unconscious) to pretend that the man can be distinguished from the office, or that the king's two bodies can be separated" (70).

Bartlet's struggle in "Take This Sabbath Day" is clearly between his morality (here strongly influenced by his religious faith) and what he perceives to be his public duty as president. As Hayton notes, Sorkin's choice to have Bartlet seek penance in the Oval Office suggests that any separation of the man from the office is unachievable, despite the character's efforts to do so. When Bartlet confesses, Sorkin reveals that the character's true failure is allowing the institution to win over the man. Choosing not to commute the execution, Bartlet separates his presidential identity from his personal one by denying the moral convictions he holds as a man and responding to the political pressures he feels as the president. While there is an element of cognition to this reading, the meaning of the president as a representative of the peoples' will, Sorkin also positions the audience to feel something for Bartlet. The character's remorse is expressed in very specific and very affective religious terms. His confession is visually dramatic; he kneels in the Oval Office, humbling himself before God and the presidency. He also spends the episode visually and mentally conflicted. The viewer watches him deep in thought, seeking answers and finally acknowledging his pain and asking for forgiveness. With this construction, Bartlet's morality is both a product of his religious training and an inherent part of his character. Sorkin uses Bartlet's remorse to neutralize his politically motivated decision. The character is not callous or coldhearted; he engages in the struggle and accepts his part in Cruz's death. Sorkin uses Bartlet's moral journey to make the character a victim who collapses under the weight of political pressure rather than a villain who calculates winning political favor. In this way, Bartlet represents a moral leader even while betraying his personal morality.

Sorkin repeats this paradox when he introduces Bartlet's multiple sclerosis into the narrative late in season two. In "17 People," Bartlet admits to Toby that he has had a form of multiple sclerosis for ten years, a secret that only seventeen people now know. As Toby begins to consider the news, he assumes a cover-up is taking place, specifically with the president's military physicians, who conduct twice-yearly exams. Leo assures him that they have not lied because the MS is in remission and does not show up in physical exams. Toby's response highlights Leo's moral lapse and frames Bartlet's misconduct as a moral issue: "Nobody lied? Is that what you've been saying to yourself over and over again for a year?" The omission is both a private and political failure, as Bartlet assigns it to his personal life and Toby reveals the larger implications:

BARTLET: I have no intention of apologizing to you, Toby.

TOBY: Would you mind if I ask why not?

BARTLET: 'Cause you're not the one with MS, a wife, three kids and airports to close. Not every part of me belongs to you. This was personal. I'm not willing to relinquish that right.

TOBY: It will appear to many, if not most, as fraud. It will appear as if you denied the voters an opportunity to decide for themselves. They're generally not willing to relinquish that right, either.

Similar to his narrative in "Take This Sabbath Day," Sorkin uses the MS plot to construct an affective frame around a political issue. Bartlet's dialogue directly connects his disease and family with presidential responsibilities. In addition, Toby's response dissolves any distinction between moral man and moral president.

In future episodes, the MS narrative grows more complex. When the other characters learn of Bartlet's deception, their reactions are intensely emotional. Sam grows visibly angry, and C. J. has a highly charged confrontation with Bartlet that reveals the rift his secret has caused in their father-daughter relationship ("Manchester Part II"). Sorkin repeats this affective tone with Leo, whose response to Bartlet's admission was initially anger, "but then I remembered that I'm a drunk and he didn't give a damn" ("Bad Moon Rising"). Leo's forgiveness is for Bartlet's private failure, just as Bartlet forgave his. Only Toby responds to the omission as an affront to the presidency, yet he too reacts emotionally. The news affects him to the point that he temporarily leaves the room after being told.

Sorkin also uses First Lady Abigail (Abbey) Bartlet (Stockard Channing) to develop the MS plot. The character's involvement adds a domestic element to the president's deception that increases the emotional context of the story. Throughout the series, Abbey Bartlet is depicted as a confident, intelligent and loving spouse. She is an accomplished physician and strong feminist as well as a presidential confidant and behind-the-scenes advisor. She has been depicted initiating debates over child labor ("The White House Pro-Am"), pushing for the president to include the Violence Against Women Act in the State of the Union Address ("Bartlet's Third State of the Union") and bringing attention to female historical figures ("And It's Surely to Their Credit"). Levine suggests that in Abbey Bartlet Sorkin "has captured, somewhat, the rise of the new first lady" (2003a, 257). This new status, Levine notes, reflects the changing role of women but is also "fraught with danger," as an activist first lady is often the target of public disapproval for disregarding traditional gender roles (255–56). Sorkin's version of "the new first lady" often includes this conflict. Several of the story lines where

Abbey is actively involved in legislation expose her amateur political skills and end with her defeat ("The White House Pro-Am;" "Bartlet's Third State of the Union"), suggesting that she is punished for stepping outside the first lady's traditional role.

While the character of Abbey is a strong representation of an independent woman, Sorkin admits that his decision to make her a physician (thereby strengthening her independent identity) was calculated to expand Bartlet's narrative. Commenting on the development of Abbey in *"The West Wing" Official Companion*, Sorkin notes that making the first lady a doctor was one way of enabling a personal view of the president that is rarely seen:

> Stockard Channing had wanted to do more episodes and ... I was thinking.... Where don't we get to see the president? We don't get to see him when he's sick in bed with the flu ... [2002, 87].

To include the character of the first lady in this intimate picture of the president, Sorkin makes her a doctor. This choice, he notes, impacted the series to a degree that was not planned:

> I thought, What if she's a doctor? If she's a doctor, I want there to be a story. I want there to be a reason to make that decision. So, it's not the flu. It's something worse than the flu ... and Abbey has to come back. And all of a sudden, simply for the sake of that episode, I made a decision that was going to affect the series for the life of the series [*ibid.*].

The decision to give Abbey a central role in Bartlet's MS story line is not only significant because it recasts her in the more traditional gender role of caregiver, it also allows Sorkin to intensify and shift the affective tone of the narrative.

In her dual role as wife and doctor, Abbey not only knows about Bartlet's MS but is also secretly administering his medication. Having defined Abbey's strength in part by her professional identity, Sorkin's decision to implicate her in Bartlet's deception weakens the character and primes her to take on a more traditional role. With her professional ethics in doubt and her medical reputation damaged, Abbey is easily positioned to save Bartlet because she has lost the only identity that defines her outside her role as first lady. Sorkin makes Abbey's loss real when she is forced to face a state medical board that controls the terms of her license. Sorkin also makes Abbey's loss an ethical one, thereby encouraging the viewer to understand her punishment as fair. He achieves this in a scene in which she expresses anger and resentment that her husband is only receiving a censure while she is faced with losing an integral part of her identity. It is Josh's assistant, Donna (Janel Maloney), who bluntly reminds her that she was also a doctor when she gave her husband drugs and failed to tell anyone ("Dead

Irish Writers"). The comment leads her to voluntarily give up her license for the duration of his administration.

Abbey's sacrifice is important because it adds a new layer of emotion to the MS plot, further distracting the viewer from evaluating Bartlet's lie as anything other than an upsetting twist. When the political implications are investigated, the viewer is already well-positioned to accept the affective tone that underlies Bartlet's presidential censure. In fact, Sorkin repeats the theme of sacrifice that he begins with Abbey. In the censure episode, "H-Con 172," Leo must testify before a congressional committee that wants to determine if Bartlet did anything unethical while running for president. Leo's testimony, the viewer learns, will eventually lead him to reveal that he was drunk when Bartlet collapsed during a campaign event, a highly embarrassing admission for the recovering alcoholic. A sympathetic Republican majority counsel offers to end the hearings immediately if Bartlet will accept a censure, a resolution that condemns the president for lying to the American people. Despite his lawyer's suggestion that the censure, by nature, is inconsequential (it is a nonbinding resolution similar to ones that support little league baseball and friendship with the people of Mongolia), Leo offers to sacrifice himself to spare Bartlet's feelings:

> This isn't that. This is 535 congressmen and senators standing up and saying the president lied and should be ashamed of himself. And this is us standing up and saying you're right. This would be the first time in history a president would be censured. Congress isn't talk radio. It's the seat of democracy. Their opinion matters and their condemnation doesn't have to come with handcuffs to be devastating to this president.

With Leo's response, Sorkin shifts the theme of the MS narrative. It began as a betrayal of both personal and political trust, but it ends as homage to loyalty and friendship. In turn, Bartlet's acceptance of the censure is a demonstration of his loyalty to Leo as well as an example of "how a man falls down." Rather than using Bartlet's confession to demonstrate the character's faults, Sorkin achieves a more affective result that highlights Bartlet as the ideal president. Bartlet tells Leo:

> I was wrong.... I may not have had sinister intent at the outset but there were plenty of opportunities for me to make it right. No one in government takes responsibility for anything anymore. We foster. We obfuscate. We rationalize. Everybody does it. That's what we say, so we come to occupy a moral safe house where everyone's to blame so no one's guilty. I'm to blame. I was wrong.

With Bartlet's acknowledgment, his right choice, Sorkin reestablishes the morality of the presidency. Bartlet recognizes the disingenuous nature of politics, rejects the "moral safe house" and rises above the ordinary. In this way, Sorkin recasts Bartlet's punishment so that it highlights the character's moral status. The audience is encouraged to see Bartlet as the ideal moral leader, despite his deception.

Sorkin's ending for the third season of the series centers on Bartlet's decision to rescind an executive order banning political assassinations. While the story is the most obvious challenge to the notion of Bartlet as a moral leader, Sorkin employs his usual affective techniques to maintain Bartlet's ethical status. From the beginning, Sorkin frames Bartlet's choice to order the murder of Sharif, the Qumari Defense Minister, as the right thing. Sharif is directly connected to a devastating terrorist attack but protected from standing trial because the evidence linking him was obtained by coercion. The dilemma initiates a debate between Leo and the leader of the Joint Chiefs. The military commander suggests that they target Sharif because international laws are not applicable. The country is in a state of war, "pregnant women are delivering bombs" and terrorists do not follow the laws of nature. To emphasize his point, he asks Leo to consider how the world would be different if assassins had been successful with Hitler ("We Killed Yamamoto"). Sharif's crimes place him outside the natural order. The narrative suggests that where the justice system has failed, Bartlet, as leader, must succeed. More than that, the president becomes the representative of a higher moral order.

Bartlet, however, is struggling with both the moral implications of his decision and the idea of breaking international law. Sorkin inserts the war metaphor into the narrative as another way to simplify the situation. This is reflected in a scene between Leo and Bartlet in which Leo suggests that the president view the problem as a "war scenario." Bartlet comments that the metaphor is a "slippery slope" because it is easy to apply—as in "the war on poverty." Leo grows impatient with Bartlet's excuses and insists that his belief in "moral absolutes" represents the "most horrifying" part of his liberalism. In the most definitive simplification of the issue, Leo responds that Sharif has "killed innocent people. He'll kill more so we have to end him.... This is justified. This is required" ("We Killed Yamamoto"). Bartlet is not convinced, and Sorkin places the character in a similar moral dilemma to that of "Take This Sabbath Day." In a conversation with Leo, his feelings about right and wrong quickly outweigh his attempt at rational reasoning:

BARTLET: This isn't a matter of religion. I recognize that there's evil in the world.

LEO: What's your objection exactly sir?

BARTLET: Doesn't this mean we join the league of ordinary nations?

LEO: That's your objection? I'm not going to have any trouble saying the pledge of allegiance tomorrow.

BARTLET: It's not my objection.

LEO: Sir?

BARTLET: It's just wrong. It's absolutely wrong.

LEO: I know but you have to do it anyway.

BARTLET: Why?

LEO: Because you won.

BARTLET: Take him ["Posse Comitatus"].

Again, Sorkin positions Bartlet between personal faith and public duty in a way that makes the character a sympathetic victim. The narrative is basic and emotive. Sharif is bad. He killed innocent people. He will kill more. The president, while a good man, must go against his nature and perform his duty.

Sorkin's successful creation of a moral president, who at times behaves immorally, depends on a specific construction of Bartlet's failures. The president's moral lapses do not alienate the viewer because he is so often constructed as a sympathetic victim of duty and politics. This construction is perhaps most evident during the fourth season when Zoey is kidnapped in retaliation for Bartlet's decision to assassinate Sharif ("Commencement"). The episode begins with the celebration of Zoey's college graduation. Bartlet delivers the commencement address, and Zoey is shown in the crowd of graduates smiling and taking a picture of her father. Later, the president and first lady are in the residence with friends and Bartlet is looking at childhood photos of his daughter, reminiscing about the quick passage of time. Leo enters the residence and tells Bartlet the terrible news. The viewer does not hear the dialogue between the two characters. Rather, a dark instrumental piece of music underscores a shot of Bartlet dropping the photo album and his drink. The shot then focuses on the liquid as it spills across the photos of Zoey. The visual impact is a powerful scene of paternal anguish. In turn, the cause for the event, Bartlet's decision to murder Sharif, is emotionally contextualized, and the president is primarily framed as a father who is suffering, rather than a politician who made a suspect moral decision. The story line continues into the final episode of season four when Bartlet becomes the ultimate victim by resigning the presidency ("Twenty-Five"). However, this event is also emotionally contextualized, as this response from Will suggests: "I think it's a fairly stunning act of patriotism and a fairly ordinary act of fatherhood" ("Twenty-Five"). Rather than a leader who ordered a murder, Bartlet is now a victim *and* a noble patriot.

In addition to characterizing the president as a victim, Sorkin often insures that the moral situations Bartlet confronts are basic. The federal prisoner executed in "Take This Sabbath Day" has committed double murder. While Sorkin hints at faulty trial procedures, the character's crime is not in doubt. Bartlet's omission that he has multiple sclerosis is framed as a plea for privacy. Sorkin implicates various characters in the deception until the president's lie is lost among a narrative of friendship and loyalty, and he weakens Bartlet's apology for the lie by framing it around patriotic rhetoric. In "Manchester Part II," Bartlet tells the staff that he is sorry but then launches into an affective speech about the greatness of past presidents and the promise his presidency holds for the future. By connecting Bartlet's act of contrition with righteous civic leadership, Sorkin reestablishes the character as a president whose moral lapse was a temporary disruption in a greater destiny. In perhaps the most confronting moral dilemma Bartlet faces—the order to assassinate a foreign defense minister—Sorkin makes the decision more palatable by connecting the man to a deadly terrorist attack ("Posse Comitatus"). While the moral situations are clear (murderers and terrorists are bad), Bartlet is admirable because his decisions are not as easily made.

The Intellectual President

> *I think Bartlet is one of those guys who didn't wake up and go, "I can't wait to be president. I need to be president. I'm on a power trip." He's a guy who was convinced by guys like me: "Mr. Bartlet, you have a great mind. You're one of the leading minds of your generation. You can best serve people by running for office." And so I think, almost against his will, he's found himself as the president of the United States.*
>
> (Rob Lowe, in an interview on *The West Wing* DVD Season One)

Typical of the campaign coverage surrounding George W. Bush during the 2000 presidential election was this subheading from a *Washington Post* story: "The Question Dogs George Bush: Is He Smart Enough?" (cited in Jamieson and Waldman 2003, 62). Bush's frequent misstatements and mispronunciations were consistently reported in the press, frequently injected into late night comedy routines and eventually became the subject of several books.[51] While both candidates Bush and Gore made verbal mistakes, only Bush was regularly discussed in the media as unintelligent.[52] Jamieson and Waldman suggest that reporters framed Bush's missteps as signs of inexperience because they understood their election role in certain terms. Specifically, "during election campaigns reporters see themselves in part as unmaskers of the hypocrisy of those who seek office" (xv). In turn, this view creates frames that "focus on strategic intent, motives and appearances" (*ibid.*). Jamieson and Waldman offer the example of press coverage of Bush during the presidential campaign and after September 11. While Bush's missteps during the campaign raised questions about his competence, press coverage of similar mistakes after the terrorist attacks were overlooked and he was recast as a forceful and competent leader, a result the authors suggest was due to the patriotic lens through which reporters were looking (130).[53]

While Jamieson and Waldman's institutional perspective recognizes reporters' perceived occupational roles as a determining factor in the creation of press frames, they neglect a significant component of the process. Framing Bush as either intellectually stunted or intellectually competent is also attributable to a basic understanding of presidential character. To the extent that Bush's intellect is an issue only when reporters decide it is (as evidenced by campaign coverage versus coverage post September 11), Jamieson and Waldman's study is convincing. The coverage certainly suggests that reporters mold the president's characteristics to meet the expectations of specific situations. Yet it is this fundamental desire to shape the perception of the president that is significant. For the press and the nation, the president should exhibit basic traits. During the 2000 election, these characteristics were honesty and intelligence. (In 1996, the traits seemed to be fidelity and integrity). The fact that these traits are arbitrarily applied is secondary to their existence as basic components of presidential character. They are only successful as measures of the candidates because the citizenry accepts them as fundamental to leadership. This is not to suggest that all American citizens believe that their president has to be intelligent or faithful to be a successful leader. Rather, the resonance that certain characteristics (smart, honest, strong) generate among many Americans for their presidential candidates suggests that various basic traits are accepted as indicative of leadership. It is this resonance that Sorkin employs in his construction of Bartlet as an intellectual leader.

Throughout the series, Sorkin uses Bartlet's intelligence for both comic and dramatic affect. He makes Bartlet's love for arcane knowledge a source of humor, a quirky eccentricity that frames the character as likeable. When Charlie is studying for a modern American history exam, Bartlet exclaims, "modern history is another word for television," and declares that he will get Charlie a copy of a speech used by George Perkins Marsh to rouse the agricultural community of Vermont in 1845 ("The Women of

Qumar"). In a Thanksgiving-themed episode, Bartlet lectures to a disinterested C. J. on the intricacies of properly seasoning a turkey, to which she replies that somewhere between anise, coriander and the other fifteen spices, she lost consciousness ("The Indians in the Lobby"). Meeting with economists in "The Crackpots and These Women," the president rattles off an impressive list of budget numbers. When one expresses amazement at his ability to recall such details, Leo responds: "The president's startlingly freakish that way." While a large part of the show's humor comes from Bartlet's enthusiasm for small details, as in one episode in which Josh refers to Bartlet's "encyclopedic knowledge of the ridiculous and dorklike" ("Enemies"), Sorkin also constructs a more serious side to Bartlet's intellect. The character holds a Ph.D. in economics, speaks Latin, is a Noble laureate and has a "once in a generation mind" ("Post Hoc, Ergo Propter Hoc"). Patrick Finn suggests that the character is an example of a "public intellectual" whose status derives, in part, from his "in-depth textual as well as historical knowledge" (2003, 106). In this way, Bartlet is "well equipped to work with, represent and stand in for America's central documents" (*ibid.*). As Finn notes, Sorkin makes the connection explicit in "What Kind of Day Has It Been" when Bartlet mentions that his ancestor signed the Declaration of Independence. Bartlet is not merely smart but rather the intellectual representative of the nation's most valued principles. Because Sorkin makes this connection, Bartlet's presidential identity absorbs his identity as a scholar patriot until intelligence is viewed as a necessary characteristic of the office. This is perhaps Sorkin's most seamless blending of the personal and the political in Bartlet's character, and it leads to one of the series' central conflicts. Bartlet's fear of appearing elitist is a recurring trait and offers strong support that Sorkin resists separating the man from the institution. The character's failure to embrace his true self, to be an intellectual force, is initially raised as an identity crisis ("Let Bartlet Be Bartlet") but reaches its climax as a psychological issue ("Night Five").[54] Both narratives rely on a strongly affective scene to communicate the struggle.

In "Let Bartlet Be Bartlet," the administration is stagnant and weak, a problem Leo attributes to Bartlet's desire for a second term. Despite the political motivation that Sorkin establishes for Bartlet, the climatic scene stresses the character's emotional state and almost reaches the level of religious testimony:

> BARTLET: I don't want to feel like this anymore.
>
> LEO: You don't have to.
>
> BARTLET: I don't want to go to sleep like this.
>
> LEO: You don't have to.

BARTLET: I want to speak.

LEO: Say it out loud. Say it to me.

BARTLET: This is more important than re-election. I want to speak now.

LEO: Say it again.

BARTLET: This is more important than re-election. I want to speak now.

The scene emphasizes the character's success in relinquishing his fear and embracing his intellectual self. Yet Sorkin achieves this by encouraging the audience to feel something about Bartlet's struggle. Bartlet's failure to speak, to be his true, intellectual self, is a personal weakness. When he admits to this failure, he is able to recapture his political strength. What prevents this scene from being a simple story of a president sacrificing meaningful action for future power is that Sorkin returns Bartlet to the struggle and makes it a deeply personal one.

In "The Two Bartlets," Sorkin revisits Bartlet's conflict over his intellectual role. The narrative suggests that Bartlet is again failing his presidential promise by refusing to be an intellectual leader. This time it is Toby who confronts Bartlet. The scene develops the back story that Sorkin alludes to in the season two finale, "Two Cathedrals," in which a flashback shows a young Bartlet in a confrontation with his verbally and physically abusive father. Sorkin also uses the scene to describe, through Toby, the two sides of Bartlet's character: "the absent-minded professor with the aw dad sense of humor, disarming, unthreatening, good for all time zones and the noble laureate still searching for salvation, lonely, frustrated lethal." The scene escalates as Toby first makes Bartlet admit his father's abuse and then offers a reason:

He didn't like you sir. That's why he hit you.... He didn't like you. You were smarter than he was.... So maybe if you get enough votes. Win one more election. You know, maybe your father....

The confrontation reduces Bartlet's intellectual characterization to an emotional plea for a father's love.

Finn suggests that part of the series' appeal is that it leaves issues unresolved, which allows audiences to decide for themselves. He argues that this "new space for political discussion" is also an inherent part of Bartlet's character (112). (For example, Bartlet is pro-choice politically but privately against it.) However, in "The Two Bartlets," Sorkin's emotional framing of Bartlet's intellectual character works to close the space for interpretation. When Toby characterizes Bartlet as an abused child whose longing for his parent's approval has followed him into adulthood, the viewer experiences a certain amount of closure. With this information, less space is available to understand Bartlet in alternative ways. In addition, the affective context of the exchange and the viewers' emotional response to the idea of an abusive parent reduces Bartlet to a wounded man whose failure to embrace his intellectual abilities is not politically motivated. Bartlet is not, as the beginning of the narrative seems to suggest, pandering to the voters. He is, in fact, the victim of emotional pain. In later episodes, Bartlet chooses to see a psychiatrist and the portrait of a vulnerable rather than calculating president is complete ("Night Five" and "Posse Comitatus").

Bartlet's status as victim, however, does not last. He ultimately embraces his intellectual image when he runs for reelection against a Republican who represents himself as the common man. Alluding to the political reality of the time (but quick to point out that his choices did not represent Al Gore and George Bush), Sorkin commented that he wanted to "dramatize that conflict [between] the know-it-all and the guy without gravitas who somehow relates to the everyman" (quoted in Elber 2002). To aid the viewer in seeing the merits of Bartlet's eventual transformation from a president ashamed of his intellectual status to one who embraces it, Sorkin frames the pursuit of education as a worthy national goal. He uses a dialogue between the president and Toby to construct scholarship as a force for good as well as reaffirm Bartlet's honorable nature. The president tells Toby:

> If a guy's a good neighbor, if he puts in a day, if every once in a while he laughs, if every once in a while he thinks about somebody else, and above all else, if he can find his way to compassion and tolerance then he's my brother. And I don't give a damn if he didn't get past finger-painting. What I can't stomach is people who are out to convince people that the educated are soft and privileged and out to make them feel like they are less than.... Especially when we know that education can be the silver bullet. The silver bullet, Toby, for crime, poverty, unemployment, drugs, hatred ["Hartsfield's Landing"].

What was previously assigned to Bartlet's personal and presidential character belongs to the country. Larger than the individual, education is the promise of a better future for all citizens. In making this connection, Sorkin allows Bartlet to be an intellectual leader without narrowing the character's appeal. Despite the character's privileged background, he is the people's president through affective rhetoric that celebrates inclusion.

In the last episode of *The West Wing*'s second season, the president attends the funeral of his secretary and friend, Mrs. Landingham. Facing the altar of the national cathedral, Bartlet confronts God with a litany of transgressions. God is a "sonofabitch" for letting Mrs. Landingham die in a car accident, "vindictive" for allowing Josh to be shot ("That was my son!") and a "feckless thug" for punishing Bartlet over a lie that might cost him the election ("Two Cathedrals"). Listing his achievements—job creation, conservation, increasing foreign trade, raising three children—he rages in Latin: "To hell with your punishments. To hell with you." In a final act of defiance, he takes a long drag from a cigarette, stubs it out on the cathedral floor and announces God's punishment: "You get Hoynes." The scene is affective on its own, but Sorkin adds to its emotional power by juxtaposing the narrative with flashbacks to Bartlet's adolescence. The viewer sees a young Mrs. Landingham and a teenage Bartlet meeting for the first time. Over several scenes, Sorkin develops a sibling relationship between the two, a point he makes explicit when Mrs. Landingham comments that Jed needs a "big sister." The flashbacks also introduce Bartlet's father, an angry man who shows disdain for his son and, in one interaction, slaps him across the face. Cutting between the character's past and present, Sorkin remains true to one of the narrative's most consistent themes: He blends the emotional pain of Bartlet the man with that of Bartlet the president until the two are difficult to distinguish.

The "Two Cathedrals" episode also usefully highlights the three basic roles of moral, paternal and intellectual leader that Sorkin uses to construct the president throughout the series. Specifically, Sorkin uses the cathedral scene to acknowledge Bartlet's paternal role, both literally and figuratively, by making reference to the character's children, his feelings toward his staff and his parenting of the country. Bartlet's angry confrontation with God offers compelling evidence that Sorkin's president is a moral man experiencing a temporary crisis of faith. Renouncing God, the character's revenge is to reject his presidential identity. Punishing God's failures in this way supports Sorkin's basic characterization of Bartlet as the rightful inheritor of a sacred mantel. Part of the scene's affectiveness lies in the idea that refusing the presidential destiny is an offense against God. The scene's emotional power also comes from the imagery Sorkin uses to symbolise Bartlet's crisis. He uses the spirit of Mrs. Landingham, who later visits Bartlet in the Oval Office to represent the character's inner thoughts. Listening to Mrs. Landingham's ghost, Bartlet begins to reconcile with God. The transformation is complete when the character steps outside the Oval Office into a driving storm. Sorkin notes that the symbolic baptism is God sending Bartlet strength, while the overall episode was designed as a "tribute to faith" (quoted in Topping 2002, 256). The "Two Cathedrals" episode also contributes to Sorkin's characterization of the president as an intellectual. The flashbacks introduce a smart young man who writes articles for the school newspaper against banning books and is persuaded to discuss the staff's pay inequities with his father. Confirming his special status and foreshadowing his presidential destiny, Mrs. Landingham tells Jed:

> Look at you. You're a boy king. You're a foot smarter than the smartest kid in the class, you're blessed with inspiration, you must know this by now, you must have sensed it.

The intellectual theme is carried through to the present when the adult Bartlet speaks fluent Latin to express his anger over the injustice he feels.

As this chapter has demonstrated, Sorkin's comments suggest that constructing Bartlet as paternal, moral and intellectual was a deliberate choice. His reasons include personal admiration for his father's qualities, a belief that compelling drama is found in the struggle between public duty and personal faith and a desire to replay a central debate of the 2000 presidential election. The character's qualities, however, also have broader associations with the president as a meaning system. As this chapter has argued, the relationship of the presidential image with patriarchy and morality was nurtured from the institution's earliest days and continues to be a central component of presidential communication. The idea that the president should possess a certain level of intelligence is similarly expressed, either subtly, as in discussions about a president's (or candidate's) lack of experience, or explicitly, as it was in the 2000 campaign. This meaning system provides a framework for Sorkin's construction of Bartlet and allows the character to posses basic, recognizable presidential traits. When Sorkin uses affective frames to communicate these defining characteristics, he intensifies their impact because Bartlet becomes more than the president. He is president and damaged adolescent; president and sympathetic victim; president and humble patriot. Each of these constructions offers the audience an emotional experience that Sorkin uses to redeem the character when he fails to act morally, paternally or intellectually. The result is a presidential representation that is not unique but rather a composite version of a learned meaning system who appears realistic only because Sorkin uses affective rhetoric to blunt the impact of the character's failures.

CHAPTER SIX

End Game

Sounds Like...

My parents took me to the theater all the time when I was a little kid.... But what I loved was the sound of dialogue; it was like symphony music to me. It was just terrific. And I wanted to make that.
(Sorkin in an interview on the *Charlie Rose Show*, October 2, 2002)

To understand *The West Wing*'s emotional representation of the president is to understand Aaron Sorkin's approach to writing. Central to this approach is the way that Sorkin conceptualizes the meaning of his scripts. As his recollection to talk show host Charlie Rose suggests, Sorkin believes that dialogue signifies impressions and meaning is more about processing associations than it is about comprehending ideas. Not having the intellectual capacity at the age of twelve to understand a sophisticated play, Sorkin relied on the sounds he heard to form meaning. Words became music and meaning became emotion. His reaction to the "symphony" was to feel "terrific."

As an adult, Sorkin's desire to recreate the music of his childhood theater experience grew into writing plays of his own. He tells Rose that when he was preparing to write *A Few Good Men*, he recruited his sister, a Navy lawyer at the time, to give him "any pieces of paper that had the jargon of [the Judge Advocate General's court] on it" (Sorkin 2002b). He remembers that he would "fall in love with phrases and the sound of things" (*ibid.*). Reading the specialized vocabulary of Navy lawyers, Sorkin decided to communicate the feelings the words conveyed to him. In his view, the point of a scene filled with unfamiliar words or idioms of a profession was not to comprehend the speech intellectually but rather to experience the words emotionally.

The process that Sorkin began with *A Few Good Men* continued when he started writing *The West Wing*. During the interview with Rose (after assuring the host that he is not politically sophisticated—"I don't know politics at all"), he explains his approach to writing the series:

> When people are talking about something, it isn't so much their position that I'm trying to imitate as the way they're presenting it. I'm just trying to phonetically recreate the sound of political sophistication and knowing what you're talking about. And oftentimes in things that I've written ... there'll be a quick passage that will go by and somebody—the studio or the producer—someone will say, "Gee, no one's going to know what these two people are talking about." I'll say, "It's not actually important that they do. What's important is that the audience say, 'Wow! These guys really know what they're talking about. That's interesting.'" And that's what I try to do [*ibid.*]

Sorkin simplifies the viewers' experience of his presidential narrative because he asks them to find meaning in associating jargon with authenticity. His characters sound like politicians because they use the specialized vocabulary of their profession. Clearly, this is a necessary technique of any drama that attempts to recreate a specific workplace. Yet Sorkin's comments suggest that he deliberately set out to communicate affective meaning through his dialogue. Having the characters quickly rattle off jargon often gives the audience a reason to invest in the emotions behind the words. If the characters' words lose intellectual meaning, they often succeed in communicating affective meaning. Sorkin often assists this outcome by disrupting the dialogue with short "snippets" or phrases that convey the personal. As one critic suggests, the show can "take on all manner of esoteric political issues and still thoroughly entertain an audience" (McCollum 2003). Thoughtfully processing the characters' debates routinely becomes secondary to experiencing their humor or their pain.

In many ways, Sorkin's writing allows *The West Wing* to become a sensory experience. The verbal pace and aural pleasure of listening to banter that is equal parts political jargon and witty asides encourages the viewer to find meaning in the sounds of political work. It is a technique recognized by at least one television critic who noted that "at its peak" the series "was about language" (Goodykoontz 2003). This language often translated as patriotism and simple conceptions of right and wrong but also depended upon a more elusive association with the presidential ideal. Just argues that the critics "overplayed *The West Wing*'s ideological component" because for many viewers

The real fantasy ... wasn't in imagining that the president was liberal—it was in imagining that the president had more ethical scruples than Bill Clinton, more intelligence than Bush and more seriousness of purpose than both put together [2003].

Sorkin's president is not only appealing as an alternative to his real life counterparts but also as a symbol of true presidential virtue. For Just, Sorkin achieves this result by stressing the themes of intelligence and selflessness and depicting the idea that "presidents ought not to merely ask the best of Americans but also to ask the best of themselves" (*ibid.*). It is an idea that has as its roots the most basic tenets of political learning.

Sorkin's presidential ideal should not be separated from the emotional processes of political learning that both shape it and make it easy to accept. Central to the feelings that Sorkin's narrative encourages for the fictional president are the basic identities with which he frames the character. Bartlet alternatively takes the roles of a father, a scholar and a moral leader. While these identities allow Sorkin to expand the character's narrative possibilities, they also resonate with political socialization. For the majority of Americans, political learning is fundamentally an emotional experience that constructs the president as a father figure, a moral leader and an intellectual. While these identities may lose their appeal as emotional learning is supplemented by cognitive reasoning, they maintain a resonance that is consistently sounded by the media. When this association is combined with the emotive characteristics of a television drama like *The West Wing*, early feelings toward the presidency may be recalled. Work in schematic theory suggests that previously formed ways of understanding the presidency inform future understandings. If this process, as it is constructed by political socialization, relies on emotions, then an affective template is created to which the presidential image may be applied and processed. Sorkin's representation of President Bartlet easily fits the template and offers a reaffirmation of basic feelings. As Just suggests, the liberal politics of the show

have always been secondary to the program's central message: that intelligence and moral purpose are the two most important attributes we ought to expect from our political leaders [*ibid.*].

If Sorkin's representation is successful, it is because he asks the audience to do nothing more than feel reconnected to a presidential ideal that most learned at an early age.

Reality Check

One of the outcomes of Sorkin's depiction of public service was that real-life politicians frequently used the show to promote an agenda. While some referred to the characters to reflect positively on themselves, others used issues raised in the narrative for publicity. For liberals, the match provided an easy alliance between politics and the personal. For those on the opposite side of Sorkin's politics, criticizing the series was also personal. Bartlet and his staff, they claimed, are too ideal, too noble, and too pure. Despite discussions on the factual accuracy of various issues, legislation and presidential actions, the realism of the series is predominately discussed in terms of how the show succeeds or fails to accurately represent what the presidency feels like for those who work in the West Wing. Levine alludes to this when he suggests that "ambition and staff politics are recurrent features of White House life that, curiously, have little place in the stories of *The West Wing*" (2003b, 45). To illustrate his point, he cites the recollections of Paul Begala, a Clinton staffer, who told a journalist that the "familial feeling was gone" when he made the transition from campaign to White House work (*ibid.*). The criticism that grounds the show's attempts at reality in emotional accuracy rather than factual truth suggests that Sorkin's affective goals are succeeding. In addition, the broadcast of the series' "Documentary Special" strengthened Sorkin's project by juxtaposing the emotional memories of real White House staff with matching scenes from the show. While documentary formats find success in communicating emotional as well as factual realism, the structure of *The West Wing*'s documentary made it difficult to distinguish the participants' truth from the show's fiction. Memory blurred with script and participants merged with characters until it was unclear whether reality was authenticating fiction or fiction was confirming fact. In turn, the series was depicted as successfully capturing some emotional truth about the presidency, despite the documentary's problematic relationship to the real.

For many critics, *The West Wing*'s relationship to reality was also directly related to how well its liberal discourse complimented the Clinton presidency. Discussing the show's ratings decline, they claimed that it failed to meet the new realities of a changed national culture led by a new president. As one critic wrote, "suddenly a newly installed conservative Republican administration made the action seem especially fictional" (Carter 2003b). Once considered an improved version of presidential reality, the show was failing to meet its obligation to reflect the leadership change. While these claims are difficult to prove, particularly when the series faced competition from highly successful reality shows, including *The Bachelor*, and suffered the loss of Rob Lowe midway through the fourth season, John Wells was quick to agree with the criticism. Discussing the perception that the show had become irrelevant, he commented:

> We need to address the fact that in our audience's mind, something really has changed in the way we look at the world and political problems and what we need from our political leaders.... We want to try to address that without making the show too ponderous or earnest [quoted in Duffy 2003].

Aside from his subtle allusion to Sorkin's narrative style, Wells' comments suggest that a main aim of the series is to reflect political reality. This reality, however, is not concerned with shifting the liberal positions of the characters. He claims that the show's characters "aren't changing but the world in which they live forces them to ... hear more of the other kind of view" (*ibid.*). Wells' plan to represent more Republican viewpoints in the series' narrative suggests that he finds the show's reflection of political reality to be central to its success. It may be argued that he is simply restoring Sorkin's early formula where the show mirrored the events of the Clinton administration (despite the writer's claims to the contrary). Yet Wells' contributions serve Sorkin's ultimate goals. His plan to reflect more political division and allow more space for "conversation" (*ibid.*) expands the show's narrative possibilities rather than shifts its ideological stance. According to Wells, the fifth season will reveal more about Bartlet's family life (Smith 2003), and the president will begin to question his past decisions and the consequences of his actions for both the country and his family (Nason 2003). While future plots of the show may reflect a reality of more Republican voices, its emotional reality will remain strong.

Character Actor

I'm just a normal guy ... gotta job to do.
(George W. Bush to Tom Brokaw, January 23, 2002)

In NBC's broadcast of the *Bush White House: Inside the Real West Wing*, Tom Brokaw takes the viewer through a typical presidential day in which Bush meets with advisors, holds meetings, exercises in the White House weight room and eventually delivers the above humble self-assessment. For some viewers, Bush's comment may be a refreshing sign of humility in the face of power. For those who appreciate the relationship between television and the president, Bush's quip is merely part of a long conversation that presidents have held with television viewers. Since Roosevelt's brief debut in 1939, presidents have attempted to harness the intimate power of television rather than be controlled by it. The difference between success and failure is often the level of skill used to balance the personal and the political, to appear both ordinary and extraordinary. When President Bush claims to be a "normal guy" with a "job to do" while sitting in the White House, he comes close to finding the balance. In *The West Wing*, Sorkin creates the same task for President Bartlet. For many viewers, a large part of the character's appeal is that they feel as if they know Bartlet. He is like them yet different; he is private person and public leader. Sheen's approach to enacting the character suggests a similar balance.

In 2000, during a panel discussion for The Museum of Television and Radio's William S. Paley Television Festival, Sheen was asked to comment on the greatest challenge he faces playing the fictional president. He responds:

> If I don't act presidential, if I just act human and allow Aaron to come through me I'm fine. When I get in the way, when I start enacting the president, it doesn't work [March 7, 2000].

Sheen's answer suggests that he only succeeds in depicting a credible president when the presidential is translated as Sorkin's vision. Central to this vision is a presidential characterization that is grounded in feelings. For Sheen, if President Bartlet is a successful character, it is because Sorkin reveals that humanity is an integral part of the presidential institution. For Sorkin, this humanity is primarily about doing the right thing. In a follow-up panel discussion held a month later, Sorkin tells the audience that his characters will usually face a weakness in themselves that must be confronted by doing "what's hard in order to do what's better" (April 3, 2000). Engaging his characters in this challenge allows Sorkin to depict the "heroic" in the struggle to overcome personal flaws (*ibid.*). When this formulation of the heroic is applied to Bartlet, the president is recognized for his ordinary traits and celebrated for moving beyond them. In this way, Sorkin makes the presidential myth accessible while maintaining its affective power.

In his work on presidential character, James Barber suggests that the presidency is "the focus for the most intense and persistent emotions in the American polity" (1992, 2). As a symbolic leader, the president must face a "climate of expectations" that includes public demands for "reassurance," "a sense of progress and action" and "legitimacy" (6).[55] Common to each of these categories is a feeling for who the president should be and how he should act. The president should transmit "a feeling that things will be alright." He should be a "take-charge man, a doer" as well as a "master politician who is above politics." Ultimately, the president should "personify our betterness in an inspiring way" (*ibid.*). Barber's categories, while totalizing, are useful summaries of the affective desires many people project onto the president. The media's contribution to this climate is significant. Real or fictional, cinematic presidents are often depicted as men of strong or weak character. Analysis of presidential press coverage (particularly during the 2000 election campaign) suggests that both candidates and presidents are subject to Barber's "climate of expectations," while television's presidents, the subjects of docudrama, documentary, satire and *The West Wing* are continually personalized. The pattern suggests that affective characterizations of presidents resonate with a large majority of the public. Formed in early political learning, these characteristics are renewed with every media representation that creates the president as a structure of feeling.

Shortly after the presidential election of 1952, electronics company RCA ran full-page newspaper advertisements that declared, "television has brought their government back to the people!" (quoted in Denton 1988, 41). The phrase suggests that RCA, in the business of selling televisions, recognized (or promoted) the idea of a public disconnection between citizen and leader that television fixed. With its intimate small screen, television could make leadership feel accessible. In a similar way, Aaron Sorkin has used television to return the president to the public by capturing a feeling about the nation's leader. Fan or critic, the viewer responded to Sorkin's presidential characterization because it resonated with a basic meaning system that constructs the president emotionally. Whether the fantasy of President Bartlet was embraced or rejected, the decision was usually based on the feelings that the character generated. While *The West Wing* under Sorkin may have "expanded possibilities for American political thinking and action" (Rollins and O'Connor 2003, 2) it also testified to the power of political socialization processes. Without the foundation laid in early political learning, the impact of Sorkin's presidential representation would have been far less pronounced. The fantasy of President Bartlet found its power in a larger presidential meaning system. Rather than contributing something new to this system, Sorkin's drama merely asked the audience to remember it.

Episodes by Season, 1999–2003

Season One

"Pilot"
22 September 1999. A. Sorkin, L. O'Donnell, P. Caddell; dir: T. Schlamme.

"Post Hoc, Ergo Propter Hoc"
29 September 1999. A. Sorkin; dir: T. Schlamme.

"A Proportional Response"
6 October 1999. A. Sorkin; dir: M. Buckland.

"Five Votes Down"
13 October 1999. A. Sorkin (teleplay), L. O'Donnell, P. Caddell (story); dir: M. Lehmann.

"The Crackpots and These Women"
20 October 1999. A. Sorkin; dir: A. Drazan.

"Mr. Willis of Ohio"
3 November 1999. A. Sorkin; dir: C. Misiano.

"The State Dinner"
10 November 1999. A. Sorkin, P. Redford; dir: T. Schlamme.

"Enemies"
17 November 1999. R. Osborn, J. Reno (teleplay), R. Cleveland, L. O'Donnell, P. Caddell (story); dir: A. Taylor.

"The Short List"
24 November 1999. A. Sorkin, P. Caddell (teleplay), A. Sorkin, D. Myers (story); dir: B. D'Elia.

"In Excelsis Deo"
15 December 1999. A. Sorkin; dir: T. Schlamme.

"Lord John Marbury"
5 January 2000. A. Sorkin, P. Caddell (teleplay), P. Caddell, L. O'Donnell (story); dir: K. Sullivan.

"He Shall, from Time to Time…"
12 January 2000. A. Sorkin; dir: A. Sanford.

"Take Out the Trash Day"
26 January 2000. A. Sorkin; dir: K. Olin.

"Take This Sabbath Day"
9 February 2000. A. Sorkin, P. Redford, L. O'Donnell; dir: T. Schlamme.

"Celestial Navigation"
16 February 2000. A. Sorkin, D. Myers, L. O'Donnell; dir: C. Misiano.

"20 Hours in L.A."
23 February 2000. A. Sorkin; dir: A. Taylor.

"The White House Pro-Am"
22 March 2000. A. Sorkin, L. O'Donnell, P. Redford; dir: K. Olin.

"Six Meetings Before Lunch"
5 April 2000. A. Sorkin; dir: C. Johnson.

"Let Bartlet Be Bartlet"
26 April 2000. A. Sorkin, P. Parnell, P. Caddell; dir: L. Innes.

"Mandatory Minimums"
3 May 2000. A. Sorkin; dir: R. Berlinger.

"Lies, Damn Lies and Statistics"
10 May 2000. A. Sorkin; dir. D. Scardino.

"What Kind of Day Has It Been?"
17 May 2000. A. Sorkin; dir: T. Schlamme.

Season Two

"In the Shadow of Two Gunmen Part I"
4 October 2000. A. Sorkin; dir: T. Schlamme.

"In the Shadow of Two Gunmen Part II"
4 October 2000. A. Sorkin; dir: T. Schlamme.

"The Midterms"
18 October 2000. A. Sorkin, L. O'Donnell, P. Caddell; dir: A. Graves.

"In This White House"
25 October 2000. A. Sorkin (teleplay), P. Parnell, A. Abner; dir: K. Olin.

"And It's Surely to Their Credit"
1 November 2000. A. Sorkin (teleplay), K. Falls, L. Glasser (story); dir: C. Misiano.

"The Lame Duck Congress"
8 November 2000. A. Sorkin (teleplay), L. O'Donnell (story); dir: J. Kagan.

"The Portland Trip"
15 November 2000. A. Sorkin (teleplay), P. Redford (story); dir: P. Barclay.

"Shibboleth"
22 November 2000. A. Sorkin (teleplay), P. Caddell (story); dir: L. Innes.

"Galileo"
29 November 2000. A. Sorkin, K. Falls; dir: A. Graves.

"Noel"
20 December 2000. A. Sorkin (teleplay), P. Parnell (story); dir: T. Schlamme.

"The Leadership Breakfast"
10 January 2001. A. Sorkin (teleplay), P. Redford (story); dir: S. Winant.

"The Drop In"
24 January 2001. A. Sorkin (teleplay), L. O'Donnell (story); dir: L. Antonio.

"Bartlet's Third State of the Union"
7 February 2001. A. Sorkin (teleplay), A. Abner, D. Myers (story); dir: C. Misiano.

"The War at Home"
14 February 2001. A. Sorkin, L. O'Donnell, P. Caddell; dir: C. Misiano.

"Ellie"
21 February 2001. A. Sorkin (teleplay), K. Falls, L. Glasser (story); dir: M. Engler.

"Somebody's Going to Emergency, Somebody's Going to Jail"
28 February 2001. A. Sorkin, P. Redford; dir: J. Yu.

"The Stackhouse Filibuster"
14 March 2001. A. Sorkin (teleplay), P. McCabe (story); dir: B. Gordon.

"17 People"
4 April 2001. A. Sorkin; dir: A. Graves.

"Bad Moon Rising"
25 April 2001. A. Sorkin (teleplay), F. Wilson (story); dir: B. Johnson.

"The Fall's Gonna Kill You"
2 May 2001. A. Sorkin (teleplay), P. Caddell (story); dir: C. Misiano.

"18th and Potomac"
9 May 2001. A. Sorkin (teleplay), L. O'Donnell (story); dir: R. Berlinger.

"Two Cathedrals"
16 May 2001. A. Sorkin; dir: T. Schlamme.

Season Three

"Isaac and Ishmael"
3 October 2001. A. Sorkin; dir: T. Schlamme.

"Manchester (Part I)"
10 October 2001. A. Sorkin; dir: T. Schlamme.

"Manchester (Part II)"
17 October 2001. A. Sorkin; dir: T. Schlamme.

"Ways and Means"
24 October 2001. A. Sorkin (teleplay), E. Attie, G. Sperling (story); dir: A. Graves.

"On the Day Before"
31 October 2001. A. Sorkin (teleplay), P. Redford, N. Chitre (story); dir: C. Misiano.

"War Crimes"
7 November 2001. A. Sorkin (teleplay), A. Abner (story); dir: A. Graves.

"Gone Quiet"
14 November 2001. A. Sorkin (teleplay), J. Dahl, L. Glasser (story); dir: J. Hutman.

"The Indians in the Lobby"
21 November 2001. A. Abner, K. Falls, A. Sorkin (teleplay), A. Abner (story); dir: P. Barclay.

"The Women of Qumar"
28 November 2001. A. Sorkin (teleplay), F. Wilson, L. Glasser, J. Dahl (story); dir: A. Graves.

"Bartlet for America"
12 December 2001. A. Sorkin; dir: T. Schlamme.

"H. Con-172"
9 January 2002. A. Sorkin (teleplay), E. Attie (story); dir: C. Misiano.

"100,000 Airplanes"
16 January 2002. A. Sorkin; dir: D. Nutter.

"The Two Bartlets"
30 January 2002. K. Falls, A. Sorkin (teleplay), G. Sperling (story); dir: A. Graves.

"Night Five"
6 February 2002. A. Sorkin; dir: C. Misiano.

"Hartsfield's Landing"
27 February 2002. A. Sorkin; dir: C. Misiano.

"Dead Irish Writers"
6 March 2002. A. Sorkin (teleplay), P. Redford (story); dir: A. Graves.

"The U.S. Poet Laureate"
27 March 2002. A. Sorkin (teleplay), L. Glasser (story); dir: C. Misiano.

"Stirred"
3 April 2002. A. Sorkin, E. Attie (teleplay), D. Myers (story); dir: J. Kagan.

"Documentary Special"
24 April 2002. W. Couturie, E. Attie, F. Wilson (interview material); dir: W. Couturie.

"Enemies Foreign and Domestic"
1 May 2002. P. Redford and A. Sorkin; dir: A. Graves.

"The Black Vera Wang"
8 May 2002. A. Sorkin; dir: C. Misiano.

"We Killed Yamamoto"
15 May 2002. A. Sorkin; dir: T. Schlamme.

"Posse Comitatus"
22 May 2002. A. Sorkin; dir: A. Graves.

Season Four

"20 Hours in America Part I"
25 September 2002. A. Sorkin; dir: C. Misiano.

"20 Hours in America Part II"
25 September 2002. A. Sorkin; dir: C. Misiano.

"College Kids"
2 October 2002. A. Sorkin (teleplay), D. Cahn, M. Goffman (story); dir: A. Graves.

"The Red Mass"
9 October 2002. A. Sorkin (teleplay), E. Attie (story); dir: V. Misiano.

"Debate Camp"
16 October 2002. A. Sorkin (teleplay), W. Sind, M. Oates Palmer (story); dir: P. Barclay.

"Game On"
30 October 2002. A. Sorkin, P. Redford; dir: A. Graves.

"Election Night"
6 November 2002. A. Sorkin (teleplay), D. Gerken, D. Handelman (story); dir: L. Linka Glatter.

"Process Stories"
13 November 2002. A. Sorkin (teleplay), P. Yoo, L. Schmidt (story); dir: C. Misiano.

"Swiss Diplomacy"
20 November 2002. E. Attie, K. Falls; dir: C. Misiano.

"Arctic Radar"
27 November 2002. A. Sorkin (teleplay), G. Sperling (story); dir: J. D. Coles.

"Holy Night"
11 December 2002. A. Sorkin; dir: T. Schlamme.

"Guns Not Butter"
8 January 2003. E. Attie, K. Falls, A. Sorkin; dir: B. D'Elia.

"The Long Goodbye"
15 January 2003. J. R. Baitz; dir: A. Graves.

"Inauguration Part I"
5 February 2003. A. Sorkin (teleplay), M. Oates Palmer, W. Sind (story); dir: C. Misiano.

"Inauguration Part II: Over There"
12 February 2003. A. Sorkin (teleplay), D. Gerken, G. Sperling (story); dir: L. Linka Glatter.

"The California 47th"
19 February 2003. A. Sorkin (teleplay), L. Schmidt, Paula Yoo (story); dir: V. Misiano.

"Red Haven's on Fire"
26 February 2003. A. Sorkin (teleplay), M. Goffman, D. Cahn (story); dir: A. Graves.

"Privateers"
26 March 2003. P. Redford, D. Cahn, A. Sorkin (teleplay), P. Redford, D. Cahn (story); dir: A. Graves.

"Angel Maintenance"
2 April 2003. E. Attie, A. Sorkin (teleplay), E. Attie, K. Falls (story); dir: J. Yu.

"Evidence of Things Not Seen"
23 April 2003. A. Sorkin (teleplay), E. Attie, D. Handelman (story); dir: C. Misiano.

"Life on Mars"
30 April 2003. A. Sorkin (teleplay), P. Redford, D. Myers (story); dir: J. D. Coles.

"Commencement"
7 May 2003. A. Sorkin; dir: A. Graves.

"Twenty Five"
14 May 2003. A. Sorkin; dir: C. Misiano.

Notes

1. Conflict between Sorkin and the show's writing staff made news in 2001 when Sorkin controversially dismissed a staff writer's contributions to a script that won an Emmy award in 2000. For a more detailed discussion of this see Sharon Waxman, "Will 'West Wing' Go Up in Smoke?" *Washington Post*, 20 July 2001.

2. A reference made by actor John Amos who plays recurring character Admiral Percy Fitzwallace (quoted in Walker 2003, np).

3. Throughout this book references to the president will be in the masculine. This usage choice reflects the fact that, to date, all U.S. presidents have been male, and the trend looks likely to continue for some time.

4. See also Cronin 1980; Hargrove 1974; Nelson 1985.

5. Throughout this discussion, political learning will be discussed in terms of childhood socialization because research suggests that childhood orientations remain relatively stable throughout adulthood for the majority of Americans. For work on adult political learning see Roberta Sigel, *Political Learning in Adulthood: A Sourcebook of Theory and Research* (Chicago: University of Chicago Press, 1999).

6. For example, voting is central to the principle of democratic governance. Many Americans do not vote, yet the political system still functions.

7. As a comprehensive review of the presidential image on film is beyond the scope of this book, this section examines some of the more popular films of the last several decades. For a comprehensive presidential filmography, see John Lawrence, "A Filmography for Images of American Presidents in Film," in *Hollywood's White House: The American Presidency in Film and History*, ed. Peter Rollins and John O'Connor (Lexington: The University Press of Kentucky, 2003), 383–402.

8. For example, Clinton plays the saxophone on a late night talk show; George W. Bush appears on various talk shows during the 2000 election campaign.

9. Paley testified in Washington in favor of broadcasting the opposition's response to presidential addresses. Foote argues that his decision to refuse airtime to the Republicans was a response to having outside sources dictate what his network's airtime would carry rather than a reversal of his original position (1990, 15).

10. This did not mean opposing views were never aired. To paraphrase Foote: In 1949, the FCC declared that the fairness doctrine was to be interpreted as part of the Communication Act of 1934, thereby compelling stations to provide an opportunity for opposing views. However, the focus of the doctrine was balancing issues rather than institutions, so when the president spoke, the networks were not obligated to present views of the opposition in Congress or the opposing party. They could choose to have their own commentators or any group they wanted provide opposing views, effectively giving the president airtime without providing it to the op-

position. As long as they balanced the issues, they were following the doctrine (22–23).

11. For example, videotape recording was introduced in 1960, improving picture quality and reduced editing time. In 1956, candidates reduced political speeches to five minutes, which guaranteed them lead-in from popular prime-time programming. This saved the preemption costs and satisfied the audience, whose entertainment programming was not interrupted (see Mickelson 1989, 58).

12. For a complete transcript of the broadcast see Schram 1987, 24–25.

13. This is not to argue that the president's speech does not also elicit familiar cues that raise emotional responses. Franklin Roosevelt's fireside chats were extremely popular and persuasive audio messages. Hinckley's study on presidential rhetoric also points to the use of familiar phrases used by consecutive presidents who recognized them as presidential. However, as the media climate has changed, the power of audio combined with visual has surpassed that of audio alone for most people when it comes to experiencing the president emotionally.

14. For example, Feuer cites a program called *Storefront Lawyers*, which centered on young attorneys working for the poor.

15. CBS objected to the character's age, marital status and the Minneapolis location. To compromise, MTM agreed to change the character to single, just ending a long-term relationship.

16. Feuer also notes that the controversial nature of *All in the Family*, a repackage of the U.K. show *'Til Death Do Us Part*, was not necessarily an innovative move on the part of CBS but a strategy to shift the network's demographics. The network desired to capture the young consumer audience but also to maintain a broad popular appeal (7).

17. The photograph was taken by George Tames on February 10, 1961, and became part of a visual essay for *New York Times Magazine*, entitled "A Day in the Life of John F. Kennedy." See *http://www.npg.si.edu/exh/travpres/jfks.htm*.

18. For Sorkin, the job of staff writers is to organize research and contribute ideas and issue-based arguments. He comments: "The most difficult part of the interview is explaining that I'm going to cramp their style creatively—almost completely, that I'm going to be writing the scripts and that they're going to be doing something else" (quoted in Welty 2000, 37).

19. The character of Charlie Young, Personal Aide to the President (Dulé Hill), is not examined as a senior member of Bartlet's staff but will be discussed in a later section on the paternal role of the president. In addition, the character of Vice President John Hoynes (Tim Matheson) will not be discussed in this book as he is generally not a prominent character in the narrative. In fact, the character resigns in "Life on Mars" after an extramarital affair is made public.

20. Sorkin furthers these ideas when he has Leo show compassion to the young woman responsible for leaking his confidential file to the congressman. A member of the human resources department, she is immediately fired but Leo asks to speak with her. It is clear from the exchange that the young woman thought she was saving the White House from the destructive behavior of an alcoholic. Leo admits that he is not sure her decision "wasn't a little bit brave" and offers her a second chance ("Take Out the Trash Day").

21. The president and his wife are at odds since his reelection announcement. She claims that they had a deal he would retire from politics after his first term due to his MS.

22. This point is also emphasized by Sam's declaration of platonic interest as well as C. J.'s comments to a reporter: "There's something commendable about Sam's behavior here..." ("A Proportional Response").

23. In practical terms, the story line allowed Sorkin to write an exit for Rob Lowe, who announced in the summer of 2002 that he was leaving the show. Lowe's departure was widely reported and attributed to his anger over not receiving the same pay rise as other cast members and his belief that the character was not playing a central role in story lines. See Gorman 2002; Armstrong 2002.

24. Sorkin continues this theme midway through season four with Sam's replacement. Will Bailey starts out as a temporary staff member who helps Toby write Bartlet's inauguration speech but quickly proves himself and is appointed Deputy Communications Director. As with Sam, Sorkin constructs Will as an idealist who is willing to speak truth to power. When Bartlet's inaction over the genocide in Kundu leads him to ponder why an African life is worth less to him than an American one, Will replies, "I don't know sir but it is" ("Inauguration Part I"). His honesty contributes to Bartlet's later decision to become involved and initiates Will into the presidential family.

25. Sam's anger over the president's lie surfaces in only two scenes from the series, but

it is weak and quickly forgotten. In one, he loses his temper with Leo in a tense meeting shortly after the news goes public and yells that some of the staff had more time to deal with the president's admission than others ("Manchester, Part I"). However, the exchange stresses the character's frustration at the fairness and timing of the disclosure rather than the admission itself. In another scene, Sam yells at Toby that the president "lied to us" but then says: "We could have gotten it done. If he had just told us in the beginning, this would've been a whole different..." ("Manchester, Part II"). For Sam, the president's omission represents a missed opportunity for his staff to help him. The president's failure is not the cover-up. Rather, it is in not trusting his aides to see him through the crisis.

26. Whitford introduced Gore at the largest rally of the campaign with the line: "I'm not a politician, I just play one on TV—kind of like George Bush" (quoted in Moore 2000, np).

27. At this time, the show's consultants were Democrats: Dee Dee Myers, former press secretary to President Clinton; Patrick Caddell, former pollster for President Carter; and Lawrence O'Donnell Jr., aide to Senator Patrick Moynihan.

28. The issue of political balance would resurface in 2003 as one of several possible reasons for Sorkin's departure. The network, many critics claimed, wanted the series to reflect more Republican viewpoints.

29. First Lady Jacqueline Kennedy made the comparison in an interview with historian Theodore H. White shortly after the president's assassination (Endewelt 1997, np).

30. In an article for *Brill's Content*, George Stephanopoulos recalls that while working as a senior adviser to President Clinton he showed Aaron Sorkin a card that contained instructions for evacuation in case of a nuclear war. The story became a plot line for the character of Josh in "The Crackpots and These Women." Similarly, Dee Dee Myers' experience of a press secretary's worst fear—being kept uninformed about a crucial military decision by the president—materialized as a story line for C. J. in "Lord John Mulbury" (Miller 2000, 93).

31. This imagery is strongest with Leo who, in "Five Votes Down," sacrifices his marriage for his work. The West Wing becomes his domestic space, where he interacts with his work family as well as his only daughter, who visits him in several episodes.

32. Sam's story line is small in this episode but does include an emphasis on the personal when he becomes angry and offended when a congressman's aide seems to make a reasonable attempt to resolve policy differences over the sentencing issue. He learns of the deception from an amused Toby and Josh, who tell him that the aide wants Sam to publicly engage in the debate so he can break the news of Sam's friendship with a call girl.

33. Misciagno defines the mythic presidency as the expectations and perceptions of the president as a strong leader (329).

34. Bartlet is also flawed, but his failures are easily forgivable and often redeemable. See chapter five for a more detailed discussion.

35. The show was directed by Oscar winner Bill Couturie (*Common Threads: Stories From the Quilt*). It won an Emmy award in 2002 for Outstanding Special Class Program.

36. Corner concedes that this merging of styles blurs the boundaries between distinct modes of documentary and claims to apply his categories with "caution" (31).

37. Interestingly, the series was actually down 31 percent among viewers 18–49 during this time period (Elber 2002, np). The drop was attributed to competition from CBS's *Amazing Race*, UPN's *The Twilight Zone* and WB's *Birds of Prey* (Berkowitz 2002, np).

38. For some members of the public this sentiment changed when Bush became president. In a study by Holbert et al., priming theory was used to examine the potential effects of the show's presidential representation on viewers' perceptions of Bush and former President Clinton. It found that the series' favorable depiction of the president led to more positive perceptions of both Bush and Clinton. However, as the authors note, its use of one episode, student participants and short-term measurement of effects limit the study. See Lance Holbert et al., "*The West Wing* as Endorsement of the US Presidency: Expanding the Bounds of Priming in Political Communication," *Journal of Communication* 53 (2003): 427–443.

39. For a more detailed discussion of this see Donnalyn Pompper, "*The West Wing*: White House Narrative That Journalism Cannot Tell," in "*The West Wing*": *The American Presidency as Television Drama*, ed. Peter Rollins and John O'Connor (Lexington: The University of Kentucky Press, 2003), 17.

40. According to Sorkin, after September 11 his writing for season three "was a continual search for what I wasn't doing that makes the

show work" (quoted in Owen 2002, np). He felt it was difficult for viewers to connect with his fictional heroes during a time when real ones were in the public eye. His comments suggest that the he did not easily dismiss the series' relationship with reality, despite his statement that "Isaac and Ishmael" was "never meant to teach anything" (quoted in Coleridge 2002, np).

41. While the election story line only covers the first six episodes of season four, Sorkin continued to evoke reality throughout the season. Two pipe bombs explode at a university in Iowa ("20 Hours in America Part II") and an African nation undergoes genocide ("Inauguration Part I," "Inauguration Part II," "Red Haven's On Fire"). For one television critic, Sorkin's rhetoric became so closely related to the Bush administration as to make Bartlet a "disorienting ... Jeckyll/Hyde" president. See Caryn James, "Shark's Pearly Teeth Gnash Near *The West Wing,*" *New York Times,* October 23, 2002.

42. The story broke on the Drudge Report website and was covered by various print, broadcast and online media sources, including the *Wall Street Journal,* where Peggy Noonan wrote a March 1, 2002, editorial about it, and *Entertainment Weekly* online, where NBC network sources were quoted as saying that Entertainment President Jeff Zucker would address Sorkin's comments during a meeting with the media.

43. For some viewers, this is the case even when they have a direct connection to the actual presidency. Joe Hagin, a deputy to George W. Bush's Chief of Staff Andrew Card, comments that "most of my friends and family relate to what I do up here by the TV show" (quoted in Lindlaw 2001, np).

44. The presidential ideal focuses on character traits rather than political ideology, an understanding evident in the comments of Republican viewers like Noonan and Luntz cited in this chapter.

45. Sheen also claimed that he had received thousands of hate emails and been verbally attacked on the street for being a traitor. The actor also said that network executives asked him to explain his position, as his high profile antiwar activities could damage the show. See Campbell 2003, 4.

46. See Michael Kimmel, *Manhood in America: A Cultural History* (New York: Free Press,

1996), for a discussion of presidential demonstrations of masculinity.

47. As the second season begins, the audience learns that the boys who shot the president belong to a racist group and were actually aiming for Charlie.

48. Clinton's response seemed to support the connection as well. Miroff notes that "the president himself adopted the language of sin and repentance in his search for public forgiveness" (1999, np).

49. In this history, Toby is already a convert, as he is on Bartlet's staff. However, Sorkin does give the character a moment of self-doubt and frustration. While Toby tells a stranger in a bar that he is a "very good" political operative, he admits that he has never won a campaign and fears he will be fired. Of the original Bartlet staff, Toby is the only one not fired. The implication is that the mission is not complete until all the faithful have been assembled.

50. In the "Pilot," the audience learns of Bartlet's personal dislike but public support for abortions. Leo tells Reverend Caldwell that the president travels the country discouraging women from having abortions but does not believe in the state's right to legislate the issue.

51. See Mark Crispin Miller, *The Bush Dyslexicon* (2001) and Jacob Weisberg, *George W. Bushisms,* (2001) and *More George W. Bushisms* (2002).

52. Gore's frame was "dishonest" although Bush also made factual errors. For a detailed examination of these press frames see Kathleen Hall Jamieson and Paul Waldman, *The Press Effect* (Oxford: Oxford University Press, 2003).

53. Sorkin's concern over this change is evident in his controversial remarks to the *New Yorker.* See chapter four.

54. The issue reoccurs briefly in the campaign story line of season four in which Josh wonders when the administration's election strategy became about "being the smartest kid in the class" ("20 Hours in American Part I") and Leo reassures the president before his debate with Ritchie that "there's no such thing as too smart" ("Game On").

55. While Barber recognizes that the climate can change with international and national events, he deems the categories as "recurring themes" (6).

Bibliography

Abelson, R., D. Kinder, M. Peters, and S. Fiske. 1982. "Affective and Semantic Components in Political Person Perception." *Journal of Personality and Social Psychology* 42: 619–30.

Abramson, P. 1967. "The Differential Political Socialization of English Secondary School Students." *Sociology of Education* 40: 246–69.

_____. 1970. "Political Socialization in English and American Secondary Schools." *The High School Journal* 54: 68–75.

Adams, W. 1984. "Media Coverage of Campaign '84: A Preliminary Report." *Public Opinion* 7 (April–May): 9–13.

Ahmed, K. 2002. "Blair Seeks *West Wing*'s Help." *Observer*, June 30. Available: http://www.guardian.co.uk/arts/news/story/0,11711,746918,00.html. (October 23, 2002).

Aldrich, J. 1980. *Before the Convention: Strategies and Choices in Presidential Nomination Campaigns*. Chicago: University of Chicago Press.

_____. 1992. "Presidential Campaigns in Party and Candidate-Centered Eras." In *Under the Watchful Eye*. Matthew McCubbins, ed. Washington, D.C.: Congressional Quarterly Press.

Alger, D. 1987. "Television Perception of Reality and the Presidential Election of '84." *PS: Political Science and Politics* 20 (winter): 49–57.

_____. 1989. *The Media and Politics*. Englewood NJ: Prentice-Hall.

Almond, G. 1960. "A Functional Approach to Comparative Politics." In *The Politics of Developing Areas*, ed. G. Almond and J. Coleman. Princeton: Princeton University Press.

Almond, G., and S. Verba. 1963. *The Civic Culture*. Princeton: Princeton University Press.

Andreyenkov, V., J. P. Robinson, and N. Popov. 1989. "News Media Use and Adolescents' Information About Nuclear Issues: A Soviet-American Comparison." *Journal of Communication* 39: 95–104.

Andrian, C. 1971. *Children and Civic Awareness*. Columbus: Charles Merrill.

Ang, I. 1985. *Watching Dallas*. London: Methuen.

Ansolabehere, S., R. Behr, and S. Iyengar. 1993. *The Media Game: American Politics in the Television Age*. New York: Macmillan.

Armstrong, M. 2002. "*West Wing*: Low Pay Sparks Lowe Exit." *Eonline*, July 24. Available: http://b4a.healthyinterest.net/news/2002_07.html. (April 20, 2005).

_____. 2003. "Comedy Central's Boffo Bush!" *Eonline*, February 20. Available: http://www.eonline.com/News/Items/0,1,8072,00.html. (February 21, 2003).

Arnston, P., and C. R. Smith. 1978. "News Distortion as a Function of Organizational Communication." *Communication Monographs* 45: 371–81.

Arterton, C. 1984. *Media Politics: The New Strategies of Presidential Campaigns*. Lexington, MA: Heath.

Atkin, C. 1981. "Communication and Political Socialization." In *Handbook of Political Communication*, ed. D. Nimmo and K. Sanders. Beverly Hills: Sage.

Atkin, C. K. and W. Gantz. 1978. "Television News and Political Socialization." *Public Opinion Quarterly* 42: 183–97.

Auster, A. 2000. "The Bacchae, the 'Missing Prince,' and Oliver Stone's Presidential Films." *Journal of Popular Film and Television* 28 (spring): 30.

Austin, E., and C. Nelson. 1993. "Influence of Ethnicity, Family Communication and Media on Adolescents' Socialization to U.S. Politics." *Journal of Broadcasting and Electronic Media* 37: 419–35.

Bailey, H., and J. Shafritz, eds. 1988. *The American Presidency: Historical and Contemporary Perspectives*. California: Brooks-Cole.

Bantz, C. R. 1979. "The Critic and the Computer: A Multiple Technique Analysis of the *ABC Evening News*." *Communication Monographs* 46: 27–39.

Barber, J. 1970. *Citizen Politics: An Introduction to Political Behavior*. Chicago: Markham.

_____. 1992. *The Presidential Character: Predicting Performance in the White House*. 4 ed. New Jersey: Prentice-Hall.

Barclay, P. 2001. "A Few Good Stories: Aaron Sorkin, Creator of *The West Wing* Talks to Paris Barclay about the Battle Between Politics and Drama—and Gays in the Bartlet White House." *The Advocate*, February 13. Available: http://www.bartlet4america.org/news/adv_sorkin_021301.html. (August 30, 2002).

Barilleaux, R. 1984. "The Presidency: Levels of Analysis." *Presidential Studies Quarterly* 14 (winter): 73–78.

Barker, D. 1988. "It's Been Real: Forms of Television Representation." *Critical Studies in Mass Communication* 5: 42–50. Available: http://www.sou.edu/polisci/hughes/469docs.barker.htm. (February 25, 2003).

Barney, C. 2003. "*West Wing* Unlikely to Soar as Before." *Contra Costa* (CA) *Times*, October 15. Available: http://www.bartlet4america.org/news/000670.html. (October 17, 2003).

Bartels, L. 1988. *Presidential Primaries and the Dynamics of Public Choice*. Princeton, NJ: Princeton University Press.

Barthes, R. 1975. *S/Z*. London: Cape.

Barton, R. L., and R. B. Gregg. 1982. "Middle East Conflict as a TV News Scenario: A Formal Analysis." *Journal of Communication*. 32 (spring): 172–85.

Baudrillard, J. 1979. *On Seduction*. Paris: Galilee.

_____. 1983. *In the Shadows of the Silent Majorities*. New York: Semiotext.

Bay, M. 1996. *The Rock*. DVD. Los Angeles: Don Simpson/Jerry Bruckheimer Films, Hollywood Pictures.

Beatty, W. 1998. *Bulworth*. DVD. Los Angeles: 20th Century Fox

Beavers, S. 2003. "*The West Wing* as a Pedagogical Tool: Using Drama to Examine American Politics and Media Perceptions of our Political System." In *'The West Wing': The American Presidency as Television Drama*, ed. P. Rollins and J. O'Connor, 175–86. Syracuse: Syracuse University Press.

Becker, H. 1993. *Malice*. DVD. Los Angeles: Castle Rock Entertainment, Columbia Pictures Corporation, New Line Cinema.

Becker, L., and D. Whitney. 1980. "Effects of Media Dependencies: Audience Assessment of Government." *Communication Research* 7: 95–120.

_____, I. Sobowale, and W. Casey. 1979. "Newspaper and Television Dependencies: Effects on Evaluations of Public Officials." *Journal of Broadcasting* 23: 465–75.

Bedell, S. 1983. *Up the Tube: Prime-Time TV and the Silverman Years*. New York: Viking.

Bennett, L. 1975. *The Political Mind and the Political Environment: An Investigation of Public Opinion and Political Consciousness*. Washington, D.C.: Heath.

Bennett, T., and J. Woollacott. 1987. *Bond and Beyond: The Political Career of a Popular Hero*. London: Macmillan.

Benoit, W. 1999. *Seeing Spots: A Functional Analysis of Presidential Television Advertisements, 1952–1996*. Westport: Praeger.

Berens, J. 2001. "Oh, Mr. Sheen." *Sydney Morning Herald*, February 3. Available: http://www.bartlet4america.org/news/smh020301.html. (August 30, 2002).

Berkowitz, B. 2002. "*West Wing* Slips in Ratings, Critics Not Worried." *Reuters*, October 11. Available: http://b4a.healthyinterest.net/news/2002_10.html. (April 4, 2005).

Bianco, R. 2001. "Glad-to-See TV: *24* and *Band of Brothers*." *USA Today*, December 28. Available: http://www.usatoday.com/life/television/2001-12-28-best-worst-tv.htm. (December 3, 2003).

Bierbaum, T. 1999. "Upscale Audiences Help *Wing*, Eye: Audiences Enjoy CBS' *The West Wing*." *Variety*, December 20. Available: http://findarticles.com. (January 20, 2000).

Bird, E., and R. Dardenne. 1989. "Myth, Chronicle and Story: Exploring the Narrative Qualities of News." In *Media, Myths and Narratives: Television and the Press*, ed. J. Carey. Beverly Hills: Sage.

Bland, E., and L. Lofaro. 2001. "Impersonating the President ... A Ha-Ha Away from Power." *Time* 19 (March): 72.

Branegan, J. 2000. "You Could Call it the Wonk Wing: NBC's Hit White House Series has Become a National Civics Lesson." *Time*, May 15. Available: http://www.jedbartlet.com/time051500.html. (January 4, 2001).

Brill, S. 2000. "Truth or Fiction, Pick One: Fictional *West Wing* Bests Many Reporters in Depicting a Nuanced Washington." *Brill's Content* 3 (March): 25.

Brunsdon, C. 1990. "Problems with Quality," *Screen* v. 31, n. 1: 67–90.

Bruzzi, S. 2000. *New Documentary: A Critical Introduction*. London: Routledge.

Buchanan, B. 1991. *Electing a President: The Markle Commission Research on Campaign '88*. Austin, Texas: University of Texas Press.

_____. 1978. *The Presidential Experience: What the Office Does to the Man*. New Jersey: Prentice-Hall.

_____. 1987. *The Citizen's Presidency: Standards of Choice and Judgment*. Washington, D.C.: Congressional Quarterly Press.

Buckingham, D. 2000. *The Making of Citizens: Young People, News and Politics*. London: Routledge.

Bundesen, C. 1990. "A Theory of Visual Attention." *Psychological Review* 97: 523–47.

Burton, T. 1996. *Mars Attacks!* DVD. Los Angeles: Warner Bros.

Byrne, B. 2002. "Will NBC Reelect *West Wing*?" *Eonline*, October 10. Available: http://www.bartlet4america.org/news/e100602.html. (October 16, 2002).

"California Assembly Mourns TV Character." 2001. *AP*, May 10. Available: http://www.bartlet4america.org.news/ap051001.html. (August 30, 2002).

Calvin, W. 1997. *How Brains Think*. London: Weidenfeld and Nicolson.

Campbell, D. 2003. "White House May Lose its Sheen of Peace." *Sydney Morning Herald*, March 5, 4.

Cannon, L. 2000. *President Reagan: The Role of a Lifetime*. New York: Public Affairs Press.

Cardman, M. 2002. "NEA Lauds Speech of Fictional TV President." *Education Daily* 35 (October 4): 1. Available: Expanded Academic ASAP (November 28, 2002).

Carey, J. 1976. "How News Media Shape Campaigns." *Journal of Communication* 26: 50–57.

Carter, B. 2002. "Trouble in *The West Wing*." *The New York Times*, October 21. Available: *http://www.b4a.healthyinterest.net/news/2002_10.html*. (April 4, 2005).

_____. 2003a. "*West Wing* Writer Quits." *The New York Times*, May 2. Available: http://www.bartlet4america.org/news/000462.html. (August 19, 2003).

_____. 2003b. "*The West Wing* Comes to Terms with the G.O.P." *The New York Times*, September 23. Available: *http://www.bartlet4america.org*/news/2003_09.html. (October 17, 2003).

Carter, R. 1998. *Mapping the Mind*. Berkeley: University of California Press.

Cavanaugh, J. 1995. *Media Effects on Voters*. Lanham, Maryland: University Press of America.

Chafee, S. H., L. S. Ward, and L. P. Tipton. 1970. "Mass Communication and Political Socialization." *Journalism Quarterly* 47: 647–59, 666.

Chaffee, S. H., and A. R. Tims. 1982. "News Media use in Adolescence: Implications for Political Cognitions." In *Communication Yearbook* 6, ed. M. Burgoon, 736–58. Beverly Hills: Sage.

Chaffee, S. H., and S. M. Yang. 1990. "Communication and Political Socialization." In *Polit-

ical Socialization, Citizenship Education and Democracy, ed. D. Ichilov. New York: Teachers College Press.

Challen, P. 2001. *Inside 'The West Wing': An Unauthorized Look at Television's Smartest Show.* Toronto: ECW Press.

Chambers, S. 2001. "Language and Politics: Agnostic Discourse in *The West Wing.*" *Ctheory*, 12 November. Available: http://www.ctheory.net/text_file?pick=317. (April 5, 2002).

———. 2003. "Dialogue, Deliberation, and Discourse: The Far-Reaching Politics of *The West Wing.*" In '*The West Wing': The American Presidency as Television Drama*, ed. P. Rollins and J. O'Connor, 83–100. Syracuse: Syracuse University Press.

———., and Finn, P. 2001. "*The West Wing*'s Digital Democracy: When Culture Becomes News." *Ctheory*, November 12. Available: http://www.ctheory.net/printer.asp?id=315. (17 December 2001).

Chase, W., ed. 1973. *Visual Information Processing.* New York: Academic Press.

Chester, E. 1969. *Radio, Television and American Politics.* New York: Sheed and Ward.

Christensen, T. 1987. *Reel Politics: American Political Movies from "Birth of a Nation" to "Platoon."* New York: Blackwell.

Cigelske, T. 2003. "Sheen Shares his Thoughts While Visiting Marquette." *AP*, September. Available: http://www.bartlet4america.org/news/2003_09.html. (October 17, 2003).

Cirino, R. 1971. *Don't Blame the People: How the News Media use Bias, Distortion and Censorship to Manipulate Public Opinion.* New York: Random House.

Clarke, P., and F. Fredin. 1978. "Newspapers, Television and Political Reasoning." *Public Opinion Quarterly* 42: 143–60.

Cleary, R. 1971. *Political Education in the American Democracy.* Scranton, PA: Intext.

Cleveland, G. 1904. *Presidential Problems.* New York: Century.

Cohen, P., and C. Gardner, eds. 1984. *It Ain't Half Racist, Mum.* London: Comedia.

Cohn, P. 2002. "Presidential Powwow." *ET Online*, April 23. Available: http://www.etonline.com/television/a10168.htm. (January 16, 2003).

Coleridge, D. 2002. "*West Wing*er Recalls 9–11 Controversy." *TV Guide*, September 9. Available: http://b4a.healthyinterest.net/news/2002_09.html. (April 14, 2005).

Comstock, G. 1991. *Television in America.* Newbury Park, CA: Sage.

Converse, P. 1975. "Public Opinion and Voting Behavior." In *Handbook of Political Science*, Vol. 4, ed. F. Greenstein and N. Polsby. Reading, MA: Addison-Wesley.

Conway, M., M. Wyckoff, E. Feldbaum, and D. Ahern. 1981. "The News Media in Children's Political Socialization." *Public Opinion Quarterly* 45: 164–78.

Corner, J. 1996. *The Art of Record: A Critical Introduction to Documentary.* Manchester: Manchester University Press.

———. 1997. "Television in Theory." *Media, Culture & Society* 19: 247–262.

Cornwell, E. 1965. *Presidential Leadership of Public Opinion.* Bloomington: Indiana University Press.

Creswell, T. 2001. "From Soap Opera to Soapbox." *HQ*, December–January, 40–5.

Cronin, T. 1974. "The Textbook Presidency and Political Science." In *Perspectives on the Presidency*, ed. S. Bach and G. Sulzner. Lexington: D. C. Heath.

———. 1980. *The State of the Presidency.* Boston: Little Brown.

Cundy, D. 1986. "Political Communication and Candidate Image: The Effect can be Substantial." In *New Perspectives on Political Advertising*, ed. L. Kaid, D. Nimmo, and K. Sanders, 210–34. Carbondale: Southern Illinois University Press.

Damasio, A. 1994. *Descartes' Error: Emotion, Reason and the Human Brain.* New York: Grosset/Putnam.

Davies, J. 1965. "The Family's Role in Political Socialization." In *Political Socialization: Its Role in the Political Process*, ed. Roberta Sigel, 11. *Annals of the American Academy of Political and Social Science*, Vol. 361. Thousand Oaks, CA: Sage.

Davis, D. 1990. "News and Politics." In *New Directions in Political Communication*, ed. D. Swanson and D. Nimmo, 147–84, Newbury Park: Sage.

Davis, R., and D. Owen. 1998. *New Media and American Politics.* New York: Oxford University Press.

Dawson, R., and K. Prewitt. 1969. *Political Socialization.* Boston: Little Brown.

De Jonge, P. 2001. "Aaron Sorkin Works his Way Through the Crisis." *The New York Times*, October 28. Available: http://www.nytimes.com/2001/10/28/magazine/28Sorkin.html. (May 6, 2002).

De Vries, B. 2002. "'President Bartlet' Urges Americans to Save Arctic Refuge." Defenders of Wildlife Press Release. January 16. Available: http://www.bbiethanol.com/news/view.cgi?article=416. (March 12, 2002).

Deggans, E. 2001. "*West Wing* Mastermind Divulges State Secrets." *St. Petersburg* (FL) *Times*, February 11. Available: http://www.bartlet4america.org/news/spt021101.html. (August 30, 2002).

Dennis, J. 1973. *Socialization to Politics: A Reader*. New York: John Wiley.

———. 1986. "Pre-Adult Learning of Political Independence: Media and Family Communication Effects." *Communication Research* 13: 401–33.

Denton, R. 1988. *The Primetime Presidency of Ronald Reagan: The Era of the Television Presidency*. Westport, CT: Praeger.

———, ed. 1994. *The 1992 Presidential Campaign: A Communication Perspective*. Westport, CT: Praeger.

———, ed. 1998. *The 1996 Presidential Campaign: A Communication Perspective*. Westport, CT: Praeger.

Devlin, L. P. 1986. "An Analysis of Presidential Television Commercials, 1952–1984." In *New Perspectives on Political Advertising*, ed. L. Kaid, D. Nimmo, and K. Sanders. Carbondale: Southern Illinois University Press.

Diamond, E., and R. Silverman. 1997. *White House to Your House: Media and Politics in Virtual America*. Cambridge, MA: MIT Press.

Diamond, E., and S. Bates. 1988. *The Spot: The Rise of Political Advertising on Television*. Cambridge, MA: MIT Press.

DiClerico, R. 1993. "The Role of Media in Heightened Expectations and Diminished Leadership Capacity." In *The Presidency Reconsidered*, ed. R. Waterman. Itasca, IL: F. E. Peacock.

Dominick, J. R. 1972. "Television and Political Socialization." *Educational Broadcasting Review* 6: 48–56.

Dover, E. D. 1994. *Presidential Elections in the Television Age: 1960–1992*. Westport, CT: Praeger.

Dovey, J. 2002. "Confession and the Unbearable Lightness of Factual." *Media International Australia*, no. 104 (August): 10–18.

Drew, D., and B. Reeves. 1980. "Learning from a Television News Story." *Communication Research* 7: 121–35.

Duffy, M. 2001. "TV 2000: *The West Wing* was the Absolute Best." *Detroit Free Press*, January 2. Available: EBSCO Host. (December 2, 2003).

———. 2003. "Series Return is a Nail-Biter Behind Scenes, Too." *Detroit Free Press*, September. Available: http://www.bartlet4america/org/news/2003_09.html. (October 17, 2003).

Dyer, R. 1989. "Quality Pleasures." *New Statesman & Society* 66 (September 8): 42–44.

Eagly, A., and S. Chaiken. 1993. *The Psychology of Attitudes*. Fort Worth, Texas: Harcourt Brace Jovanovich.

Easton, D., and J. Dennis. 1969. *Children in the Political System*. New York: McGraw-Hill.

———, and R. Hess. 1962. "The Child's Political World." *Midwest Journal of Political Science* 6 (August): 235–36.

Eastwood, C. 1983. *Sudden Impact*. DVD. Los Angeles: The Malpaso Company, Warner Bros.

———. 1997. *Absolute Power*. DVD. Los Angeles: Castle Rock Entertainment, Columbia Pictures Corporation, Malpaso Productions.

Edelman, M. 1988. *Constructing the Political Spectacle*. Chicago: University of Chicago Press.

Edwards, B. 2003. "Martin Sheen's West Wing Fantasy: Actor Says TV Drama Has a Role to Play in Trying Times." Transcript. 23 January. *National Public Radio*. <http://www.npr.org/templates/story/story.php?storyId=942641> (27 January 2003).

Edwards, G. 1983. *The Public Presidency: The Pursuit of Popular Support*. New York: St. Martin's Press.

Efron, E. 1971. *The News Twisters*. Los Angeles: Nash.

Ehman, L. 1969. "An Analysis of the Relationships of Selected Educational Variables with the Political Socialization of High School Students." *American Educational Research Journal* 6: 559–80.

Elber, L. 2001. "TV Shows Hum with Walden's Tunes." *AP*, March 5. Available: http://www.dearsally.org/felicity/articles/030501_walden_associatedpress.html. (October 16, 2002).

———. 2002. "*West Wing* Walks Fine Line of Fiction, Political Reality." *AP*, April 23. Available: http://www.sfgate.com. (January 16, 2003).

———. 2002. "*West Wing* at Ratings Crossroads." *AP*, October 22. Available: http://b4a.healthyinterest.net/news/2002_10.html.

Ellis, R, ed. 1998. *Speaking to the People: The Rhetorical Presidency in Historical Perspective*. Amherst: University of Massachusetts Press.

Emmerich, R. 1996. *Independence Day*. DVD. Los Angeles: 20th Century Fox, Centropolis Entertainment.

Endewelt, A. n.d. *The Story Behind Camelot*. Available: http://www.more.abcnews.go.com/sections/us/camelot_jackie/. (February 24, 2003).

Entman, R. 1989. *Democracy Without Citizens: Media and the Decay of American Politics*. New York: Oxford University Press.

Erickson, P. 1985. *Reagan Speaks: The Making of an American Myth*. New York: New York University Press.

Evans, H. 1988. *Campaign! Forty Years of TV in American Elections*. Produced by Illumination for Channel 4. Directed by D. Ash. Videocassette.

Ezell, P. 2003. "The Sincere Sorkin White House, or, the Importance of Seeming Earnest." In *'The West Wing': The American Presidency as Television Drama*, ed. P. Rollins and J. O'Connor, 159–74. New York: Syracuse University Press.

Faber, R., and M. Storey. 1984. "Recall of Information from Political Advertising." *Journal of Advertising* 13: 39–44.

"Fans Get Look Inside *West Wing*." 2001. *Zap2it.com*, January 16. Available: http://www.bartlet4america.org. News archive. (August 30, 2002).

Feuer, J. 1984. "MTM Enterprises: An Overview." In *MTM: Quality Television*, ed. J. Feuer, P. Kerr, and T. Vahimagi, 1–32. London: BFI.

———. 1984. "The MTM Style." In *MTM: Quality Television*, ed. J. Feuer, P. Kerr, and T. Vahimagi, 33–60. London: BFI.

Feuerherd, P. 2000. "The Last Word: A *Wing* and a Prayer." *Commonweal* 127 (March 10): 47. Available: Expanded Academic ASAP. (May 11, 2001).

Fields, W. 1996. *Union of Words: A History of Presidential Eloquence*. New York: Free Press.

Finn, P. 2001. "Remediating Democracy: The Public Intellectual, Hypertext and *The West Wing*." *Ctheory*, November 12. Available: http://www.ctheory.net/text_file.asp?pick=316. (April 5, 2002).

———. 2003. "*The West Wing*'s Textual President: American Constitutional Stability and the New Public Intellectual in the Age of Information." In *'The West Wing': The American Presidency as Television Drama*, ed. P. Rollins and J. O'Connor, 101–24. Syracuse, NY: Syracuse University Press.

Fisher, W. R. 1982. "Romantic Democracy, Ronald Reagan and Presidential Heroes." *Western Journal of Speech Communication* 46: 299–310.

Fisher, B. 2001. "Behind the Scenes at *The West Wing* with Cinematographer Tom Del Ruth, ASC." *Kodak.com*. Available: http://www.bartlet4america.org/news/kodak.html. (15 January 2001).

Fiske, J. 1987. *Television Culture*. New York: Routledge.

Fitzwater, M. 2000. Interview by T. Smith, September 8. *NewsHour with Jim Lehrer*. Available: http://www.pbs.org/newshour/media/west_wing/fitzwater.html. (September 3, 2002).

Fixx, J, ed. 1972. *The Mass Media and Politics*. New York: Arno Press.

Flacks, R. 1967. "The Liberate Generation: An Exploration of the Roots of Student Protest." *Journal of Social Issues* 23: 52–75.

Foote, J. 1990. *Television Access and Political Power: The Networks, the Presidency and the 'Loyal Opposition.'* New York: Praeger.

Friend, T. 2002. "*West Wing* Watch: Snookered by Bush." *The New Yorker* 78 (March 4): 30–32. Available: Expanded Academic ASAP. (February 21, 2003).

Garramone, G. 1983. "Issue Versus Image Orientation and Effects of Political Advertising." *Communication Research* 10: 59–76.

Garramone, G., and C. Atkin. 1986. "Mass Communication and Political Socialization: Specifying the Effects." *Public Opinion Quarterly* 50: 76–86.

_____., C. Atkin, B. Pinkleton, and R. Cole. 1990. "Effects of Negative Political Advertising on the Political Process." *Journal of Broadcasting and Electronic Media* 34 (summer).

Gazzaniga, M. 1992. *Nature's Mind: The Biological Roots of Thinking, Emotions, Sexuality, Language and Intelligence.* Harmondsworth, England: Penguin.

Geis, M. L. 1987. *The Language of Politics.* New York: Springer-Verlag.

Gelderman, C. 1997. *All the Presidents' Words: The Bully Pulpit and the Creation of the Virtual Presidency.* New York: Walker.

Gerbner, G. 1960. "Mass Communications and the Citizenship of Secondary School Youth." In *The Adolescent Citizen,* ed. F. Patterson, 179–205. New York: Free Press.

Gerbner, G., L. Gross, M. Morgan, and N. Signorielli. 1982. "Charting the Mainstream: Television's Contributions to Political Orientations." *Journal of Communication* 32 (spring): 100–27.

_____. 1984. "Political Correlates of Television Viewing." *Public Opinion Quarterly* 48: 283–300.

Gilberg, S., C. Eyal, M. McCombs, and D. Nicholas. 1980. "The State of the Union Address and the Press Agenda." *Journalism Quarterly* 57 (winter): 584–88.

Gitlin, T. 1980. *The Whole World is Watching: Mass Media in the Making and Unmaking of the New Left.* Berkeley: University of California Press.

Glasgow University Media Group. 1976. *Bad News.* London: Routledge and P. Kegan.

_____. 1980. *More Bad News.* London: Routledge and P. Kegan.

Glass, D. 1985. "Evaluating Presidential Candidates: Who Focuses on their Personal Attributes?" *Public Opinion Quarterly* 49: 517–34.

Glynn, I. 1999. *An Anatomy of Thought: The Origin and Machinery of the Mind.* New York: Oxford University Press.

Godmilow, J. 1997. "How Real is the Reality in Documentary Film? Jill Godmilow, in Conversation with Ann-Louise Shapiro." *History & Theory: Studies in the Philosophy of History* 36 (December): 80–101.

Goethals, G. 1986. "TV Faith: Rituals of Secular Life." *Christian Century* (April 23): 414. Available: http://www.religion-online.org/cgi-bin/relsearchd.dll/showarticle? itemid=1036. (April 2, 2003).

Goodykoontz, B. 2003. "*West Wing* Small Talk was Big Draw." *Arizona Republic,* July 29. Available: http://www.bartlet4america.org/news/2003_07.html. (October 17, 2003).

Gorman, S. 2002. "Actor Rob Lowe Leaving *The West Wing.*" *Reuters,* July 24. Available: http://b4a.healthyinterest.net/news/2002_07.html. (April 20, 2005).

Graber, D. 1986. "Mass Media and Political Images in Elections." *Research in Micropolitics* 1: 127–59.

_____. 1989. *Mass Media and American Politics.* Washington, D.C.: Congressional Quarterly Press.

_____. 2001. *Processing Politics: Learning from Television in the Internet Age.* Chicago: University of Chicago Press.

Greenstein, F. 1960. "The Benevolent Leader: Children's Images of Political Authority." *American Political Science Review* 59: 934–45.

_____. 1965. *Children and Politics.* New Haven, CT: Yale University Press.

_____. 1968. "Political Socialization." In *International Encyclopedia of the Social Sciences,* Vol. 1, ed. D. Sills. New York: Macmillan.

_____. 2000. *The Presidential Difference: Leadership Styles from FDR to Clinton.* New York: Martin Kessler Books/Free Press.

Greenstein, F., L. Berman, A. Felzenberg, and D. Lidtke. 1977. *Evolution of the Modern Presidency: A Bibliographical Survey.* Washington, D.C.: American Enterprise for Public Policy Research.

Gregory, R. 1997. *Eye and Brain: The Psychology of Seeing.* 5th ed. Princeton, N.J.: Princeton University Press.

Griffin, M. 1992. "Looking at TV News: Strategies for Research." *Communication* 13: 121–141.

Griffith, D.W. 1915. *The Birth of a Nation.* DVD. Los Angeles: Image Entertainment Inc.

Grossman, M., and M. Kumar. 1981. *Portraying the President: The White House and the News Media.* Baltimore: Johns Hopkins University Press.

Gunter, B. 1987. *Poor Reception: Misunderstanding and Forgetting Broadcast News.* Hinsdale: Erlbaum.

———. 1993. "The Audience and Quality in Television Broadcasting." *Media Information Australia* 70 (November): 53–60.

Hahn, D. 1987. "The Media and the Presidency: Ten Propositions." *Communications Quarterly* 35: 254–66.

Halberstam, D. 1979. *The Powers That Be.* New York: Knopf.

Hallin, D. 1991. *Sound Bite News: Television Coverage of Elections, 1968–1988.* Washington, D.C.: Woodrow Wilson International Center for Scholars, Media Studies Project.

Hargrove, E. 1974. *Power of the Modern Presidency.* Philadelphia: Temple University Press.

Hart, R. 1987. *The Sound of Leadership: Presidential Communication in the Modern Age.* Chicago: University of Chicago Press.

———. 1994. *Seducing America: How Television Charms the Modern Voter.* Oxford: Oxford University Press.

Hart, R., D. Smith-Howell, and J. Llewellyn 1991. "The Mindscape of the Presidency: *Time* magazine, 1945–1985." *Journal of Communication* 41 (summer): 6–25.

Hart, R., P. Jerome, and K. McCombs. 1984. "Rhetorical Features of Newscasts about the President." *Critical Studies in Mass Communication* 1: 260–286.

Haught, N. 2001. "A True Believer in *The West Wing.*" *Atlanta Journal-Constitution,* March 31. Available: http://www.bartlet4america.org/news/ajc033101.html. (August 30, 2002).

Hayton, H. "The King's Two Bodies: Identity and Office in Sorkin's *West Wing.*" In *"The West Wing": The American Presidency as Television Drama.* Peter Rollins and John O'Connor, eds. Syracuse: Syracuse University Press, 2003.

Heale, M. J. 1982. *The Presidential Quest: Candidates and Images in American Political Culture, 1787–1852.* New York: Longman.

Heclo, H. 1977. *Studying the Presidency: A Report to the Ford Foundation.* New York: Ford Foundation Press.

Henry, J. 1963. "Attitude Organization in Elementary School Classrooms." In *Education and Culture,* ed. G. Spindler, 192–93. New York: Holt.

Herman, L. 2003. "Bestowing Knighthood: The Visual Aspects of Bill Clinton's Camelot Legacy." In *Hollywood's White House: The American Presidency in Film and History.* Peter Rollins and John O'Connor, eds. Lexington, Kentucky: The University Press of Kentucky.

Hess, R., and D. Easton. 1960. "The Child's Changing Image of the President." *Public Opinion Quarterly* 24 (winter): 632–44.

———. 1962. "The Role of the Elementary School in Political Socialization." *The School Review* 70: 257–65.

———, and J. Torney. 1967. *The Development of Political Attitudes in Children.* New York: Anchor.

Hill, D., and J. Weingrad. 1986. *Saturday Night: A Backstage History of 'Saturday Night Live.'* New York: Vintage Books.

Hinckley, Barbara. 1990. *The Symbolic Presidency: How Presidents Portray Themselves.* New York: Routledge.

Hinds, J. 2000a. "Bartlet 2000: The Fictional President from *The West Wing* has Real-Life Appeal." *Detroit Free Press,* October 1. Available: http://www.freep.com/entertainment/tvandradio/bartlet1_20001001.htm. (January 15, 2003).

———. 2000b. "*West Wing* Chief Looks Like a Winner." *Detroit Free Press,* October 6. Available: http://www.freep.com/entertainment/tvandradio/west6_20001006.htm. (January 15, 2003).

Hirsch, H. 1971. *Poverty and Politicization: Political Socialization in an American Sub-Culture.* New York: The Free Press.

Hobson, D. 1982. '*Crossroads*': *The Drama of a Soap Opera*. London: Methuen.

Hoekstra, D. 1982. "The Textbook Presidency Revisited." *Presidential Studies Quarterly* 12: 162.

Hofstetter, C., and C. Zukin. 1979. "TV Network News and Political Advertising." *Journalism Quarterly* 56: 106–15, 152.

Hofstetter, R. 1976. *Bias in the News: Network Television Coverage of the 1972 Election Campaign*. Columbus: Ohio State University Press.

Hollander, N. 1971. "Adolescents and the War: The Sources of Socialization." *Journalism Quarterly* 48 (autumn): 472–79.

Hope, D. 2002. *Behind the Scenes with Thomas Schlamme*. Available: http://www.geocities. com/westwing01/wwcredits_schlamme.html. (October 16, 2002).

Hutcheson, R. 1988. *God in the White House: How Religion has Changed the Modern Presidency*. New York: Macmillan.

Hyman, H. 1959. *Political Socialization*. Glencoe: Free Press.

Iyengar, S., and D. Kinder. 1986. "More than Meets the Eye: TV News, Priming and Public Evaluations of the President." In *Public Communication and Behavior*, Vol. 1, ed. G. Comstock, 135–74. Orlando: Academic Press.

Jackson, D. 2002. *Entertainment and Politics: The Influence of Popular Culture on Young Adult Political Socialization*. New York: P. Lang.

James, C. 1999. "All the President's Quips: Levity at the White House." *New York Times*, September 22, E1. Available: http://www.nytimes.com. (April 11, 2003).

Jamieson, K. 1984. *Packaging the Presidency: A History and Criticism of Presidential Campaign Advertising*. New York: Oxford University Press.

———. 1986. "The Evolution of Political Advertising in America." In *New Perspectives on Political Advertising*, ed. L. Kaid, D. Nimmo, and K. Sanders, 1–20. Carbondale: Southern Illinois University Press.

———, ed. 1996. "The Media and Politics." *Annals of the American Academy of Political and Social Science*, Vol. 546. Thousand Oaks, CA: Sage.

———. 1997. *The Interplay of Influence: News, Advertising, Politics and the Mass Media*. Belmont: Wadsworth.

Jamieson, K. H., and P. Waldman. 2003. *The Press Effect: Politicians, Journalists and the Stories That Shape the Political World*. New York: Oxford University Press.

Jennings, K., and R. Niemi. 1968. "Patterns of Political Learning." *Harvard Educational Review* 38 (summer): 443–67.

Jennings, M. K., and K. Langton. 1969. "Mothers Versus Fathers: The Formation of Political Orientations Among Young Americans." *Journal of Politics* 31: 329–58.

Johnson-Cartee, K., and G. Copeland. 1991. *Negative Political Advertising*. Hillsdale, NJ: Lawrence Golbaum.

Johnston, A. 1990. "Trends in Political Communication: A Selective Review of Research in the 1980's." In *New Directions in Political Communication*, ed. D. Swanson and D. Nimmo, 329–62. Newbury Park: Sage.

Joseph, P. 2000. "Sometimes Real Life is Better than Television." *Picturing Justice.com*. July 8. Available: http://www.usfca.edu/pj/west-wing-joseph.htm. (January 17, 2003).

Joslyn, R. 1984. *Mass Media and Elections*. Reading, MA: Addison-Wesley.

———. 1986. "Political Advertising and the Meaning of Elections." In *New Perspectives on Political Advertising*, ed. L. Kaid, D. Nimmo, and K. Sanders, 139–83. Carbondale: Southern Illinois University Press.

Jurkowitz, M. 2001. "A Freaky Twist on Reality Television." *Boston Globe*, March 1. Available: http://www.bartlet4america.org. News archive. (August 30, 2002).

Just, M., D. Alger, and M. Kern, eds. 1996. *Crosstalk: Citizens, Candidates and the Media in a Presidential Campaign*. Chicago: University of Chicago Press.

Just, R. 2003. "Cerebral Vortex: How Aaron Sorkin, the Brains Behind TV's Smartest Show, Got the Last Laugh." *The American Prospect Online*, May 16. Available: http://www. bartlet4america.org/news/2003_05.html. (October 17, 2003).

Kagay, M., and G. Caldeira. 1975. '*I like the look of his face*': *Elements of Electoral Choice, 1952–1972*. San Francisco: American Political Science Association Annual Meeting.

Kaid, L., and A. Johnston. 2000. *Videostyle in Presidential Campaigns: Style and Content of Televised Political Advertising.* Westport, CT: Praeger.

Kaid, L., D. Nimmo, and K. Sanders, eds. 1986. *New Perspectives on Political Advertising.* Carbondale: Southern Illinois University Press.

Kann, M. 1996. "Manhood, Immortality, and Politics During the American Founding." *The Journal of Men's Studies* 5 (November): 79. Available: Expanded Academic ASAP. (May 12, 2003).

Kaplan, D. 2002. "Rob's Lowe Blow." *New York Post,* July 24. Available: http://b4a.healthyinterest.net/news/2002_07.html. (April 20, 2005).

Katz, E. 1957. "The 'Two-Step Flow' of Communication: An Up-to-Date Report on an Hypothesis." *Public Opinion Quarterly* 21 (spring): 61–78.

Katz, E., and P. Lazarsfeld. 1955. *Personal Influence.* New York: Free Press.

Kellner, D. "Baudrillard: A New McLuhan?" *Illuminations: The Critical Theory Website.* Available: http://www.uta.edu/huma/illuminations/kell26.htm. (February 21, 2002).

Keogh, J. 1972. *President Nixon and the Press.* New York: Funk & Wagnalls.

Kern, M. 1989. *Thirty-Second Politics: Political Advertising in the 1980's.* New York: Praeger.

Kernall, S. 1997. *Going Public: New Strategies of Presidential Leadership.* 3d ed. Washington, D.C.: Congressional Quarterly Press.

_____, and G. C. Jacobson. 1987. "Congress and the Presidency as News in the Nineteenth Century." *Journal of Politics* 49: 1016–35.

Kessel, J. 1988. *Presidential Campaign Politics: Coalition Strategies and Citizen Response.* Homewood, IL: Dorsey Press.

Key, V. O. 1961. *Public Opinion and American Democracy.* New York: Knopf.

Kinder, D., and R. Abelson. 1981. *Appraising Presidential Candidates: Personality and Affect in the 1980 Campaign.* San Francisco: American Political Science Association Annual Meeting.

Klapper, J. 1960. *The Effects of Mass Communication.* New York: Free Press.

Kohrs-Campbell, K., and K. Hall-Jamieson. 1990. *Deeds Done in Words: Presidential Rhetoric and the Genres of Governance.* Chicago: University of Chicago Press.

Kosslyn, S. 1994. *Image and Brain: The Resolution of the Imagery Debate.* Cambridge, Mass.: MIT Press.

Kraus, S., and D. Davis 1976. *The Effects of Mass Communication on Political Behavior.* University Park: The Pennsylvania State University Press.

Kubota, A., and R. Ward. 1970. "Family Influence and Political Socialization in Japan: Some Preliminary Findings in Comparative Perspective." *Comparative Political Studies* 3: 140–75.

Kubrick, S. 1964. *Dr. Strangelove or: How I Learned to Stop Worrying and Love the Bomb.* DVD. Great Britain: Hawk Films Limited.

Kuo, C. 1985. "Media Use, Interpersonal Communication and Political Socialization: An Interactional Model Analysis Using LISREL." In *Communication Yearbook* 9, ed. M. McLaughlin, 625–41. Beverly Hills: Sage.

Lambert, M. 2000. *Insights: Interview with W. G. Snuffy Walden Composing Scores for 'The West Wing' and Other Shows,* December. Available: http://www.mel-lambert.com/Writer/Interviews/MIX.Snuffy_Walden.html. (October 16, 2002).

Lane, B. 2001. "Giving Voice to Place: Three Models for Understanding American Sacred Space." *Religion and American Culture* 11 (winter): 53. Available: Expanded Academic ASAP. (November 11, 2002).

Lane, C. 2003. "The White House Culture of Gender and Race in *The West Wing*: Insights from the Margins." In *'The West Wing': The American Presidency as Television Drama,* ed. P. Rollins and J. O'Connor, 32–41. Syracuse: Syracuse University Press.

Lane, R. 1959. *Political Life: How and Why People Get Involved in Politics.* New York: Free Press.

Lane, R. E. 1966. "Adolescent Influence, Rebellion and Submission: Patterns of Political Maturation in the U.S. and Germany." *Revue Francaise de Sociologie* 7: 598–618.

Lang, K., and G. Lang. 1966. "The Mass Media in Voting." In *Reader in Public Communication,* ed. B. Berelson and M. Janowitz. New York: Free Press.

_____. 1984. *Politics and Television Re-Viewed.* Beverly Hills: Sage.

Langton, K. 1969. *Political Socialization*. New York: Oxford University Press.
_____, and M. K. Jennings. 1968. "Political Socialization and the High School Civics Curriculum." *American Political Science Review* 62: 852–67.
Lasswell, H. D. 1960. *Psychopathology and Politics*. New York: Viking.
Last, J. 2000. "*The West Wing* Could Only be Left Wing." *Salon.com*, May 1. Available: http://www.bartlet4america.org/news/sal050100.html. (August 30, 2002).
LeDoux, J. 1996. *The Emotional Brain: The Mysterious Underpinnings of Emotional Life*. New York: Simon and Schuster.
Lehmann, C. 2001. "The Feel-Good Presidency: The Pseudo-Politics of *The West Wing*." *The Atlantic Monthly* (March). Available: http://www.theatlantic.com. (May 6, 2002).
Leibiger, S. 2003. "George Washington, *The Crossing*, and Revolutionary Leadership." In *Hollywood's White House: The American Presidency in Film and History*, ed. P. Rollins and J. O'Connor, 19–29. Lexington: University Press of Kentucky.
Levesque, J. 2000. "Aaron Sorkin is a Man of Many Words." *Seattle Post-Intelligencer*, March 7. Available: http://www.seattlepi.nwsource.com/tv/sork07.shtml. (October 16, 2002).
Levine, M. 1961. "Social Climates and Political Socialization." *Public Opinion Quarterly* 265, no. 4: 596–606.
_____. 2003a. "The Transformed Presidency: People and Power in the real West Wing." In '*The West Wing': The American Presidency as Television Drama*, ed. P. Rollins and J. O'Connor, 235–58. Syracuse: Syracuse University Press.
_____. 2003b. "*The West Wing* (NBC) and the West Wing (D.C.): Myth and Reality in Television's Portrayal of the White House." In '*The West Wing': The American Presidency as Television Drama*, ed. P. Rollins and J. O'Connor, 42–62. Syracuse: Syracuse University Press.
Levinson, B. 1997. *Wag the Dog*. DVD. Los Angeles: Baltimore Pictures, New Line Cinema, Punch Productions Inc., Tribeca Productions.
Lewis, A. 2001. "*The West Wing*: An Insider Calls it the Insider's View of Democracy as We Hope It Can Be." *Television Quarterly* 32 (spring). Available: http://www. emmyonline. org/tvq/articles/32-1-6.asp. (January 16, 2003).
Liebes, T. 1992. "Television, Parents and the Political Socialization of Children." *Teachers College Record* 94: 73–86.
Lindlaw, S. 2001. "*West Wing* Cast Gets Special Tour." *AP*, April 29. Available: http:// www.bartlet4america.org/news/ap042901.html. (August 30, 2002).
Lippman, L. 2000. "*The West Wing*: The Lovable Liberal Behind Bush's Victory." *The New York Times*, December 31. Available: http://www.jedbartlet.com/nyt123100.html. (January 4, 2001).
Litt, E., ed. 1966. *The Political Imagination*. Glenview: Scott-Foresman.
Livingston, C. D. 1986. "The Televised Presidency." *Presidential Studies Quarterly* 16: 22–30.
Lockhart, J. 2000. Interview by T. Smith, September 13. *NewsHour with Jim Lehrer*. Available: http://www.pbs.org/newshour/media/west_wing/lockhart.html. (September 3, 2002).
Loewen, J. 1995. *Lies My Teacher Told Me: Everything Your American History Textbook Got Wrong*. New York: Touchstone.
Lowi, T. 1985. *The Personal President*. New York: Cornell University Press.
Lowry, B. 2003. "The Tale of Rob Lowe's Wild Ride." *Los Angeles Times*, February 19. Available: http://www.bartlet4america.org/news/000336.html. (February 28, 2003).
Luhmann, N. 2000. *The Reality of the Mass Media*. Cambridge, England: Polity Press.
Lumet, S. 1964. *Fail-Safe*. DVD. Los Angeles: Columbia Pictures Corporation.
Luntz, F. 2002. "President Bartlet, Please Take Me Back." *The New York Times*, December 28, A19. Available: ProQuest. (January 16, 2003).
Macarthur, C. 1981. "Historical Drama." In *Popular Television and Film*, ed. T. Bennett, S. Boyd-Bowman, C. Mercer, and J. Woollacott, 288–302. London: British Film Institute/ Open University Press.
Marc, D. 1997. *Comic Visions: Television Comedy and American Culture*. 2d ed. Malden, MA: Blackwell.
Marcus, G., R. Neuman, and M. Mackuen. 2000. *Affective Intelligence and Political Judgment*. Chicago: University of Chicago Press.

McCabe, C. 1981. "Days of Hope." In *Popular Television and Film*, ed. T. Bennett, S. Boyd-Bowman, C. Mercer, and J. Woollacott, 310–19. London: British Film Institute/Open University Press, London.

McClosky, H., and H. Dahlgren. 1959. "Primary Group Influence on Party Loyalty." *American Political Science Review* 53: 757–76.

McCollum, C. 2003. "Television: Righting the Ship of State." *San Jose Mercury News*, September. Available: http://www.bartlet4america.org/news/2003_09.html. (October 17, 2003).

McCombs, M. 1967. "Editorial Endorsements: A Study of Influence." *Journalism Quarterly* 44 (autumn): 545–48.

McCubbins, M., ed. 1992. *Under the Watchful Eye: Managing Presidential Campaigns in the Television Era*. Washington, D.C.: Congressional Quarterly Press.

McGinniss, J. 1969. *The Selling of the President, 1968*. New York: Trident Press.

McGuire, M. 2002. "Sorkin Returns to Old *Wing*." *Timesunion.com*, September 24. Available: http://b4a.healthyinterest.net/news/2002_09.html. (April 15, 2005).

McLuhan, M., and F. Quentin. 1967. *The Medium is the Message*. New York: Touchstone.

McQuail, D. 1986. "From Bias to Objectivity and Back: Competing Paradigms for News Analysis and a Pluralistic Alternative." In *Studies in Communication*, Vol. 3, ed. T. McCormack, 1–36. Greenwich: JAI Press.

Meadow, R., and L. Sigelman. 1982. "Some Effects and Non-Effects of Campaign Commercials: An Experimental Study." *Political Behavior* 4: 163–75.

Meadowcroft, J. 1986. "Family Communication Patterns and Political Development: The Child's Role." *Communication Research* 13: 603–24.

Medhurst, M., ed. 1996. *Beyond the Rhetorical Presidency*. College Station: Texas A&M University Press.

Melcher, R. 2001. "The Virtual President." *Ctheory*. March 21. Available: http://www.ctheory.net/text_file.asp?pick=229. (April 5, 2002).

Mendelsohn, H., and G. O'Keefe. 1976. *The People Choose a President*. New York: Praeger.

Mercer, G. 1971. *Political Learning and Political Education*. Ph.D. diss., University of Strathclyde.

Merelman, R. 1971. *Political Socialization and Educational Climates: A Study of Two School Districts*. New York: Holt, Rinehart and Winston.

Merriam, C. 1931. *The Making of Citizens*. Chicago: University of Chicago Press.

Merrill, J. 1965. "How *Time* Stereotyped Three U.S. Presidents." *Journalism Quarterly* 42 (Autumn): 563–70.

Meyrowitz, J. 1985. *No Sense of Place: The Impact of Electronic Media on Social Behavior*. New York: Oxford University Press.

Mickelson, S. 1989. *From Whistle Stop to Sound Bite: Four Decades of Politics and Television*. New York: Praeger.

Middleton, D., and D. Edwards, eds. 1990. *Collective Remembering*. London: Sage.

Miller, E. 2001. "The Children of Light: Josiah Bartlet in *The West Wing*." *Christianity Today* 45 (October 1): 73. Available: Expanded Academic ASAP Plus. (April 2, 2003).

Miller, M. 2000. "Real White House: Can a Smart TV Show Inspire Interest in Public Life in Ways Real Politics Brought to Us by the Real Press Corps Can't? *Brill's Content* 3 (March): 88–95, 113.

Millington, B., and R. Nelson. 1987. *Boys from the Blackstuff: The Making of TV Drama*. Gloucestershire, England: Comedia Publications.

Millman, J. 1999, "...But I Play One on TV." *Salon.com*, November 1. Available: http://www.salon.com/ent/col/mill/1999/11/01/westwing. (August 30, 2002).

———. 2000. "The POTUS with the Mostest." *Salon.com*, October 18. Available: http://www.salon.com/ent/col/mill/2000/10/18/west_wing/index.html?pn=3. (August 31, 2002).

Minow, N., J. Martin, and L. Mitchell. 1973. *Presidential Television*. New York: Basic Books.

Miroff, B. 1999. "The Contemporary Presidency: Moral Character in the White House: From Republican to Democrat." *Presidential Studies Quarterly* 29 (September): 708. Available: Expanded Academic ASAP. (May 27, 2003).

Misciagno, P. 1996. "Rethinking the Mythic Presidency." *Political Communication* 13 (July–September): 329–344.

Mitchell, W. 1962. *The American Polity: A Social and Cultural Interpretation.* New York: Free Press.

Moore, F. 2000. "Whitford Loves Just Joshin.'" *AP*, December 20. Available: http://www.jedbartlet.com/ap122000.html. (January 4, 2001).

Morley, D. 1990. "The Construction of Everyday Life: Political Communication and Domestic Media." In *New Directions in Political Communication*, ed. D. Swanson and D. Nimmo. Newbury Park: Sage.

Morton, W. 1996. *The Cerebral Code.* Cambridge, Mass.: MIT Press.

Mulgan, G., ed. 1990. "Television's Holy Grail: Seven Types of Quality." In *The Question of Quality: The Broadcasting Debate*, n. 6: 4–32. London: BFI.

Mullen, L. 1997. "The President's Visual Image from 1945 to 1947: An Analysis of Spatial Configurations in News Magazine Photographs." *Presidential Studies Quarterly* 27 (Fall): 819. Available: Expanded Academic ASAP. (February 25, 2003).

Murphy, M., and M. Schwed. 2003. "Broken Wing: The Strange Drama Behind the Sudden Exit of *West Wing* Creator Aaron Sorkin." *TV Guide*, May 28. Available: http://www.bartlet4america.org/news/2003_05.html. (October 17, 2003).

Nason, P. 2003. "Analysis: *West Wing*'s Fresh Start." *UPI Hollywood Reporter*, September 23. Available: http://www.bartlet4america.org/news/2003_09.html. (October 17, 2003).

Nelson, M., ed. 1985. *The Election of 1984.* Washington, D.C.: Congressional Quarterly Press.

Neustadt, R. 1960. *Presidential Power: The Politics of Leadership.* New York: Wiley.

Newcomb, H. 1974. *TV: The Most Popular Art.* New York: Anchor Books.

Newcomb, T. 1958. "Attitude Development as Function of Reference Groups." In *Readings in Social Psychology*. 3d ed. E. Maccoby, T. Newcomb, and E. Hartley, eds., 265–75. New York: Holt.

Newman, W. R. 1986. *The Paradox of Mass Politics: Knowledge and Opinion in the American Electorate.* Cambridge, MA: Harvard University Press.

Nichols, B. 1991. *Representing Reality: Issues and Concepts in Documentary.* Bloomington: Indiana University Press.

———. 1994. *Blurred Boundaries: Questions of Meaning in Contemporary Culture.* Bloomington: Indiana University Press.

Nimmo, D. 1978. *Political Communication and Public Opinion in America.* Santa Monica: Goodyear.

Nimmo, D., and K. Sanders, eds. 1981. *Handbook of Political Communication.* Beverly Hills: Sage.

Nissen, B. 2000. "A Presidential Sheen." *CNN.com*, August 29. Available: http://www.bartlet4america.org/news/cnn081800.html. (August 30, 2002).

Nixon, R. 1952. "Checker's Speech." Transcript, September 23. Available: http://www.nixonlibrary.org/TheNixons/archive/checkers.pdf. (December 3, 2003).

Noonan, P. 2002. "Break Out the Bubbly: Why Shouldn't Aaron Sorkin Tells us What he Thinks of President Bush?" *Wall Street Journal*, March 1. Available: http://www.opinionjournal.com/columnists/pnnoonan/?id=105001705. (February 14, 2003).

Nowlan, J., and M. Montray. 1984. "Broadcast Advertising and Party Endorsements in a Statewide Primary." *Journal of Broadcasting* 28: 361–63.

Oppenheimer, J. 2000. "The Halls of Power." *American Cinematographer*, October. Available: http://www.bartlet4america.org/news/amc1000.html. (August 30, 2002).

Owen, R. 2002. "Aaron Sorkin Wants to Put Fun Back into *West Wing*." *Pittsburgh Post-Gazette*, September 24. Available: http://b4a.healthyinterest.net/news/2002_09.html. (April 15, 2005).

Pakula, A. 1976. *All the President's Men.* DVD. Los Angeles: Warner Bros., Wildwood.

Paletz, D. 1999. *The Media in American Politics: Contents and Consequences.* New York: Longman.

Paletz, D. L., and R. M. Entman 1981. *Media Power Politics.* New York: Free Press.

———. 1984. "Accepting the System." In *Media Power in Politics*, ed. D. Graber, 81–88. Washington, D.C.: Congressional Quarterly Press.

Parry-Giles, T., and S. Parry-Giles. 1996. "Political Scopophilia, Presidential Campaigning, and the Intimacy of American Politics." *Communication Studies* 47: 191–205. Available: ProQuest. (May 12, 2003).

———. 2002. "*The West Wing*'s Prime-Time Presidentiality: Mimesis and Catharsis in a Postmodern Romance." *Quarterly Journal of Speech* 88 (May): 209–227.

Paterson, R. 1998. "Drama and Entertainment." In *Television: An International History*, ed. A. Smith with R. Paterson. Oxford: Oxford University Press.

Patterson, T. 1980. *The Mass Media Election: How Americans Choose Their President.* New York: Praeger.

———. 1982. "Television and Election Strategy." In *The Communication Revolution in Politics*, ed. G. Benjamin. New York: The Academy of Political Science.

———, and R. McClure. 1976. *The Unseeing Eye: The Myth of Television Power in National Elections.* New York: G. W. Putnam.

Peterson, S., and A. Somit. 1982. "Cognitive Development and Childhood Political Socialization." *American Behavioral Scientist* 25: 313–34.

Peterson, W. 1997. *Air Force One.* DVD. Los Angeles: Beacon Communications LLC, Columbia Pictures Corporation, Radiant Productions.

Pew Research Center for the People and the Press. 1998. *American News Habits. 1998 Media Consumption*, Sec. 3. Available: http://www.people-press.org/med98/pt.htm. (March 26, 2001).

Pierard, R., and Linder, R. 1988. *Civil Religion and the Presidency.* Grand Rapids, MI: Academic Books.

Pierson, F. 1995. *Truman.* DVD. Los Angeles: Home Box Office, Spring Creek Productions.

Piccalo, G., and L. Roug. 2002. "Fund-Raiser Takes Flight with *West Wing*'s Help." *Los Angeles Times*, October 4. Available: http://b4a.healthyinterest.net/news/2002_ 10.html. (April 17, 2005).

Pinner, F. 1965. "Parental Overprotection and Political Distrust." *Annals of the American Academy of Political and Social Science*, vol. 361: 58–70.

Pious, R. 2000. "Moral Action and Presidential Leadership." *Society* 37 (September): 14. Available: Expanded Academic ASAP. (May 27, 2003).

Plissner, M. 1999. *The Control Room: How Television Calls the Shots in Presidential Elections.* New York: Free Press.

Podhoretz, J. 2003. "The Liberal Imagination." In '*The West Wing': The American Presidency as Television Drama*, ed. P. Rollins and J. O'Connor, 222–34. Syracuse: Syracuse University Press.

Pollard, J. 1964. *The Presidents and the Press: Truman to Johnson.* Washington, D.C.: Public Affairs Press.

Pompper, D. 2003. "*The West Wing*: White House Narratives that Journalism Cannot Tell." In '*The West Wing': The American Presidency as Television Drama*, ed. P. Rollins and J. O'Connor, 17–31. Syracuse: Syracuse University Press.

Poniewozik, J. 2001. "*West Wing*: Terrorism 101." *Time*, October 4. Available: http://www.time.com/time/columnist/poniewozik/article/0,9565,178042,00.html (August 30, 2002).

Pranger, R. 1968. *The Eclipse of Citizenship: Power and Participation in Contemporary Politics.* New York: Holt.

Prewitt, K., G. Von der Muhll, and D. Court. 1970. "School Experience and Political Socialization: A Study of Tanzanian Secondary School Students." *Comparative Political Studies* 3: 203–25.

Pye, L. 1965. "Introduction: Political Culture and Political Development." In *Political Culture and Political Development*, ed. L. Pye and S. Verba. Princeton: Princeton University Press.

Ranney, A. 1983. *Channels of Power: The Impact of Television on American Politics.* New York: Basic Books.

Reaves, J. 2000. "I'll Take My Reality with a Generous Dollop of Fiction, Please." *Time*, July 20. Available: http://www.bartlet4america.org/news/time072000.html. (August 30, 2002).

Reiner, R. 1995. *The American President.* DVD. Los Angeles: Castle Rock Entertainment, Columbia Pictures Corporation, Universal Pictures, Wildwood Enterprises.

Riccards, M. 1973. *The Making of the American Citizenry: An Introduction to Political Socialization*. New York: Chandler.

Richardson-Hayton, H. 2003. "The King's Two Bodies: Identity and Office in Sorkin's *West Wing*." In *'The West Wing': The American Presidency as Television Drama*, ed. P. Rollins and J. O'Connor, 63–79. Syracuse: Syracuse University Press.

Robinson, J., and M. Levy. 1986. *The Main Source: Learning from Television News*. Beverly Hills: Sage.

Robinson, J. P. 1967. "World Affairs Information and Mass Media Exposure." *Journalism Quarterly* 44: 23–30.

_____. 1972. "Mass Communication and Information Diffusion." In *Current Perspectives in Mass Communication Research*, ed. F. G. Kline and P. J. Tichenor. Beverly Hills: Sage.

_____, E. Chivian, and J. Tudge. 1989. "News Media Use and Adolescents' Attitudes about Nuclear Issues: An American-Soviet Comparison." *Journal of Communication* 39: 105–13.

Robinson, M. 1981. "The Media in 1980: Was the Message the Message?" In *The American Elections of 1980*, ed. A. Ranney, 179–80. Washington, D.C.: American Enterprise Institute.

_____. 1987. "News Media Myths and Realties: What the Networks Did and Didn't Do in the 1984 General Campaign." In *Elections in America*, ed. K. Lehman Schlozman, 143–70. Boston: Allen & Unwin.

Robinson, M., and A. Ranney, eds. 1984. *The Mass Media in Campaign '84*. Washington, D.C.: American Enterprise Institute.

_____, and M. Sheehan. 1983. "Traditional Ink vs. Modern Video Versions of Campaign '80." In *Television Coverage of the 1980 Presidential Campaign*, ed. W. Adams. Norwood, NJ: Ablex.

_____. 1983. *Over the Wire and on TV: CBS and UPI in Campaign '80*. New York: Russell Saye.

Rochelle, W. 1999. "The Literary Presidency." *Presidential Studies Quarterly* 29: (June): 407. Available: ProQuest. (May 11, 2001).

Rogin. M. P. 1987. *Ronald Reagan, The Movie and Other Episodes in Political Demonology*. California: University of California Press.

Rollins, P., and J. O'Connor, eds. 2003. *'The West Wing': The American Presidency as Television Drama*. Syracuse: Syracuse University Press.

Rommel-Ruiz. 2003. "Redeeming Lincoln, Redeeming the South: Representations of Abraham Lincoln in D.W. Griffith's *The Birth of a Nation* (1915) and Historical Scholarship." In *Hollywood's White House: The American Presidency in Film and History*, ed. P. Rollins and J. O'Connor, 76–95. Lexington: University Press of Kentucky.

Roosevelt, T. 1913. *An Autobiography*. Best Books.

Rosentiel, T. 1992. *Strange Bedfellows: How Television and the Presidential Candidates Changed American Politics*. New York: Hyperion.

Rossiter, C. 1960. *The American Presidency*. New York: Harcourt-Brace.

Rothman, S., and R. Lerner. 1989. *Politics and the Media: A TV Revolution*. Current (March–April): 4–11.

Rubin, A. M. 1976. "Television in Children's Political Socialization." *Journal of Broadcasting* 20: 51–9.

Saenz, Michael. "Television Viewing as a Cultural Practice." *Television: The Critical View*. Ed. Horace Newcomb. New York and Oxford: Oxford University Press, 1994. 573–86.

Sanchez, J. M. 1996. "Old Habits Die Hard: The Textbook Presidency is Alive and Well." *PS: Political Science and Politics* 29 (March): 63. Available: ProQuest. (May 11, 2001).

Schlamme, T. 2000. Interview by T. Smith, September 16. *NewsHour with Jim Lehrer* Available: http://www.pbs.org/newshour/media/west_wing/schlamme.html. (September 3, 2002).

Schlesinger, A. 1974. *The Imperial Presidency*. New York: Popular Library.

Schmertz, H. 1986. "The Media and the Presidency." *Presidential Studies Quarterly* 16 (winter): 11–21.

Schram, M. 1987. *The Great American Video Game: Presidential Politics in the Television Age*. New York: William Morrow.

Schram, S. F. 1991. "The Post-Modern Presidency and the Grammar of Electronic Electioneering." *Critical Studies in Mass Communication* 8: 210–216.

Scott, T. 1998. *Enemy of the State*. DVD. Los Angeles: Don Simpson/Jerry Bruckheimer Films, Jerry Bruckheimer Films, Scott Free Productions, Touchstone Pictures.

Seib, P. 1987. *Who's in Charge? How the Media Shape News and Politicians Win Voters*. Dallas: Taylor.

Seitz, M., and A. Sepinwall. 2003. "*The West Wing* Loses its Founding Fathers." *Star-Ledger*, May 2. Available: http://www.bartlet4america.org/news/2003_05.html. (October 17, 2003).

Sepinwall, A. 2002. "Exit Poll: *West Wing* is Sinking. Why?" *NJ.com*. Available: htpp://www.bartlet4america.org/news/2002_11.html. (February 28, 2003).

Seymour-Ure, C. 1982. *The American President: Power and Communication*. New York: St. Martin's Press.

Shapiro, R., and L. Jacobs. 2000. "Polling and Pandering." *Society* 37 (September): 11. Available: Expanded Academic ASAP. (May 27, 2003).

Sharrett, C. 1996. "The Belly of the Beast: Oliver Stone's *Nixon* and the American Nightmare." *Cineaste* 22 (winter): 4–5.

Sheen, M. 2003. Interview by B. Edwards, January 28. *National Public Radio* transcript. Available: http://www.npr.com. (February 28, 2003).

Shister, G. 2002. "Real Presidents, but no Bushes, on Special *West Wing*." *Philadelphia Inquirer*, April 22. Available: http://www.phillycom. (January 16, 2003).

Shyles, L. 1984. "The Relationship of Images, Issues and Presentational Methods in Televised Spot Advertisements for 1980's American Presidential Primaries." *Journal of Broadcasting* 28: 405–21.

_____. 1986. "The Televised Political Spot Advertisement: Its Structure, Content and Role in the Political System." In *New Perspectives on Political Advertising*, ed. L. Kaid, D. Nimmo, and K. Sanders, 107–38. Carbondale: Southern Illinois University Press.

Sidey, H. 2002. "Washington's Hottest Spot for 100 Years: A West Wing Office Means Power, Glory and a Chance to Boost Future Earnings." *Time*, 160 (18 November). Available: Expanded Academic ASAP. (November 28, 2002).

Smith, A. 2003. "John Wells at the Helm of *West Wing*." *Providence* (RI) *Journal*, September. Available: http://www.bartlet4america.org/news/2003_09.html. (October 17, 2003).

Smith, C. R. 1977. "Television News as Rhetoric." *Western Journal of Speech Communication* 41: 147–59.

Smith, G. 2003. "The Left Takes Back the Flag: The Steadicam, the Snippet, and the Song in *The West Wing*'s 'In Excelsis Deo.'" In '*The West Wing*': *The American Presidency as Television Drama*, ed. P. Rollins and J. O'Connor, 125–35. Syracuse: Syracuse University Press.

Smith, M. B., J. S. Brunner, and R. W. White. 1956. *Opinions and Personality*. New York: John Wiley.

Smoller, F. 1986. "The Six O'Clock Presidency: Patterns of Network News Coverage in Major Newspapers." *Journalism Quarterly* 16: 31–49.

Sniderman, P., R. Brody, and P. Tetlock, eds. 1991. *Reasoning and Choice: Explorations in Political Psychology*. Cambridge, MA: Cambridge University Press.

Sorkin, A. 2000. Interview by T. Smith, September 27. *NewsHour with Jim Lehrer*. Available: http://www.pbs.org/newshour/media/west_wing/sorkin.html. (September 3, 2002).

_____. 2002a. '*The West Wing*' *Scriptbook: Six Teleplays*. New York: Newmarket Press.

_____. 2002b. Interview by Charlie Rose. *The Charlie Rose Show*. Transcript. October 2. Available: http://www.bartlet4america.org/news/cr100202.html. (October 16, 2002).

Spector, B. 1985. "A Clash of Cultures: *The Smothers Brothers* vs. CBS Television." In *American History/American Television: Interpreting the Video Past*, ed. J. O'Connor, 159–183. New York: Frederick Ungar.

Spitz, B. 2001. "*The West Wing*er: Behind the Scenes with *West Wing* creator Aaron Sorkin." *Delta Sky*, April. Available: http://www.bartlet4america.org/news/delta0401. html. (August 30, 2002).

Stanley, H., and R. Niemi. 1998. *Vital Statistics on American Politics 1997–1998*. Washington, D.C.: Congressional Quarterly Press.

Stanwood, E. 1898, 1912. *A History of the Presidency*. Boston and New York: Houghton Mifflin

Company [1916]. 2 v. [v. 1] From 1788 to 1897.—[v. 2] From 1897–1916. Vol. 1 first published separately in 1898; continuation to 1909 published in 1912.

Starr, A. 2000. "To Tell the Truth." *New York Times Magazine*, October 22. Available: http://www.bartlet4america.org/news/nytm/102200.html. (August 30, 2002).

Stein, M. 1969. *When Presidents Meet the Press*. New York: Messner.

Stempel, G., and J. Windhauser, eds. 1991. *The Media in the 1984 and 1988 Presidential Campaigns*. Westport, CT: Greenwood Press.

Stoddart, S. "*The Adams Chronicles*: Domesticating the American Presidency." In *Hollywood's White House: The American Presidency in Film and History*, ed. P. Rollins and J. O'Connor, 30–49. Lexington: University Press of Kentucky.

Stone, O. 1995. *Nixon*. DVD. Los Angeles: Cinergi Pictures Entertainment Inc., Hollywood Entertainment, Illusion Entertainment.

Stuckey, M., and F. Antczak. 1998. "The Rhetorical Presidency: Deepening Vision, Widening Exchange." *Communication Yearbook* 21: 405–41.

Stuttaford, A. 2003. "The President of the Left: No, He's Not President. Martin Sheen Only Plays One on TV. But...." *National Review* 55 (March 24). Available: Expanded Academic ASAP Plus. (April 23, 2003).

Sullivan, D., and R. Masters. 1988. "'Happy warriors': Leaders' Facial Displays, Viewer's Emotions and Political Support." *American Journal of Political Science* 32, no. 2: 345–68.

Swanson, D., and D. Nimmo, eds. 1990. *New Directions in Political Communication: A Resource Book*. Newbury Park: Sage.

Swanson, D. L. 1977. "And That's the Way it Was? Television Covers the 1976 Presidential Campaign." *Quarterly Journal of Speech* 63: 239–48.

Taft, W. H. 1911. *Four Aspects of Civic Duty*. Best Books.

Taylor, P. 1990. *See How They Run: Electing the President in an Age of Mediocracy*. New York: Knopf.

Tebbel, J., and S. Watts. 1985. *The Press and the Presidency*. New York: Oxford University Press.

Television and the Presidency. 1980. VHS. Los Angeles: CBS Television, Roger Ailes.

Thomas, N., and Pika, J. 1997. *The Politics of the Presidency*. Washington, D.C.: Congressional Quarterly Press.

Thurber, J., C. Nelson, and D. Dulio, eds. 2000. *Crowded Airwaves: Campaign Advertising in Elections*. Washington, D.C.: Brookings Institution Press.

Tims, A. 1986. "Family Political Communication and Social Values." *Communication Research* 13: 5–18.

Tooley, J., and J. Schrof. 1989. "Picture-Perfect Chiefs." *U.S. News & World Report* 107, no. 2 (10 July): 62.

Topping, K. 2002. '*The West Wing': Inside Bartlet's White House*. London: Virgin Books.

Tuchman, G. 1978. *Making News: A Study in the Construction of Reality*. New York: Free Press.

Tucker, K. 2000. "Meet the Prez." *Entertainment Weekly*, February 25. Available: http://www.bartlet4america.org/news/ew022500.html. (August 30, 2002).

Tulis, J. 1987. *The Rhetorical Presidency*. Princeton, NJ: Princeton University Press.

Unattributed. 2002. "'President Bartlet' Urges Americans to Help Save Arctic Refuge." *US Newswire*, January 15. Available Expanded Academic ASAP Plus. (April 23, 2003).

Volgy, T., and J. Schwarg. 1984. "Misreporting and Vicarious Political Participation at the Local Level." *Public Opinion Quarterly* 48: 757–65.

Walker, D. 2003. "Stars and Strife." *New Orleans Times-Picayune*, August 9. Available: http://www.bartlet4america.org/news/2003_08.html. (October 17, 2003).

Warner Brothers. 2002. '*The West Wing': The Official Companion*. New York: Pocket Books.

Wasby, S. L. 1966. "The Impact of the Family on Politics: An Essay and Review of the Literature." *The Family Life Coordinator* 15: 3–23.

Waterman, R., R. Wright, and G. St. Clair. 1999. *The Image-is-Everything Presidency: Dilemmas in American Leadership*. Boulder, CO: Westview Press.

Wattenberg, M. 1984. *The Decline of American Political Parties, 1952–1980*. Cambridge, Mass.: Harvard University Press.

Waxman, S. 2000. "Inside *The West Wing*'s New World." *George* magazine, November. Available: http://www.jedbartlet.com/george1100.html. (January 4, 2001).

Weaver, D., D. Graber, M. McCombs, and C. Eyal. 1981. *Media Agenda-Setting in Presidential Elections*. New York: Praeger.

Weiner, A. 2003. "*The West Wing*: New Commander-in-Chief John Wells Talks Exclusively about Getting NBC's White House Drama in Order." *Entertainment Weekly*, September 6. Available: http://www.bartlet4america. org/news/2003_09.html. (October 17, 2003).

Weinraub, B. 2000. "*The West Wing*: Leader of the Free World (Free TV, That Is)." *The New York Times*, October 17. Available: http://www.bartlet4america.org/news/nyt101700.html. (August 30, 2002).

Welty, T. 2000. "Aaron Sorkin: Making the Rules." *Script* 6 (September–October): 34–37, 62–64.

West, D. 1997. *Air Wars: Television Advertising in Election Campaigns, 1952–1996*. Washington D.C.: Congressional Quarterly Press.

White, T. 1983. *America in Search of Itself: The Making of the President 1956–1980*. London: Johnathan Cape.

_____. 1984. *Television and the Presidency*. Produced by R. Ailes and J. Harrison. Directed by R. Ailes. 90 minutes. Videocassette.

William S. Paley Television Festival. 2000. VHS. 7 March and 3 April. Los Angeles: The Museum of Television and Radio.

Wilson, W. 1914. [2001]. *The New Freedom: A Call for the Emancipation of the Generous Energies of a People*. Virginia: Patrick Henry University Press.

Wolff, M. 2000. "Our Remote-Control President." *New York Magazine*, December 4. Available: http://www.jedbartlet.com/nym120400.html. (January 4, 2001).

Wren, C. 1999. "The Inside Dope." *Commonweal* 126 (December 3): 17. Available: Expanded Academic ASAP Plus (April 2, 2003).

Ziblatt, D. 1965. "High School Extracurricular Activities and Political Socialization." *Annals of the American Academy of Political and Social Science*, Vol. 361. Thousand Oaks, CA: Sage.

Zimmer, T. 1983. "Local News Exposure and Local Government Alienation." *Social Science Quarterly* 64: 634–40.

Zukin, C. 1981. "Mass Communication and Public Opinion." In *Handbook of Political Communication*, ed. D. Nimmo and K. Sanders. Beverly Hills: Sage.

Note: Videotapes of *That Was The Week That Was, The Arsenio Hall Show, The Jack Paar Program, The Bush White House: Inside the Real West Wing*, and the William S. Paley Television Festival were screened April 16–19, 2003 at the Museum of Television and Radio, Beverly Hills, California.

Index